41 A
AF521522

MARINE LAW

MARINE LAW

J. THANNAPAN

ANMOL PUBLICATIONS PVT. LTD.
NEW DELHI - 110 002 (INDIA)

ANMOL PUBLICATIONS PVT. LTD.

H.O.: 4374/4B, Ansari Road, Darya Ganj,
New Delhi-110 002 (India)
Ph.: 23278000, 23261597

B.O.: No. 1015, Ist Main Road, BSK IIIrd Stage
IIIrd Phase, IIIrd Block
Bangalore - 560 085 (India)
Visit us at: www.anmolpublications.com

Marine Law
© 2007

ISBN 978-81-261-3205-8

PRINTED IN INDIA

Printed at Mehra Offset Press, Delhi.

Contents

Preface

With more than two-thirds of the world's surface covered by water, the seas have played a vital role in the development of the international community. Throughout history, states have used the oceans as a means of protection, as a source of food, and as a means to advance national interests. Some coastal states have relied upon the oceans as a protective buffer between them and their enemies, while other states have depended upon the free navigation of the seas to promote fishing and trade with other states. However a particular state uses the oceans, the navies and coast guards of maritime states are fundamental components in promoting and protecting a state's national interests on the water.

That maritime states share common interests is not surprising. In the past, those shared interests were generally restricted to the rights and responsibilities of free navigation. Today, however, in a world marked by fast-evolving marine technology and an explosion in maritime commerce and trade, those interests have expanded substantially. The modern maritime state is faced with many issues including coastal defense, navigation, regulation of shipping, search and rescue, marine environmental protection, vessel traffic management, customs, immigration, anti-smuggling enforcement, and boating safety.

Regulation of the oceans and coastal regions by maritime states has grown more complex in the twentieth century. Over the last 30 years, the number of newly independent maritime states, as well as the number of international maritime conventions, has proliferated. Many of these new states are developing new systems of law and are confronting legal and maritime issues they have never faced before. To effectively deal with these issues, these maritime states are developing a maritime regulatory infrastructure flexible enough to allow them to respond to the variety of issues which arise from the use of the seas.

International law and the requirements and rights it imposes on individual states is constantly evolving. On November 16, 1994, the 1982 United Nations International Convention on the Law of the Sea (LOS Convention), entered into force. Over 65 nations have ratified the convention which establishes a reasonable balance between the rights and obligations of coastal and flag states. Though the LOS Convention is only binding on those states who have ratified it, the Convention has an important influence on states who have not done so. The LOS Convention is viewed by the international community as a highly persuasive source of customary international law for many, though not all, of the issues it covers. To manage their maritime affairs and fulfill the obligations imposed by the Convention and other sources of international law, maritime states need a legal and organizational infrastructure.

The United States recognizes its special responsibility to those states which are embracing free markets and new systems of government for the first time. As part of this effort, the United States supports the International Maritime Organization's proposals to assist maritime states in implementing international conventions.

I have dealt with all the critical issues of maritime law keeping view of the general readers.

Author

Chapter 1

Maritime Law and the Ship

THE LEGAL DEFINITION OF A SHIP

A ship is a large, sea-going watercraft. A ship usually has sufficient size to carry its own boats, such as lifeboats, dinghies, or runabouts. A rule of thumb saying (though it doesn't always apply) goes: "a boat can fit on a ship, but a ship can't fit on a boat". Consequently submarines are referred to as "boats", because early submarines were small enough to be carried aboard a ship in transit to distant waters. Another type of large vessel which is traditionally called a boat is the Great Lakes freighter. Often local law and regulation will define the exact size (or the number of masts) which a boat requires to become a ship.

During the age of sail, ship signified a ship-rigged vessel, that is, one with three or more masts, usually three, all square-rigged. Such a vessel would normally have one fore and aft sail on her aftermost mast which was usually the mizzen. Almost invariably she would also have a bowsprit but this was not part of the definition. The same economic pressures which increased sizes to the point of carrying four or five masts, also introduced the fore and aft rig to larger vessels, so few ship-rigged vessels were built with more than three masts. The five-masted Preussen was the outstanding example, but the big German ships and barques were built partly for prestige reasons.

Nautical means related to sailors, particularly customs and practices at sea. Naval is the adjective pertaining to ships, though in common usage it has come to be more particularly associated with the noun 'navy'.

A watercraft is a vehicle, vessel or craft designed to move across (or through) water for pleasure, recreation, physical exercise, commerce, transport of people and goods, and military missions. It is derived from the term "craft" which was used as term to describe all types of water going vessels. (The term craft has since been expanded to include all types of vessels which travel on water (watercraft), in air (aircraft) and in space (spacecraft).)

Most watercraft would be described as either a ship or a boat. However, there are a number of craft which many people would consider neither a ship nor a boat, such as: canoes, kayaks, rafts, barges, catamarans, hydrofoils, windsurfers, surfboards (when used as a paddle board), underwater robots, torpedos and jet skis.

Although ships are typically larger than boats, the distinction between those two categories is not one of size per se.

- Ships typically are large ocean-going vessel. Boats are smaller and travel most often on inland or costal waters.
- A rule of thumb says "a boat can fit on a ship, but a ship can't fit on a boat", and a ship usually has sufficient size to carry its own boats, such as lifeboats, dinghies, or runabouts.
- Local law and regulation may define the exact size (or the number of masts) that distinguishes a ship from a boat.
- Traditionally submarines were called "boats", perhaps reflecting their cramped conditions: small size reduces the need for power, and thus the need to surface or snorkel for a supply of the air that running diesel engines requires; in contrast, nuclear-powered

submarines' reactors supply abundant power without consuming air, and such craft are large, much roomier, and classed as ships.

- A ship is any floating craft that transports cargo for the purpose of earning revenue; in that context, a passenger ship's "cargo" is its passengers. However, neither fishing boats nor ferries are considered ships, though both carry cargo (their catch of the day or passengers) and ferries carry lifeboats.

The term "watercraft" (unlike such terms as aircraft or spacecraft) is rarely used to describe any specific individual object: Rather the term serves to unify the category that ranges from jet skis to Aircraft carriers.

Measuring Ships

One can measure ships in terms of overall length, length of the waterline, beam (breadth), depth (distance between the crown of the weather deck and the top of the keelson), draft (distance between the highest waterline and the bottom of the ship) and tonnage. A number of different tonnage definitions exist; most measure volume rather than weight, and are used when describing merchant ships for the purpose of tolls, taxation, etc.

In Britain until the Samuel Plimsoll Merchant Shipping Act of 1876, ship-owners could load their vessels until their decks were almost awash, resulting in a dangerously unstable condition. Additionally, anyone who signed onto such a ship for a voyage and, upon realizing the danger, chose to leave the ship, could end up in Prison jail.

Samuel Plimsoll, a member of Parliament, realised the problem and engaged some engineers to derive a fairly simple formula to determine the position of a line on the side of any specific ship's hull which, when it reached the surface of the water during loading of cargo, meant the ship had reached its maximum safe loading level. To this day, that mark, called the "Plimsoll Mark", exists on ships' sides, and consists of a circle with a horizontal line through the centre. Because different types of water, (summer, fresh, tropical fresh, winter north Atlantic) have different densities, subsequent regulations required painting a group of lines forward of the Plimsoll mark to indicate the safe depth (or freeboard above the surface) to which a specific ship could load in water of various densities. Hence the "ladder" of lines seen forward of the Plimsoll mark to this day.

Propulsion

Pre Mechanisation

Until the application of the steam engine to ships in the early 19th century, oars propelled galleys or the wind propelled sailing ships. Before mechanisation, merchant ships always used sail, but as long as naval warfare depended on ships closing to ram or to fight hand-to-hand, galleys dominated in marine conflicts because of their maneuverability and speed. The Greek navies that fought in the Peloponnesian War used triremes, as did the Romans contesting the Battle of Actium. The use of large numbers of cannon from the 16th century meant that maneuverability took second place to broadside weight; this led to the dominance of the sail-powered warship.

Steam Propulsion

The development of the steamship became a complex process, the first commercial success accruing to Robert Fulton's North River Steamboat (often called Clermont) in the US in 1807, followed in Europe by the 45-foot Comet of 1812. Steam propulsion progressed considerably over the rest of the 19th century. Notable developments included the condenser, which reduced the requirement for fresh water, and the multiple expansion engine, which improved efficiency. As the means of transmitting the engine's power, the paddle wheel gave way to the more efficient screw propeller. The marine steam turbine developed by Sir Charles Algernon Parsons, brought the power to weight ratio down. He had achieved publicity by demonstrating it unofficially in the 100-foot Turbinia at the Spithead naval review in 1897. This facilitated a generation of high-speed liners in the first half of the 20th century and rendered the reciprocating steam engine out of date, in warships.

Most new ships since around 1960 have been built with diesel engines. Rising fuel costs have almost led to the demise of the steam turbine, with many ships being re-engined to improve fuel efficiency. One high profile example was the 1968 built Queen Elizabeth 2 which had her turbines replaced with a diesel-electric propulsion plant in 1986. The last major passenger ship built with steam turbines was the Fairsky, launched in 1984. Some specialised merchant ships have also been built with steam turbines since then, notably Liquefied Natural Gas (LNG) and coal carriers where part of the cargo has been used as fuel for the boilers.

LNG Carriers

LNG carriers in particular have remained a stronghold for steam , and new ships continue to be built with steam turbines in this high growth area of shipping. This is because the Natural Gas is stored in a liquid state in cryogenic vessels onboard these ships. A small amount of "boil off" of gas is required to maintain the pressure and temperature inside the vessels to within operating limits. The "boil off" gas provides the fuel for the ship's boilers, which provide steam for the turbines- the simplest method of dealing with the gas. Technology to operate internal combustion engines (modified marine two stroke diesel engines) on this gas has improved however, so these engines are beginning to appear in LNG carriers; with their greater thermal efficiency, less gas is burnt. Also, developments have been made in the process of re-liquefying "boil off" gas, enabling it to be returned to the cryogenic tanks.

The financial returns on LNG are potentially greater than the cost of the marine grade fuel oil burnt in conventional diesel engines, so the re-liquefaction process is starting to be used on diesel engine propelled LNG carriers. Another factor driving the switch from turbines to diesel engines for LNG carriers is the shortage of steam turbine qualified sea going engineers. With the lack of turbine powered ships in other shipping sectors, and the rapid increase in size of the worldwide LNG fleet, not enough have been trained to meet the demand. It may be that the days of the last stronghold for steam turbine propulsion systems are numbered, despite all but sixteen of the orders for new LNG carriers at the end of 2004 being for steam turbine propelled ships.

Diesel Propulsion

The marine diesel engine first came into use in 1903 when the river tanker Vandal was brought into service by Branobel. At the same time it was the first diesel electric ship. It soon offered even greater efficiency than the steam turbine but for many years had an inferior power-to-space ratio. About this period too, heavy fuel oil came into more general use and began to replace coal as the fuel of choice in steamships. Its great advantages were the convenience, the reduction in manning owing to the removal of the need for trimmers and stokers, and the reduction in space required for fuel bunkers. Diesel engines today are broadly classified according to their operating cycle (two-stroke or four-stroke), their construction (crosshead, trunk, or opposed piston) and their speed (slow speed, medium speed or high speed). Most modern larger merchant ships use either slow speed, two stroke, crosshead engines, or medium speed, four stroke, trunk engines. Some smaller vessels may operate high speed diesel engines. The operating ranges of the different speed types are as follows;

- Slow speed- any engine with a maximum operating speed up to 300 revs/minute, although most large 2 stroke slow speed diesel engines operate below 120 revs/minute. Some very long stroke engines have a maximum speed of around 80 revs/minute. The largest, most powerful engines in the world are slow speed, two stroke, crosshead diesels.
- Medium speed- any engine with a maximum operating speed in the range 300- 900 revs/ minute. Many modern 4 stroke medium speed diesel engines have a maximum operating speed of around 500 rpm.

- High speed- any engine with a maximum operating speed above 900 revs/ minute

As modern ships' propellers are at their most efficient at the operating speed of most slow speed diesel engines, ships with these engines do not generally require gearboxes. Usually such propulsion systems consist of either one or two propeller shafts each with its own direct drive engine. Ships propelled by medium or high speed diesel engines may have one or two (sometimes more) propellers, commonly with one or more engines driving each propeller shaft through a gearbox. Where more than one engine is geared to a single shaft, each engine will most likely drive through a clutch, allowing engines not being used to be disconnected from the gearbox while others continue to operate. This arrangement allows maintenance to be carried out while under way at sea. Diesel electric is another propulsion system that has been around for a long time, but is becoming more common. By having the engines drive alternators, which supply electricity to motors driving the propellers, gearboxes and clutches can be dispensed with and greater flexibility gained in the positioning of the engines, while still providing the step down in speed required for a medium speed engine to efficiently drive a ships propeller.

The size of the different types of engines is an important factor in selecting what will be installed in a new ship. Slow speed two stroke engines are much taller, but the foot print required- length and width- is smaller than that required for four stroke medium speed diesel engines. As space higher up in passenger ships and ferries is at a premium, these ships tend to use multiple medium speed engines resulting in a longer, lower engine room than that required for two stroke diesel engines. Multiple engine installations also gives greater redundancy in the event of mechanical failure of one or more engines and greater efficiency over a wider range of operating conditions.

Other Propulsion Systems

Many warships built since the 1960s have used gas turbines for propulsion, as have a few passenger ships, like the jetfoil. Most recently, the Queen Mary 2 has had gas turbines installed in addition to diesel engines. Because of their poor thermal efficiency, it is common for ships using them to have diesel engines for cruising with gas turbines reserved for when higher speeds are required. Some warships and a few modern cruise ships have also utilised steam turbines to improve the efficiency of gas turbines in a combined cycle. In such a combined cycle, where waste heat from a gas turbine is used to create steam for driving a steam turbine, thermal efficiency can be the same or slightly greater than that of diesel engines. However, the grade of fuel required for gas turbines is much more expensive than that required for diesel engines so running costs are higher.

A few ships have used nuclear reactors (like Arktika class icebreaker with 75,000 shaft horsepower), but this is not a separate form of propulsion; the reactor heats steam to drive the turbines. Nonetheless, it has caused concerns about safety and waste disposal. It has become usual only in large aircraft carriers, where the space previously used for ship's bunkerage could then be used instead to bunker aviation fuel, and in submarines, where the ability to run submerged at high speed and in relative quiet for long periods holds obvious advantage. A few cruisers have also employed nuclear power; as of 2006, the only ones remaining in service are the Russian Kirov class.

THE MARITIME LAW

Admiralty law usually referred to as maritime law is a distinct body of law which governs maritime questions and offenses. Under conventions of international law, the flag flown by a ship generally determines the source of law to be applied in admiralty cases, regardless of which court has personal jurisdiction over the parties.

Admiralty law was introduced into England by Eleanor of Aquitaine while she was acting as regent for her son King Richard the Lionhearted. She had earlier established admiralty law on the island of Oleron (where it was published as the Rolls of Oleron) in her own lands (but she is often referred to in admiralty law books as "Eleanor of Guyenne"), having learned about it in the eastern Mediterranean while on Crusade with her first husband, King Louis VII of France. In England special courts, admiralty courts handle all admiralty cases. These courts do not use the common law of England, but are civil law courts based upon the Corpus Juris Civilis of Justinian.

In the United States, admiralty is under the jurisdiction of the federal courts. However, admiralty courts in the United States are courts of limited jurisdiction, so state courts have concurrent jurisdiction in admiralty when state law claims are at issue. Moreover, state courts may have jurisdiction in admiralty when the matters being adjudicated are local in nature.

Background

Sea-borne transport being one of the most ancient channels of commerce, rules for resolution of disputes involving maritime trade developed very early in recorded history. Classical sources of this law include the Rhodian law, of which no primary written specimen has survived, but which is alluded to in other legal texts: Roman and Byzantine legal codes, and the customs of the Hanseatic League.

Admiralty law was introduced into England by Eleanor of Aquitaine while she was acting as regent for her son, King Richard the Lionheart. She had earlier established admiralty law on the island of Oleron (where it was published as the Rolls of Oleron) in her own lands (although she is often referred to in admiralty law books as "Eleanor of Guyenne"), having learned about it in the eastern Mediterranean while on Crusade with her first husband, King Louis VII of France. In England, special admiralty courts handle all admiralty cases. These courts do not use the common law of England, but are civil law courts based upon the Corpus Juris Civilis of Justinian.

Admiralty Courts were a prominent feature in causing the American Revolution. For example, the phrase in the Declaration of Independence "For depriving us in many cases, of the benefits of Trial by Jury" refers to the practice of Parliament giving the Admiralty Courts jurisdiction to enforce The Stamp Act in the American Colonies. Because the Stamp Act was unpopular, a colonial jury was unlikely to convict a colonist of its violation. Since Admiralty Courts do not grant trial by jury, a colonist accused of violating the Stamp Act could be tried before a judge of the Admiralty Courts without a jury.

Admiralty law became part of the law of the United States as it was gradually introduced through admiralty cases arising after the adoption of the U.S. Constitution in 1789. Many American lawyers who were prominent in the American Revolution were admiralty and maritime lawyers in their private lives. Those include Alexander Hamilton in New York and John Adams in Massachusetts.

In 1787 Thomas Jefferson, who was then ambassador to France, wrote to James Madison proposing that the U.S. Constitution, then under consideration by the States, be amended to include "trial by jury in all matters of fact triable by the laws of the land [as opposed the law of admiralty] and not by the laws of Nations [i.e. not by the law of admiralty]." The result was the Sixth Amendment to the U.S. Constitution.

International Conventions

Prior to the mid-1970s, most international conventions concerning maritime trade and commerce originated in a private organization of maritime lawyers known as the Comite Maritime International (International Maritime Committee or CMI). Founded in 1897, the CMI was responsible for the drafting of numerous international conventions including the Hague Rules (International Convention on Bills of Lading), the Visby Amendments (amending the Hague Rules), the Salvage Convention and many others. While the CMI continues to function in an advisory capacity, many of its functions have been taken over by the International Maritime Organization, which was established by the United Nations in 1958 but did not become truly effective until about 1974.

The IMO has prepared numerous international conventions concerning maritime safety including the Safety of Life at Sea Convention (SOLAS), the Standards for Training, Certification, and Watchkeeping (STCW), the Collision Regulations (COLREGS), Martime Pollution Regulations (MARPOL), Maritime Search and Rescue Convention (SAR) and others. The United Nations Convention on the Law of the Sea (UNCLOS) defined a treaty regarding protection of the marine environment and various maritime boundaries.

Once adopted, the international conventions are enforced by the individual nations which are signatories, either through their local Coast Guards, or through their courts.

In the United States

Jurisdiction

Article III, Section 2 of the United States Constitution granted original jurisdiction to U.S. federal courts over admiralty and maritime matters. However, most admiralty cases in the United States can be brought in either federal or state court.

The federal and state courts have concurrent jurisdiction over most admiralty and maritime claims pursuant to the terms of a federal statute known as the "Savings to Suitors. Under the Savings to Suitors clause, certain remedies are exclusively limited to being filed in the federal courts. Those include suits seeking to arrest ships to enforce maritime mortgages and liens, petitions to limit a shipowner's liability to the value of a ship after a major accident, and actions seeking to partition ownership of a ship. However, the vast majority of maritime actions, such as suits for damage to cargo, injuries to seamen, collisions between vessels, wake damage, and maritime pollution cases may be brought in either state court or federal court.

In federal courts in the United States, there is generally no right to trial by jury in admiralty cases. Congress has created an exception in seamen's personal injury actions brought under the Jones Act where a jury trial is permitted.

In state courts, the right to trial by jury is determined by the law of the state where the case is brought. Consequently, admiralty cases brought in state courts can be tried before a jury.

Applicable Law

A state court hearing an admiralty or maritime case is required to apply the admiralty and maritime law, even if it conflicts with the law of the state, under a doctrine known as the "reverse-Erie doctrine." The "Erie doctrine" says that federal courts hearing state actions must apply state law. The "reverse-Erie doctrine" says that state courts hearing admiralty cases must apply federal admiralty law. This can make a big difference; for example, U.S. maritime law recognizes the concept of joint and several liability among tortfeasors, while many states do not. Under joint and several liability, where two or more people create a single injury or loss, all are equally liable, even if they only contributed a small amount. A state court hearing an admiralty case would be required to apply the doctrine of joint and several liability even if its state had outlawed the concept.

Here are some basic principles of maritime law in the United States:

Limitation of Shipowner's Liability

One of the unique aspects of maritime law is the ability of a shipowner to limit its liability to the value of a ship after a major accident. An example of the use of the Limitation Act is the sinking of the RMS Titanic in 1912. Even though the Titanic had never been to the United States, upon her sinking the owners rushed into the federal courts in New York to file a limitation of liability proceeding. The Limitation Act provides that if an accident happens due to a circumstance which is beyond the "privity and knowledge" of the ship's owners, the owners can limit their liability to the value of the ship after it sinks.

After the Titanic sank, the only portion of the ship remaining were the life boats which had a collective value of about $3000. The owners of the Titanic were successful in showing that the sinking occurred without their privity and knowledge, and therefore, the families of the deceased passengers, as well as the surviving passengers who lost their personal belongings, were entitled to split the $3000 value of the remaining lifeboats.

In the era of modern communications, continued need for the Limitation Act is questionable. The theory behind the Act was that a shipowner who properly equipped and crewed a ship shouldn't be liable for something that happens when the ship is out of his control. Modern ships are seldom out of the control of their shoreside owners, but the Act remains a viable protection to them.

The Limitation Act doesn't just apply to large ships. It can be used to insulate a motorboat owner from liability when he loans his boat to another who then has an accident. Even jet ski owners have been able to successfully utilize the Limitation Act to insulate themselves from liability.

Cargo Claims

Claims for damage to cargo shipped in international commerce are governed by the Carriage of Goods by Sea Act, which is the U.S. enactment of the Hague Rules. Some of its key features is that a shipowner is liable for cargo damaged from "hook to hook", meaning from loading to discharge, unless it is exonerated under one of 13 exceptions to liability such as "Act of God", inherent nature of the goods, errors in navigation and management of the ship (not the cargo), etc. A shipowner is generally entitled to limit its liability to $500 per package. The statute of limitations is one year.

Personal Injuries to Seamen

Seamen are compensated for injuries sustained aboard ship by three separate concepts: the principle of maintenance and cure, the doctrine of unseaworthiness, and the Jones Act. The principle of maintenance and cure requires a shipowner to pay for medical care, and provide basic living expenses for any seaman injured on a ship, regardless of whether the shipowner is at fault. It is similar in some ways to workers' compensation. The doctrine of unseaworthiness makes a shipowner liable if a seaman is injured because the ship, or any appliance of the ship, is "unseaworthy," meaning defective in some way. The Jones Act incorporates the Federal Employers Liability Act (FELA), which governs injuries to railway workers. A shipowner is liable to a seaman in the same way as a railroad operator is liable to its employees who are injured due to the negligence of the employer. The statute of limitation is 3 years.

Not every worker injured onboard a vessel is a "seaman" entitled to Jones Act, unseaworthiness, and maintenance and cure. To be a seaman a worker must work 30% or more of his time onboard a specific vessel or a fleet of vessels "under common ownership or control." With few exceptions, all non-seamen injured over navigable waters are covered instead by the Longshore and Harbor Workers' Compensation Act, 33 U.S.C. § 901 et seq., a powerful form of workers' compensation.

Maintenance and Cure

The doctrine of maintenance and cure is rooted in the Article VI of the Rules of Oleron promulgated in about 1160 A.D. The obligation to "cure" requires a shipowner to provide medical care, free of charge, to a seaman injured in the service of the ship, until the seaman has reached "maximum medical cure." The concept of "maximum medical cure" is more extensive than the concept "maximum medical improvement." The obligation to "cure" a seaman includes the obligation to provide him with medications and medical devices which improve his ability to function, even if they don't "improve" his actual condition. They may include long term treatments permit him to continue to function well. Common examples include prostheses, wheelchairs, and pain medications.

The obligation of "maintenance" requires the shipowner to provide a seaman with his basic living expenses while he is convalescing. Once a seaman is able to work, he is expected to maintain himself. Consequently, a seaman can lose his right to maintenance, while the obligation to provide cure is ongoing.

Personal Injuries to Passengers

Shipowners owe a duty of reasonable care to passengers. Consequently, passengers who are injured aboard ships may bring suit the same as if they had been injured ashore through the negligence of a third party. The passenger bears the burden of proving that the shipowner was negligent. While the statute of limitations is generally three years, suits against cruise lines must usually be brought within one year because of limitations contained in the passenger ticket. Most cruise line passenger tickets also have provisions requiring that suit to be brought in either Miami, Florida or Seattle, Washington.

Maritime Liens and Mortgages

Banks which loan money to purchase ships, vendors who supply ships with necessaries like fuel and stores, seamen who are due wages, and many others have a lien against the ship to guarantee payment. To enforce the lien, the ship must be arrested or seized. This is one of those remedies which must be brought in federal court and cannot be done in state court.

Salvage and Treasure Salvage

When property is lost at sea and rescued by another, the rescuer is entitled to claim a salvage award on the salved property. There is no "life salvage." All mariners have a duty to save the lives of others in peril without expectation of reward. Consequently salvage law applies only to the saving of property.

There are two types of salvage: contract salvage and pure salvage, which is sometimes referred to as "merit salvage." In contract salvage the owner of the property and salvor enter into a salvage contract prior to the commencement of salvage operations and the amount that the salvor is paid is determined by the contract. The most common salvage contract is called a "Lloyds Open Form Salvage Contract."

In pure salvage, there is no contract between the owner of the goods and the salvor. The relationship is one which is implied by law. The salvor of property under pure salvage must bring his claim for salvage in federal court, which will award salvage based upon the "merit" of the service that was performed.

Pure salvage claims are divided into "high-order" and "low-order" salvage. In high-order salvage, the salvor exposes himself to the risk of injury or damage to his equipment in order to salvage the damaged ship. Examples of high-order salvage are boarding a sinking ship in heavy weather, boarding a ship which is on fire, raising a ship or boat which has already sunk, or towing a ship which is in the surf away from the shore. Low-order salvage occurs where the salvor is exposed to little or no personal risk. Examples of low-order salvage include towing another vessel in calm seas, supplying a vessel with fuel, or pulling a vessel off a sand bar. Salvors performing high order salvage receive substantially greater salvage award than those performing low order salvage.

In both high- and low-order salvage the amount of the salvage award is based first upon the value of the property saved. If nothing is saved, or if additional damages is done, there will be no award. The other factors to be considered are the skills of the salvor, the peril to which the salvaged property was exposed, the value of the property which was risked in effecting the salvage, the amount of time and money expended in the salvage operation etc.

A pure or merit salvage award will seldom exceed 50 percent of the value of the property salved. The exception to that rule is in the case of treasure salvage. Because sunken treasure has generally been lost for hundreds of years, while the original owner (or insurer, if the vessel was insured) continues to have an interest in it, the salvor or finder will generally get the majority of the value of the property.

While sunken ships from the Spanish Main (such as Nuestra Señora de Atocha in the Florida Keys) are the most commonly thought of type of treasure salvage, other types of ships including German submarines from World War II which can hold valuable historical artifacts, American Civil War ships (the USS Maple Leaf in the St. Johns River, and the USS

Monitor in Chesapeake Bay), and sunken merchant ships (the SS Central America off of Cape Hatteras) have all been the subject of treasure salvage awards. Due to refinements in side-scanning sonars, many ships which were previously missing are now being located and treasure salvage is now a less risky endeavor than it was in the past, although it is still highly speculative.

Maritime Law of Common Law Countries

Most of the common law countries (including Pakistan, Singapore, India, Canada, and many other Commonwealth of Nations countries) follow the English statutes and case laws. India still follows the old Victorian law i.e. Admiralty Court Act, 1861 [24 Vict c 10]. Though Pakistan has its own statutes i.e. Admiralty Jurisdiction of High Courts Ordinance, 1980 (Ordinance XLII of 1980), it still follows English case laws. One reason is that the Pakistani law is somewhat replica of old English admiralty law as enunciated in Administration of Justice Act, 1956. The current statute dealing with the Admiralty jurisdiction of the England and Wales High Court is Supreme Court Act, 1981. This statue is based on International Arrest Convention 1952.

Admiralty Courts assume jurisdiction by virtue of the presence of the vessel in its territorial jurisdiction irrespective of whether the vessel is national or not and whether registered or not and wherever the residence or domicile or their owners may be. A vessel is usually arrested by the court to retain jurisidiction. State owned vessels are usually immune from arrest.

CARRIAGE LAW

Carriage of Goods

The bulk of maritime commercial activity involves carriage of goods. The most important document used in this type of transaction is the bill of lading. A bill of lading is basically a contract of carriage but a very special one. Since ocean bills are negotiable, they control possession of the goods and allow for the financing of the movement of merchandise and commodities around the world. The good faith purchaser of a bill of lading, or holder in due course, is given privileged status. The debt is said to be "merged" with the instrument, which means that when the instrument is discharged, so is the underlying debt. It also means that only payment to a holder of the bill or note (someone in physical possession) will discharge the debt. Even payment to a thief will discharge the debt. Creditors of a holder in order to reach an instrument to collect their credits need attach the paper itself as opposed to serving garnishment process on the holder.

The most important mercantile shipping terms for the sale of goods are three: F.O.B., C.I.F. and F.A.S. In a F.O.B. (Free on Board) shipment, the risk passes to buyer at the F.O.B. point. The F.O.B. point can be the seller's factory or warehouse. In that case, the sale price quoted does not include freight which is the responsibility of the buyer as is the risk from the warehouse onward. If, however, the term is F.O.B. point of destination, seller bears the risk during transit and is responsible for payment of the freight. The term F.A.S. (Free Alongside) followed by "vessel" at some specific port is a variation of F.O.B. The sale is consummated when the seller delivers the goods alongside the vessel. The difference between the terms "F.O.B. vessel" and "F.A.S. vessel" is that in the F.O.B. the seller bears the risk until the loading has been completed. C.I.F. stands for Cost, Insurance, Freight, a term followed by the port of destination. "C.I.F. London", for example, would mean that the quoted price would include the price of the goods plus freight up to London and insurance.

A contract for the sale of goods by documents requires the buyer to pay (or accept) drafts on presentation of documents, without inspection of the goods. This type of arrangement is mostly used in international transactions. The goods move under a negotiable bill of lading. In order to get the goods the buyer has to get the bill; he only gets the bill after payment or acceptance. Another important instrument used in international transactions is the letter of credit. That instrument is an official promise by a bank to pay money to the customer for whom it has issued the credit. The buyer is the bank's customer for whose account the letter of credit is issued by the bank (issuer) and the seller is the beneficiary. The reason for the extensive use of letters of credit is that the seller, who is required to ship goods to distant or foreign locations, is protected by the bank's promise more than by the buyer's obligations under the contract.

One of the most important issues dealt with by maritime law is the loss for lost or damaged goods. The basic statute regulating the subject is the Carriage of Goods by Sea Act of 1936 (also known as Cogsa). The thrust of Cogsa, which followed the Harter Act of 1893 and the Hague Rules, was to prevent shipowners from contracting out of the duty to use care to put his vessel in good shape for the voyage, or the duty to properly care for the goods aboard. If he did however provide a seaworthy vessel, he would not be liable for those in charge of the vessel. Cogsa only applies to foreign trade. Its application is also limited to the period running from the time when the goods are loaded until they are discharged from the ship. In those areas where Cogsa does not apply, Harter is still applicable law. Also, pursuant to Cogsa, every bill of lading incorporates the statute. It is allowed to contract out of Cogsa's terms but only by increasing the shipowner's liabilities and not by decreasing them.

Among the duties of a carrier are the exercise of due diligence to 1) make the vessel seaworthy; 2) properly equip, supply and man the vessel; 3) make the holds, cooling compartments and al other areas where the goods are to be stored, fit and safe for their reception, preservation and carriage. Once the due care is given, the law protects the carrier by stating in Section 4 (1) of Cogsa that:

"Neither the carrier nor the ship shall be liable for loss or damage arising or resulting from unseaworthiness unless caused by want of due diligence on the part of the carrier to make the ship seaworthy, and to secure that the ship is properly manned, equipped, and supplied, and to make the holds, refrigerating and cool chambers, and all other parts of the ship in which goods are carried fit and safe for their reception, carriage and preservation in accordance with the provision of paragraph (1) of section 3. Whenever loss or damage has resulted from unseaworthiness, the burden of proving the exercise of due diligence shall be on the carrier or other persons claiming exemption under this section."

Section 4(2) of Cogsa lists the causes for which the carrier shall not be liable. The most important is 4(2)a:

"Act, neglect or default of the master, mariner, pilot, or the servants of the carrier in the navigation or in the management of the ship"

Sections 4(2) b through p list other causes of damagee which are excepted. Fire, for example, is excepted unless caused by the actual fault or privity of the carrier. The perils of the sea are also excepted. A carrier is also not liable for acts of God or, as stated in the statute, " for any accident as to which he can show that it is due to natural causes, directly and exclusively, without human intervention, and that it could not have been prevented by any amount of foresight and pains and care reasonably to be expected of him."

Other exceptions related to human force include: acts of war; acts of public enemies; arrest or restraint of princes; seizure under legal process; quarantine restrictions; riots and civil commotions; strikes; lockouts or stoppages of work; acts or omissions of the owner or shipper of the goods; losses arising from inherent defect of the goods or insufficiency of packing. Section 4(2) provides a catchall exception as follows:

"Neither the carrier nor the ship shall be responsible for loss or damage arising or resulting from.......any other cause arising without the actual fault and privity of the carrier and without the fault or neglect of the agents or servants of the carrier, but the burden of proof shall be on the person claiming the benefit of this exception to show that neither the actual fault or privity of the carrier nor the fault or neglect of the agents or servants of the carrier contributed to the loss or damage."

The effect of deviation is addressed by Cogsa in Section 4(4) to the effect that a deviation does not breach the Act or the carriage contract if it is undertaken to save life or property at sea. a deviation undertaken to load or unload cargo or passengers is not deemed reasonable and is therefore in breach.

Suits based on cargo loss or damage or other breach of the contract of carriage, are within the admiralty jurisdiction. Actions in personam may be brought either in federal court under the admiralty jurisdiction or in state courts under the saving clause. It should be noted, however, that maritime liens arising out of the shipper-carrier relation may be enforced only in federal court under admiralty jurisdiction.

Chapter 2

Nationality and Registration of a Ship

Flag State

Flag State refers to that authority under which a country exercises regulatory control over the Commercial vessel which is registered under its flag. This involves the inspection, certification, and issuance of safety and pollution prevention documents.

In the United States, the Coast Guard under the authority of various federal laws, regulations, and international conventions and treaties, the Officer in Charge Marine Inspections is responsible for the inspection of U.S. flag vessels to ensure compliance with minimum safety and security standards. These inspections are carried out by Marine Inspectors at different times during the life of the vessel, depending on the type of ship and the ship's area of operation. This authority extends to U.S. Flag vessels operating throughout the world.

Port State

Port State refers to that authority under which a country exercises regulatory control over the commercial vessel which is registered under another country's flag. This authority only exists while those vessels are operating within that country's territorial waters. United States territorial waters extend out to 12 miles (22.2 km). The Coast Guard carries out this responsibility under the Port State Control (PSC) Initiative.

The United States Coast Guard verifies that all foreign flagged vessels operating in U.S. waters are in substantial compliance with international conventions, as well as all applicable U.S. laws/regulations and treaties. Coast Guard personnel performing this mission are referred to as Port State Control Officers (PSCO).

FLAG OF CONVENIENCE

A flag of convenience is a flag of one country, flown by a ship owned by a citizen of another country. The ship owner can thereby often avoid taxes and make registration easier; the country providing the flag charges money for that service. The International Transport Workers' Federation (ITF) maintains a list of countries that use their flag for this purpose.

The use of a flag of convenience in order to take advantage of another nation's laxer registration standards is frowned upon for two reasons: The practice causes nations with stricter requirements to lose income and safety/work conditions of shipboard employees may suffer. However, many nations under the International Ship and Port Facility Security Code (ISPS) require minimum standards for vessels entering their national waters. In the case of the United States, the Coast Guard requires inspections on at least an annual basis and may deny entry to American waters based on defects not corrected.

Ships at sea fly a national flag called an ensign. Under conventions of international law, the flag flown by a ship determines the source of law to be applied in admiralty cases, regardless of which court has personal jurisdiction over the parties.

Cheap registration fees, low taxes, and freedom from labor laws or safety standards are motivating factors for many flags of convenience. Fishing boat owners who use a flag of convenience can also ignore their home countries' conservation agreements. To quote William Langewiesche's The Outlaw Sea:

"No one pretends that a ship comes from the home port painted on its stern, or that it has ever been anywhere near. Panama is the largest maritime nation on earth, followed by bloody Liberia, which hardly exists. No coastline is required either. There are ships that hail from La Paz, in landlocked Bolivia. There are ships that hail from the Mongolian desert. Moreover, the registries themselves are rarely based in the countries whose names they carry: Panama is considered to be an old-fashioned "flag" because its consulates handle the paperwork and collect the registration fees, but "Liberia" is run by a company in Virginia, "Cambodia" by another in South Korea, and the proud and independent "Bahamas" by a group in the City of London."

Supporters of flags of convenience argue that where a vessel is engaged in international trade it should be free to register in the jurisdiction which best suits its commercial model. Jurisdictions which are criticised as offering flags of convenience also often have relatively sophisticated maritime codes, and courts which are versed in maritime law and admiralty matters. Registering vessels in such jurisdictions where they can be mortgaged effectively and the mortgagee's property rights respected facilitates the financing of such vessels. Forcing vessels to register in jurisdictions with unsophisticated maritime laws or where mortgaging the vessel is difficult to do effectively, or worse yet, where the vessel becomes vulnerable to compulsory acquisition causes unnecessary disruption and increased expense in an already volatile international shipping market. Critics of the ITF sometimes suggest that the ITF's past militant policies (including the "blacking" of ships using non-unionised labour) has more to do with the drive to using flags of convenience than a desire for cheaper registration fees. In 2004 the ITF said that it would consider whether the ships flagged in the United Kingdom should be deemed to be flying flags of convenience on a "case-by-case" basis, a stance that is very difficult to square with the traditional criticisms of flags of convenience.

Criticisms of flags of convenience are rarely repeated with respect to registration of aircraft, to which similar considerations apply, but which employ fewer people, and form part of a less unionised industry.

THE LAW AND FLAGS

Section 1. General Provisions

Article 86

Application of the Provisions of this Part

The provisions of this Part apply to all parts of the sea that are not included in the exclusive economic zone, in the territorial sea or in the internal waters of a State, or in the archipelagic waters of an archipelagic State. This article does not entail any abridgement of the freedoms enjoyed by all States in the exclusive economic zone in accordance with article 58.

Article 87

Freedom of the High Seas

1. The high seas are open to all States, whether coastal or land-locked. Freedom of the high seas is exercised under the conditions laid down by this Convention and by other rules of international law. It comprises, inter alia, both for coastal and land-locked States:
   (a) freedom of navigation;
   (b) freedom of overflight;
   (c) freedom to lay submarine cables and pipelines, subject to Part VI;
   (d) freedom to construct artificial islands and other installations permitted under international law, subject to Part VI;
   (e) freedom of fishing, subject to the conditions laid down in section 2;
   (f) freedom of scientific research, subject to Parts VI and XIII.
2. These freedoms shall be exercised by all States with due regard for the interests of other States in their exercise of the freedom of the high seas, and also with due regard for the rights under this Convention with respect to activities in the Area.

Article 88

Reservation of the High Seas for Peaceful Purposes

The high seas shall be reserved for peaceful purposes.

Article 89

Invalidity of Claims of Sovereignty Over the High Seas

No State may validly purport to subject any part of the high seas to its sovereignty.

Article 90

Right of Navigation

Every State, whether coastal or land-locked, has the right to sail ships flying its flag on the high seas.

Article 91

Nationality of Ships

1. Every State shall fix the conditions for the grant of its nationality to ships, for the registration of ships in its territory, and for the right to fly its flag. Ships have the nationality of the State whose flag they are entitled to fly. There must exist a genuine link between the State and the ship.
2. Every State shall issue to ships to which it has granted the right to fly its flag documents to that effect.

Article 92

Status of Ships

1. Ships shall sail under the flag of one State only and, save in exceptional cases expressly provided for in international treaties or in this Convention, shall be subject to its exclusive jurisdiction on the high seas. A ship may not change its flag during a voyage or while in a port of call, save in the case of a real transfer of ownership or change of registry.
2. A ship which sails under the flags of two or more States, using them according to convenience, may not

claim any of the nationalities in question with respect to any other State, and may be assimilated to a ship without nationality.

Article 93

Ships Flying the Flag of the United Nations, its Specialized Agencies

The preceding articles do not prejudice the question of ships employed on the official service of the United Nations, its specialized agencies or the International Atomic Energy Agency, flying the flag of the organization.

Article 94

Duties of the Flag State

1. Every State shall effectively exercise its jurisdiction and control in administrative, technical and social matters over ships flying its flag.
2. In particular every State shall:
   - (a) Maintain a register of ships containing the names and particulars of ships flying its flag, except those which are excluded from generally accepted international regulations on account of their small size; and
   - (b) Assume jurisdiction under its internal law over each ship flying its flag and its master, officers and crew in respect of administrative, technical and social matters concerning the ship.
3. Every State shall take such measures for ships flying its flag as are necessary to ensure safety at sea with regard, inter alia, to:
   - (a) the construction, equipment and seaworthiness of ships;
   - (b) the manning of ships, labour conditions and the training of crews, taking into account the applicable international instruments;

(c) the use of signals, the maintenance of communications and the prevention of collisions.

4. Such measures shall include those necessary to ensure:

(a) that each ship, before registration and thereafter at appropriate intervals, is surveyed by a qualified surveyor of ships, and has on board such charts, nautical publications and navigational equipment and instruments as are appropriate for the safe navigation of the ship;

(b) that each ship is in the charge of a master and officers who possess appropriate qualifications, in particular in seamanship, navigation, communications and marine engineering, and that the crew is appropriate in qualification and numbers for the type, size, machinery and equipment of the ship;

(c) that the master, officers and, to the extent appropriate, the crew are fully conversant with and required to observe the applicable international regulations concerning the safety of life at sea, the prevention of collisions, the prevention, reduction and control of marine pollution, and the maintenance of communications by radio.

5. In taking the measures called for in paragraphs 3 and 4 each State is required to conform to generally accepted international regulations, procedures and practices and to take any steps which may be necessary to secure their observance.

6. A State which has clear grounds to believe that proper jurisdiction and control with respect to a ship have not been exercised may report the facts to the flag State. Upon receiving such a report, the flag State shall investigate the matter and, if appropriate, take any action necessary to remedy the situation.

7. Each State shall cause an inquiry to be held by or before a suitably qualified person or persons into every marine casualty or incident of navigation on the high seas involving a ship flying its flag and causing loss of life or serious injury to nationals of another State or serious damage to ships or installations of another State or to the marine environment. The flag State and the other State shall cooperate in the conduct of any inquiry held by that other State into any such marine casualty or incident of navigation.

Article 95

Immunity of Warships on the High Seas

Warships on the high seas have complete immunity from the jurisdiction of any State other than the flag State.

Article 96

Immunity of Ships used only on Government Non-commercial Service

Ships owned or operated by a State and used only on government non-commercial service shall, on the high seas, have complete immunity from the jurisdiction of any State other than the flag State.

Article 97

Penal Jurisdiction in Matters of Collision or any other Incident of Navigation

1. In the event of a collision or any other incident of navigation concerning a ship on the high seas, involving the penal or disciplinary responsibility of the master or of any other person in the service of the ship, no penal or disciplinary proceedings may be instituted against such person except before the judicial or administrative authorities either of the flag State or of the State of which such person is a national.

2. In disciplinary matters, the State which has issued a master's certificate or a certificate of competence or licence shall alone be competent, after due legal process, to pronounce the withdrawal of such certificates, even if the holder is not a national of the State which issued them.
3. No arrest or detention of the ship, even as a measure of investigation, shall be ordered by any authorities other than those of the flag State.

Article 98

Duty to Render Assistance

1. Every State shall require the master of a ship flying its flag, in so far as he can do so without serious danger to the ship, the crew or the passengers:
   (a) to render assistance to any person found at sea in danger of being lost;
   (b) to proceed with all possible speed to the rescue of persons in distress, if informed of their need of assistance, in so far as such action may reasonably be expected of him;
   (c) after a collision, to render assistance to the other ship, its crew and its passengers and, where possible, to inform the other ship of the name of his own ship, its port of registry and the nearest port at which it will call.
2. Every coastal State shall promote the establishment, operation and maintenance of an adequate and effective search and rescue service regarding safety on and over the sea and, where circumstances so require, by way of mutual regional arrangements cooperate with neighbouring States for this purpose.

Article 99

Prohibition of the Transport of Slaves

Every State shall take effective measures to prevent and punish the transport of slaves in ships authorized to fly its flag and to prevent the unlawful use of its flag for that purpose. Any slave taking refuge on board any ship, whatever its flag, shall ipso facto be free.

Article 100

Duty to Cooperate in the Repression of Piracy

All States shall cooperate to the fullest possible extent in the repression of piracy on the high seas or in any other place outside the jurisdiction of any State.

Article 101

Definition of Piracy

Piracy consists of any of the following acts:

(a) any illegal acts of violence or detention, or any act of depredation, committed for private ends by the crew or the passengers of a private ship or a private aircraft, and directed:

  (i) on the high seas, against another ship or aircraft, or against persons or property on board such ship or aircraft;

  (ii) against a ship, aircraft, persons or property in a place outside the jurisdiction of any State;

(b) Any act of voluntary participation in the operation of a ship or of an aircraft with knowledge of facts making it a pirate ship or aircraft;

(c) Any act of inciting or of intentionally facilitating an act described in subparagraph (a) or (b).

Article 102

Piracy by a Warship, Government Ship or Government Aircraft whose Crew has Mutinied

The acts of piracy, as defined in article 101, committed by a warship, government ship or government aircraft whose crew has mutinied and taken control of the ship or aircraft are assimilated to acts committed by a private ship or aircraft.

Article 103

Definition of a Pirate Ship or Aircraft

A ship or aircraft is considered a pirate ship or aircraft if it is intended by the persons in dominant control to be used for the purpose of committing one of the acts referred to in article 101. The same applies if the ship or aircraft has been used to commit any such act, so long as it remains under the control of the persons guilty of that act.

Article 104

Retention or Loss of the Nationality of a Pirate Ship or Aircraft

A ship or aircraft may retain its nationality although it has become a pirate ship or aircraft. The retention or loss of nationality is determined by the law of the State from which such nationality was derived.

Article 105

Seizure of a Pirate Ship or Aircraft

On the high seas, or in any other place outside the jurisdiction of any State, every State may seize a pirate ship or aircraft, or a ship or aircraft taken by piracy and under the control of pirates, and arrest the persons and seize the property on board. The courts of the State which carried out the seizure may decide upon the penalties to be imposed, and may also determine the action to be taken with regard to the ships, aircraft or property, subject to the rights of third parties acting in good faith.

Article 106

Liability for Seizure without Adequate Grounds

Where the seizure of a ship or aircraft on suspicion of piracy has been effected without adequate grounds, the State making the seizure shall be liable to the State the nationality of which is possessed by the ship or aircraft for any loss or damage caused by the seizure.

Article 107

Ships and Aircraft Which are Entitled to Seize on Account of Piracy

A seizure on account of piracy may be carried out only by warships or military aircraft, or other ships or aircraft clearly marked and identifiable as being on government service and authorized to that effect.

Article 108

Illicit Traffic in Narcotic Drugs or Psychotropic Substances

1. All States shall cooperate in the suppression of illicit traffic in narcotic drugs and psychotropic substances engaged in by ships on the high seas contrary to international conventions.
2. Any State which has reasonable grounds for believing that a ship flying its flag is engaged in illicit traffic in narcotic drugs or psychotropic substances may request the cooperation of other States to suppress such traffic.

Article 109

Unauthorized Broadcasting from the High Seas

1. All States shall cooperate in the suppression of unauthorized broadcasting from the high seas.
2. For the purposes of this Convention, "unauthorized broadcasting" means the transmission of sound radio or television broadcasts from a ship or installation on the high seas intended for reception by the general public contrary to international regulations, but excluding the transmission of distress calls.
3. Any person engaged in unauthorized broadcasting may be prosecuted before the court of:
   (a) the flag State of the ship;
   (b) the State of registry of the installation;
   (c) the State of which the person is a national;

(d) any State where the transmissions can be received; or

(e) any State where authorized radio communication is suffering interference.

4. On the high seas, a State having jurisdiction in accordance with paragraph 3 may, in conformity with article 110, arrest any person or ship engaged in unauthorized broadcasting and seize the broadcasting apparatus.

Article 110

Right of Visit

1. Except where acts of interference derive from powers conferred by treaty, a warship which encounters on the high seas a foreign ship, other than a ship entitled to complete immunity in accordance with articles 95 and 96, is not justified in boarding it unless there is reasonable ground for suspecting that:

(a) the ship is engaged in piracy;

(b) the ship is engaged in the slave trade;

(c) the ship is engaged in unauthorized broadcasting and the flag State of the warship has jurisdiction under article 109;

(d) the ship is without nationality; or

(e) though flying a foreign flag or refusing to show its flag, the ship is, in reality, of the same nationality as the warship.

2. In the cases provided for in paragraph 1, the warship may proceed to verify the ship's right to fly its flag. To this end, it may send a boat under the command of an officer to the suspected ship. If suspicion remains after the documents have been checked, it may proceed to a further examination on board the ship, which must be carried out with all possible consideration.

3. If the suspicions prove to be unfounded, and provided that the ship boarded has not committed

any act justifying them, it shall be compensated for any loss or damage that may have been sustained.

4. These provisions apply mutatis mutandis to military aircraft.
5. These provisions also apply to any other duly authorized ships or aircraft clearly marked and identifiable as being on government service.

Article 111

Right of Hot Pursuit

1. The hot pursuit of a foreign ship may be undertaken when the competent authorities of the coastal State have good reason to believe that the ship has violated the laws and regulations of that State. Such pursuit must be commenced when the foreign ship or one of its boats is within the internal waters, the archipelagic waters, the territorial sea or the contiguous zone of the pursuing State, and may only be continued outside the territorial sea or the contiguous zone if the pursuit has not been interrupted. It is not necessary that, at the time when the foreign ship within the territorial sea or the contiguous zone receives the order to stop, the ship giving the order should likewise be within the territorial sea or the contiguous zone. If the foreign ship is within a contiguous zone, as defined in article 33, the pursuit may only be undertaken if there has been a violation of the rights for the protection of which the zone was established.
2. The right of hot pursuit shall apply mutatis mutandis to violations in the exclusive economic zone or on the continental shelf, including safety zones around continental shelf installations, of the laws and regulations of the coastal State applicable in accordance with this Convention to the exclusive economic zone or the continental shelf, including such safety zones.

3. The right of hot pursuit ceases as soon as the ship pursued enters the territorial sea of its own State or of a third State.
4. Hot pursuit is not deemed to have begun unless the pursuing ship has satisfied itself by such practicable means as may be available that the ship pursued or one of its boats or other craft working as a team and using the ship pursued as a mother ship is within the limits of the territorial sea, or, as the case may be, within the contiguous zone or the exclusive economic zone or above the continental shelf. The pursuit may only be commenced after a visual or auditory signal to stop has been given at a distance which enables it to be seen or heard by the foreign ship.
5. The right of hot pursuit may be exercised only by warships or military aircraft, or other ships or aircraft clearly marked and identifiable as being on government service and authorized to that effect.
6. Where hot pursuit is effected by an aircraft:
   (a) the provisions of paragraphs 1 to 4 shall apply mutatis mutandis;
   (b) the aircraft giving the order to stop must itself actively pursue the ship until a ship or another aircraft of the coastal State, summoned by the aircraft, arrives to take over the pursuit, unless the aircraft is itself able to arrest the ship. It does not suffice to justify an arrest outside the territorial sea that the ship was merely sighted by the aircraft as an offender or suspected offender, if it was not both ordered to stop and pursued by the aircraft itself or other aircraft or ships which continue the pursuit without interruption.
7. The release of a ship arrested within the jurisdiction of a State and escorted to a port of that State for the purposes of an inquiry before the competent

authorities may not be claimed solely on the ground that the ship, in the course of its voyage, was escorted across a portion of the exclusive economic zone or the high seas, if the circumstances rendered this necessary.

8. Where a ship has been stopped or arrested outside the territorial sea in circumstances which do not justify the exercise of the right of hot pursuit, it shall be compensated for any loss or damage that may have been thereby sustained.

Article 112

Right to Lay Submarine Cables and Pipelines

1. All States are entitled to lay submarine cables and pipelines on the bed of the high seas beyond the continental shelf.
2. Article 79, paragraph 5, applies to such cables and pipelines.

Article113

Breaking or Injury of a Submarine Cable or Pipeline

Every State shall adopt the laws and regulations necessary to provide that the breaking or injury by a ship flying its flag or by a person subject to its jurisdiction of a submarine cable beneath the high seas done wilfully or through culpable negligence, in such a manner as to be liable to interrupt or obstruct telegraphic or telephonic communications, and similarly the breaking or injury of a submarine pipeline or high-voltage power cable, shall be a punishable offence. This provision shall apply also to conduct calculated or likely to result in such breaking or injury. However, it shall not apply to any break or injury caused by persons who acted merely with the legitimate object of saving their lives or their ships, after having taken all necessary precautions to avoid such break or injury.

Article 114

Breaking or injury by owners of a submarine cable or pipeline of another submarine cable or pipeline.

Every State shall adopt the laws and regulations necessary to provide that, if persons subject to its jurisdiction who are the owners of a submarine cable or pipeline beneath the high seas, in laying or repairing that cable or pipeline, cause a break in or injury to another cable or pipeline, they shall bear the cost of the repairs.

Article 115

Indemnity for Loss Incurred in Avoiding Injury to a Submarine Cable or Pipeline

Every State shall adopt the laws and regulations necessary to ensure that the owners of ships who can prove that they have sacrificed an anchor, a net or any other fishing gear, in order to avoid injuring a submarine cable or pipeline, shall be indemnified by the owner of the cable or pipeline, provided that the owner of the ship has taken all reasonable precautionary measures beforehand.

Section 2. Conservation and Management of the living Resources of the High Seas

Article 116

Right to Fish on the high Seas

All States have the right for their nationals to engage in fishing on the high seas subject to:

(a) their treaty obligations;

(b) the rights and duties as well as the interests of coastal States provided for, inter alia, in article 63, paragraph 2, and articles 64 to 67; and

(c) the provisions of this section.

Article 117

Duty of States to Adopt with Respect to their Nationals Measures for the Conservation of the Living Resources of the high Seas

All States have the duty to take, or to cooperate with other States in taking, such measures for their respective nationals as may be necessary for the conservation of the living resources of the high seas.

Article118

Cooperation of States in the Conservation and Management of Living Resources

States shall cooperate with each other in the conservation and management of living resources in the areas of the high seas. States whose nationals exploit identical living resources, or different living resources in the same area, shall enter into negotiations with a view to taking the measures necessary for the conservation of the living resources concerned. They shall, as appropriate, cooperate to establish subregional or regional fisheries organizations to this end.

Article119

Conservation of the Living Resources of the high Seas

1. In determining the allowable catch and establishing other conservation measures for the living resources in the high seas, States shall:
   (a) take measures which are designed, on the best scientific evidence available to the States concerned, to maintain or restore populations of harvested species at levels which can produce the maximum sustainable yield, as qualified by relevant environmental and economic factors, including the special requirements of developing States, and taking into account fishing patterns, the interdependence of stocks and any generally recommended international minimum standards, whether subregional, regional or global;
   (b) take into consideration the effects on species associated with or dependent upon harvested species with a view to maintaining or restoring populations of such associated or dependent species above levels at which their reproduction may become seriously threatened.
2. Available scientific information, catch and fishing effort statistics, and other data relevant to the

conservation of fish stocks shall be contributed and exchanged on a regular basis through competent international organizations, whether subregional, regional or global, where appropriate and with participation by all States concerned.

3. States concerned shall ensure that conservation measures and their implementation do not discriminate in form or in fact against the fishermen of any State.

Article120

Marine Mammals

Article 65 also applies to the conservation and management of marine mammals in the high seas.

DIFFERENT SEA FLAGS

The United States Flag

The flag of the United States was first adopted by resolution of the Continental Congress, June 14, 1777:

Resolved, That the flag of the thirteen United States be thirteen stripes, alternate red and white: that the union be thirteen stars, white in a blue field, representing a new constellation.

This 13-star, 13-stripe design remained in effect until 1795, when two additional stars and stripes were added to mark the admission to the Union of Vermont and Kentucky. From that point on, it was unchanged, despite the admission of further states, until 1818, when the number had reached 20. After much debate, Congress decided to abandon the idea of adding a stripe for each new state and instead adopted the law that determines the design of the flag today:

Be it enacted by the Senate and House of Representatives of the United States of America, in Congress assembled, That from and after the fourth day of July next, the flag of the United States be thirteen horizontal stripes, alternate red and white: that the union be twenty stars, white in a blue field.

Sec. 2. And be it further enacted, That on the admission of every new state into the Union, one star be added to the union of the flag; and that such addition shall take effect on the fourth day of July then next succeeding such admission.

Act of April 4, 1818, ch. 34, 3 Stat. 415

Although it has been reenacted several times in connection with the codification of federal statutes (most recently in 1947), the substance of the 1818 law is still in effect and may be found in Title 4, United States Code, Sections 1 and 2:

Sec. 1. Flag; stripes and stars on. The flag of the United States shall be thirteen horizontal stripes, alternate red and white; and the union of the flag shall be forty-eight stars, white in a blue field.

Sec. 2. Same; additional stars. On the admission of a new State into the Union one star shall be added to the union of the flag; and such addition shall take effect on the fourth day of July then next succeeding such admission.

It may be noted that the statute gives relatively little guidance on the precise design of the flag: the correct proportions between hoist and fly, the size of the canton (union), the arrangement of the stars, the shades of red and blue, or even whether the stripes are seven red and six white or vice versa. Traditionally, there was great variety in these aspects of flag design, with only the Navy, Army, and federal civilian departments subject to more precise regulation, which they issued in the form of departmental orders and directives. The earliest of these was a circular from the Board of Navy Commissioners in 1818 prescribing the arrangement of the stars and the sequence of the stripes for the 20-star ensign enacted by Congress that year. In the early 20th century, several officers noted the desirability of a single standard design and a set of standard flag sizes for government use, and in 1912 President Taft issued an executive order setting 10:19 as the standard ratio for hoisted flags and prescribing the precise sizes and arrangements of the flag's component parts. Since then, each time a new state is admitted, a new executive order is issued, the one currently in effect being President Eisenhower's Executive Order No. 10834 of August. 21, 1959. The color shades used in flags procured for government and military use are set by a federal procurement specification issued by the General Services Administration.

There is some question whether the requirements of the executive order apply outside the Executive Branch of the Federal Government. In 1998, Congress added to the Flag Code (Title 4, U.S. Code, Sec. 5 et seq) the proviso that "The flag of the United States for the purpose of this chapter shall be defined according to sections 1 and 2 of this title and Executive Order 10834 issued pursuant thereto." But this language on its face would rule most actual U.S. flags out of coverage by the Flag Code, since very few flags in public use conform to the 10:19 proportions set by the Executive Order. Clearly Congress cannot have intended that due respect and honor need not be paid to a Stars and Stripes manufactured in four by six or three by five foot sizes. I conclude from this that, notwithstanding this addition to the Code, private citizens and agencies outside the Federal Executive Branch remain at liberty to use flags of any design consistent with the terms of the 1818 law if they so desire.

Sea Flags in International Law

The display of national flags on the high seas is regulated by customary international law, articles 90-94 of the UN Convention on the Law of the Sea (to which the United States is not a party), and article 5 of the 1958 Geneva Convention on the High Seas, "each State shall fix the conditions for the grant of its nationality to ships, for the registration of ships in its territory, and for the right to fly its flag." Further, "each State shall issue to ships to which it has granted the right to fly its flag documents to that effect." Flying a country's flag constitutes a claim by the vessel flying it that it possesses the nationality of the flag (NWP 1-14M, The Commander's Handbook on the Law of Naval Operations), and therefore, as the U.S. District Court for Oregon ruled in the case of The Fideliter in 1869, "it is of importance to all maritime powers that the national character borne by a ship [i.e., in the flag she displays] should be her true character" (8 F.Cas. 1177). Accordingly, most countries have implemented the obligations in the by explicit legislation.

Sea Flags in U.S. Domestic Law

Unlike most other countries, the right of American ships and boats to fly the American flag is not explicitly spelled out by law or regulation. It stems rather from a combination of the laws determining what constitutes a vessel with American nationality, judicial precedent, and the customary international law that gives vessels of a particular nationality the right to display that flag.

The first law governing the nationality of vessels in the United States, "An Act for Registering and Clearing Vessels" (1 Stat. 55) was enacted on September 1, 1789. It provided that only a ship built in the United States, owned by an American citizen, and under the command of an American master could be registered, and being registered "shall be deemed and taken to be, and denominated, a ship or vessel of the United States." Three years later, "An Act Concerning the Registering and Recording of Ships or Vessels" (1 Stat. 287) added that registered vessels of the United States were "entitled to the benefits and privileges appertaining to such ships or vessels." Under customary international law, one of those privileges is flying the United States flag.

Under the current statutory authority on documentation of American vessels, the Vessel Documentation Act of 1980, ships and boats of more than five measurement tons are eligible to be documented by the U.S. Coast Guard. The Coast Guard considers that documentation to provide authoritative evidence of a vessel's U.S. nationality. Not all vessels over five tons are required to be documented, however; those not involved in trade are exempt.

What, then, of the right to fly the flag aboard undocumented vessels, whether above or below the five-ton threshold? The Assistant Attorney General of the United

States, arguing the case of Billings v. United States before the Supreme Court in 1914, stated that "A yacht belonging to a citizen of the United States, even though not a vessel of the United States in the sense that it is entitled to registry or enrollment, yet flies the American flag, and is the object of peculiar protection by the United States" (232 U.S. 261). Furthermore, the right of free expression guaranteed by the first amendment to the Constitution would also guarantee to any U.S. citizen the right to fly the American (or any other) flag.

Sea Flags and the Law of Naval Warfare

According to The Commander's Handbook on the Law of Naval Operations, international law defines a warship as a ship belonging to the armed forces of a nation bearing the external markings distinguishing the character and nationality of such ships, under the command of a commissioned officer, and manned by a crew under regular military discipline. Most countries use flags, at least in part, as the external markings required. In the United States Navy and Coast Guard, these "distinctive markings" are the commission pennant, command pennant, or admiral's flag; the Coast Guard ensign in the case of a Coast Guard cutter; and the Geneva Convention Red Cross flag in the case of a hospital ship.

During wartime, if a vessel operates under an enemy flag, it by definition possesses "enemy character" and may be attacked as an enemy ship. By contrast, flying a neutral ship is not a definitive proof of a ship's neutral character, as an enemy ship may be flying a neutral flag as a ruse. For this reason, one of the rights of a belligerent warship is the right of "visit and search." There are specific rules on how this right is exercised, including the requirement that the warship exercising the right hoist its national flag before summoning the suspect vessel to lie to for boarding. If a neutral merchant ship, the summoned vessel is required to follow instructions and display her colors as well. If it is in fact an enemy ship and tries to get away, it is subject to attack. Refusing to heed the instructions of a warship under these conditions is tantamount to an admission of enemy status and entitles the warship to use force.

As in the days of sail, an enemy warship signals its readiness to surrender by "striking its colors," that is, hauling down her national ensign. Once an enemy warship "has clearly indicated a readiness to surrender," the attack must be discontinued. One may not fire upon a ship that has struck its colors.

False Colours

In warfare at sea, it is permissible for a belligerent warship to fly the flag of a country other than its own in order to deceive an enemy into believing that it is neutral or even a ship of the enemy's own navy.

White Flag (Flag of Truce)

In addition, customary international law recognizes that a white flag indicates a request for a cease-fire, negotiation, or surrender. Use of the white flag to gain a military advantage is an act of perfidy under the laws of war. In the naval context, as explained in NTP-13(B), Flags, Pennants and Customs:

When displayed from any conspicuous place of hoist, [the flag of truce] indicates a desire to send a communication, but the truce does not exist until the hoist has been replied to. A belligerent may decline to receive the flag of truce. If blank guns are fired while a flag of truce is displayed, the ship, boat or party nearing it must stop and not approach nearer. Bearers of the flag of truce are inviolable provided they do not act improperly. Should they do so, or should the flag be used improperly to obtain information, the bearers may become subject to capture and punished as spies.

Cartel ships, vessels used to transport exchanged prisoners of war or to carry envoys, are identified by the display of flags as mutually agreed by the belligerent parties. This display normally includes flying the flag of truce at some specified point of hoist on the cartel ship.

Geneva Convention Flags (Red Cross, Red Crescent, etc.)

Under the 1949 Geneva Conventions and previous international agreements, a white flag with a red cross (or, in the case of Islamic countries, a red crescent) is the recognized symbol of protected medical and religious persons and activities. Ships and installations flying these flags or otherwise marked with these symbols are exempt from attack. Their misuse in order to injure, kill, or capture the enemy is an act of perfidy under the laws of warfare.

Foreign Flags on U.S. Ships

Courtesy Ensigns

Many countries require either as a matter law or of customary practice that foreign vessels in their territorial waters display the host country's flag. This flag is known as a "courtesy ensign." When a host country has a merchant ensign that differs from its national flag used ashore, it is the merchant ensign that is displayed as the courtesy ensign. According to The Commander's Handbook on the Law of Naval Operations, however, "a warship cannot be required to fly the flag of the host nation." U.S. policy is that public vessels, including warships as well as civilian-manned ships belonging to the Military Sealift Command and other U.S. government vessels, enjoy sovereign immune status, that they are exempt from the jurisdiction of any other state. Because complying with a coastal state's regulations purporting to require the display of its flag in its waters or ports could be construed as an admission that the U.S. public vessel is subject to the coastal state's jurisdiction, all U.S. public vessels are forbidden from flying courtesy ensigns.

Foreign Ensigns While Rendering Honors

As described at the page on Navy flag ceremonies, a Navy or Coast Guard ship firing a salute in honor of a foreign country or a foreign officer or dignitary does fly that country's naval ensign at a masthead as prescribed by Navy Regulations. This practice is sometimes misinterpreted as a violation of the U.S. Flag Code, as it seems to involve placing a foreign flag above that of the United States. In fact, the Flag Code has no bearing on naval flag practice; by its own terms the Flag Code applies only to "civilians or civilian groups or organizations as may not be required to conform with regulations promulgated by one or more executive departments of the Government of the United States." Furthermore, the Flag Code speaks of displaying a foreign flag "equal, above, or in a position of superior prominence or honor to, or in place of" the American flag. On a ship, the place of superior prominence and honor is the flagstaff at the stern (when not under way) or the gaff (when under way). Any masthead is a place of inferior honor to either of these. Moreover, both the Coast Guard and the Navy have stated that "above" in the nautical context means at a higher level at the same point of hoist, given the distinctive arrangement of the masts and rigging used for nautical flag display.

Dressing and Full-Dressing in Honor of Foreign Festivities

As with salutes, a ship that is dressed or full-dressed for a foreign festivity or solemnity flies that country's naval ensign at the head of the mainmast. As with flags displayed for salutes, this practice does not contravene the Flag Code's prohibition against displaying a foreign flag "above" the American flag, whether the ship dressed is a warship or a merchant vessel.

UNITED NATIONS CONVENTION ON CONDITIONS FOR REGISTRATION OF SHIPS

Recalling General Assembly resolution 35/56 of 5 December 1980, the annex to which contains the International Development Strategy for the Third United Nations Development Decade, which called, inter alia , in paragraph 128, for an increase in the participation by developing countries in world transport of international trade.

Recalling also that according to the 1958 Geneva Convention on the High Seas and the 1982 United Nations

Convention on the Law of the Sea there must exist a genuine link between a ship and a flag State and conscious of the duties of the flag State to exercise effectively its jurisdiction and control over ships flying its flag in accordance with the principle of the genuine link.

Believing that to this end a flag State should have a competent and adequate national maritime administration.

Believing also that in order to exercise its control function effectively a flag State should ensure that those who are responsible for the management and operation of a ship on its register are readily identifiable and accountable.

Believing further that measures to make persons responsible for ships more readily identifiable and accountable could assist in the task of combating maritime fraud.

Reaffirming, without prejudice to this Convention, that each State shall fix the conditions for the grant of its nationality to ships, for the registration of ships in its territory and for the right to fly its flag.

Prompted by the desire among sovereign States to resolve in a spirit of mutual understanding and co-operation all issues relating to the conditions for the grant of nationality to, and for the registration of, ships.

Considering that nothing in this Convention shall be deemed to prejudice any provisions in the national laws and regulations of the Contracting Parties to this Convention, which exceed the provisions contained herein.

Recognizing the competences of the specialized agencies and other institutions of the United Nations system as contained in their respective constitutional instruments, taking into account arrangements which may have been concluded between the United Nations and the agencies, and between individual agencies and institutions in specific fields, Have agreed as follows:

Article 1

Objectives

For the purpose of ensuring or, as the case may be, strengthening the genuine link between a State and ships flying its flag, and in order to exercise effectively its jurisdiction and control over such ships with regard to identification and accountability of shipowners and operators as well as with regard to administrative, technical, economic and social matters, a flag State shall apply the provisions contained in this Convention.

Article 2

Definitions

For the purposes of this Convention:

"Ship" means any self-propelled sea-going vessel used in international seaborne trade for the transport of goods, passengers, or both with the exception of vessels of less than 500 gross registered tons;

"Flag State" means a State whose flag a ship flies and is entitled to fly;

"Owner" or "shipowner" means, unless clearly indicated otherwise, any natural or juridical person recorded in the register of ships of the State of registration as an owner of a ship;

"Operator" means the owner or bareboat charterer, or any other natural or juridical person to whom the responsibilities of the owner or bareboat charterer have been formally assigned;

"State of registration" means the State in whose register of ships a ship has been entered;

"Register of ships" means the official register or registers in which particulars referred to in article 11 of this Convention are recorded;

"National maritime administration" means any State authority or agency which is established by the State of registration in accordance with its legislation and which, pursuant to that legislation, is responsible, inter alia , for the implementation of international agreements concerning maritime transport and for the application of rules and standards concerning ships under its jurisdiction and control;

"Bareboat charter" means a contract for the lease of a ship, for a stipulated period of time, by virtue of which the lessee has complete possession and control of the ship, including the right to appoint the master and crew of the ship, for the duration of the lease;

"Labour-supplying country" means a country which provides seafarers for service on a ship flying the flag of another country.

Article 3

Scope of Application

This Convention shall apply to all ships as defined in article 2.

Article 4

General Provisions

1. Every State, whether coastal or land-locked, has the right to sail ships flying its flag on the high seas.
2. Ships have the nationality of the State whose flag they are entitled to fly.
3. Ships shall sail under the flag of one State only.
4. No ships shall be entered in the registers of ships of two or more States at a time, subject to the provisions of paragraphs 4 and 5 of article 11 and to article 12.
5. A ship may not change its flag during a voyage or while in a port of call, save in the case of a real transfer of ownership or change of registry.

Article 5

National Maritime Administration

1. The flag State shall have a competent and adequate national maritime administration, which shall be subject to its jurisdiction and control.

2. The flag State shall implement applicable international rules and standards concerning, in particular, the safety of ships and persons on board and the prevention of pollution of the marine environment.
3. The maritime administration of the flag State shall ensure:
   (a) That ships flying the flag of such State comply with its laws and regulations concerning registration of ships and with applicable international rules and standards concerning, in particular, the safety of ships and persons on board and the prevention of pollution of the marine environment;
   (b) That ships flying the flag of such State are periodically surveyed by its authorized surveyors in order to ensure compliance with applicable international rules and standards;
   (c) That ships flying the flag of such State carry on board documents, in particular those evidencing the right to fly its flag and other valid relevant documents, including those required by international conventions to which the State of registration is a Party;
   (d) That the owners of ships flying the flag of such State comply with the principles of registration of ships in accordance with the laws and regulations of such State and the provisions of this Convention.
4. The State of registration shall require all the appropriate information necessary for full identification and accountability concerning ships flying its flag.

Article 6

Identification and Accountability

1. The State of registration shall enter in its register of ships, inter alia , information concerning the ship and

its owner or owners. Information concerning the operator, when the operator is not the owner, should be included in the register of ships or in the official record of operators to be maintained in the office of the Registrar or be readily accessible to him, in accordance with the laws and regulations of the State of registration. The State of registration shall issue documentation as evidence of the registration of the ship.

2. The State of registration shall take such measures as are necessary to ensure that the owner or owners, the operator or operators, or any other person or persons who can be held accountable for the management and operation of ships flying its flag can be easily identified by persons having a legitimate interest in obtaining such information.
3. Registers of ships should be available to those with a legitimate interest in obtaining information contained therein, in accordance with the laws and regulations of the flag State.
4. A State should ensure that ships flying its flag carry documentation including information about the identity of the owner or owners, the operator or operators or the person or persons accountable for the operation of such ships, and make available such information to port State authorities.
5. Log-books should be kept on all ships and retained for a reasonable period after the date of the last entry, notwithstanding any change in a ship's name, and should be available for inspection and copying by persons having a legitimate interest in obtaining such information, in accordance with the laws and regulations of the flag State. In the event of a ship being sold and its registration being changed to another State, log-books relating to the period before such sale should be retained and should be available for inspection and copying by persons having a

legitimate interest in obtaining such information, in accordance with the laws and regulations of the former flag State.

6. A State shall take necessary measures to ensure that ships it enters in its register of ships have owners or operators who are adequately identifiable for the purpose of ensuring their full accountability.
7. A State should ensure that direct contact between owners of ships flying its flag and its government authorities is not restricted.

Article 7

Participation by Nationals in the Ownership and/or Manning of Ships

With respect to the provisions concerning manning and ownership of ships as contained in paragraphs 1 and 2 of article 8 and paragraphs 1 to 3 of article 9, respectively, and without prejudice to the application of any other provisions of this Convention, a State of registration has to comply either with the provisions of paragraphs 1 and 2 of article 8 or with the provisions of paragraphs 1 to 3 of article 9, but may comply with both.

Article 8

Ownership of Ships

1. Subject to the provisions of article 7, the flag State shall provide in its laws and regulations for the ownership of ships flying its flag.
2. Subject to the provisions of article 7, in such laws and regulations the flag State shall include appropriate provisions for participation by that State or its nationals as owners of ships flying its flag or in the ownership of such ships and for the level of such participation. These laws and regulations should be sufficient to permit the flag State to exercise effectively its jurisdiction and control over ships flying its flag.

Article 9

Manning of Ships

1. Subject to the provisions of article 7, a State of registration, when implementing this Convention, shall observe the principle that a satisfactory part of the complement consisting of officers and crew of ships flying its flag be nationals or persons domiciled or lawfully in permanent residence in that State.
2. Subject to the provisions of article 7 and in pursuance of the goal set out in paragraph 1 of this article, and in taking necessary measures to this end, the State of registration shall have regard to the following:
   (a) the availability of qualified seafarers within the State of registration;
   (b) multilateral or bilateral agreements or other types of arrangements valid and enforceable pursuant to the legislation of the State of registration;
   (c) the sound and economically viable operation of its ships.
3. The State of registration should implement the provision of paragraph 1 of this article on a ship, company or fleet basis.
4. The State of registration, in accordance with its laws and regulations, may allow persons of other nationalities to serve on board ships flying its flag in accordance with the relevant provisions of this Convention.
5. In pursuance of the goal set out in paragraph 1 of this article, the State of registration should, in co-operation with shipowners, promote the education and training of its nationals or persons domiciled or lawfully in permanent residence within its territory.
6. The State of registration shall ensure:
   (a) that the manning of ships flying its flag is of such a level and competence as to ensure compliance

with applicable international rules and standards, in particular those regarding safety at sea;

(b) that the terms and conditions of employment on board ships flying its flag are in conformity with applicable international rules and standards;

(c) that adequate legal procedures exist for the settlement of civil disputes between seafarers employed on ships flying its flag and their employers;

(d) that nationals and foreign seafarers have equal access to appropriate legal processes to secure their contractual rights in their relations with their employers.

Article 10

Role of flag States in respect of the management of shipowning companies and ships

1. The State of registration, before entering a ship in its register of ships, shall ensure that the shipowning company or a subsidiary shipowning company is established and/or has its principal place of business within its territory in accordance with its laws and regulations.
2. Where the shipowning company or a subsidiary shipowning company or the principal place of business of the shipowning company is not established in the flag State, the latter shall ensure, before entering a ship in its register of ships, that there is a representative or management person who shall be a national of the flag State, or be domiciled therein. Such a representative or management person may be a natural or juridical person who is duly established or incorporated in the flag State, as the case may be, in accordance with its laws and regulations, and duly empowered to act on the shipowner's behalf and account. In particular, this representative or management person should be

available for any legal process and to meet the shipowner's responsibilities in accordance with the laws and regulations of the State of registration.

3. The State of registration should ensure that the person or persons accountable for the management and operation of a ship flying its flag are in a position to meet the financial obligations that may arise from the operation of such a ship to cover risks which are normally insured in international maritime transportation in respect of damage to third parties. To this end the State of registration should ensure that ships flying its flag are in a position to provide at all times documents evidencing that an adequate guarantee, such as appropriate insurance or any other equivalent means, has been arranged.

Furthermore, the State of registration should ensure that an appropriate mechanism, such as a maritime lien, mutual fund, wage insurance, social security scheme, or any governmental guarantee provided by an appropriate agency of the State of the accountable person, whether that person is an owner or operator, exists to cover wages and related monies owed to seafarers employed on ships flying its flag in the event of default of payment by their employers. The State of registration may also provide for any other appropriate mechanism to that effect in its laws and regulations.

Article 11

Register of Ships

1. A State of registration shall establish a register of ships flying its flag, which register shall be maintained in a manner determined by that State and in conformity with the relevant provisions of this Convention. Ships entitled by the laws and regulations of a State to fly its flag shall be entered in this register in the name of the owner or owners or, where national laws and regulations so provide, the bareboat charterer.

2. Such register shall, inter alia , record the following:
   (a) the name of the ship and the previous name and registry if any;
   (b) the place or port of registration or home port and the official number or mark of identification of the ship;
   (c) the international call sign of the ship, if assigned;
   (d) the name of the builders, place of build and year of building of the ship;
   (e) the description of the main technical characteristics of the ship;
   (f) the name, address and, as appropriate, the nationality of the owner or of each of the owners; and, unless recorded in another public document readily accessible to the Registrar in the flag State:
   (g) the date of deletion or suspension of the previous registration of the ship;
   (h) the name, address and, as appropriate, the nationality of the bareboat charterer, where national laws and regulations provide for the registration of ships bareboat chartered-in;
   (i) the particulars of any mortgages or other similar charges upon the ship as stipulated by national laws and regulations.
3. Furthermore, such register should also record:
   (a) if there is more than one owner, the proportion of the ship owned by each;
   (b) the name, address and, as appropriate, the nationality of the operator, when the operator is not the owner or the bareboat charterer.
4. Before entering a ship in its register of ships a State should assure itself that the previous registration, if any, is deleted.

5. In the case of a ship bareboat chartered-in a State should assure itself that right to fly the flag of the former flag State is suspended. Such registration shall be effected on production of evidence, indicating suspension of previous registration as regards the nationality of the ship under the former flag State and indicating particulars of any registered encumbrances.

Article 12

Bareboat Charter

1. Subject to the provisions of article 11 and in accordance with its laws and regulations a State may grant registration and the right to fly its flag to a ship bareboat chartered-in by a charterer in that State, for the period of that charter.
2. When shipowners or charterers in States Parties to this Convention enter into such bareboat charter activities, the conditions of registration contained in this Convention should be fully complied with.
3. To achieve the goal of compliance and for the purpose of applying the requirements of this Convention in the case of a ship so bareboat chartered-in the charterer will be considered to be the owner. This Convention, however, does not have the effect of providing for any ownership rights in the chartered ship other than those stipulated in the particular bareboat charter contract.
4. A State should ensure that a ship bareboat chartered-in and flying its flag, pursuant to paragraphs 1 to 3 of this article, will be subject to its full jurisdiction and control.
5. The State where the bareboat chartered-in ship is registered shall ensure that the former flag State is notified of the deletion of the registration of the bareboat chartered ship.
6. All terms and conditions, other than those specified in this article, relating to the relationship of the

parties to a bareboat charter are left to the contractual disposal of those parties.

Article 13

Joint ventures

1. Contracting Parties to this Convention, in conformity with their national policies, legislation and the conditions for registration of ships contained in this Convention, should promote joint ventures between shipowners of different countries, and should, to this end, adopt appropriate arrangements, inter alia , by safeguarding the contractual rights of the parties to joint ventures, to further the establishment of such joint ventures in order to develop the national shipping industry.
2. Regional and international financial institutions and aid agencies should be invited to contribute, as appropriate, to the establishment and/or strengthening of joint ventures in the shipping industry of developing countries, particularly in the least developed among them.

Article 14

Measures to Protect the Interests of Labour-Supplying Countries

1. For the purpose of safeguarding the interests of labour-supplying countries and of minimizing labour displacement and consequent economic dislocation, if any, within these countries, particularly developing countries, as a result of the adoption of this Convention, urgency should be given to the implementation, inter alia , of the measures as contained in Resolution 1 annexed to this Convention.
2. In order to create favourable conditions for any contract or arrangement that may be entered into by shipowners or operators and the trade unions of seamen or other representative seamen bodies,

bilateral agreements may be concluded between flag States and labour-supplying countries concerning the employment of seafarers of those labour-supplying countries.

Article 15

Measures to Minimize Adverse Economic Effects

For the purpose of minimizing adverse economic effects that might occur within developing countries, in the process of adapting and implementing conditions to meet the requirements established by this Convention, urgency should be given to the implementation, inter alia , of the measures as contained in Resolution 2 annexed to this Convention.

Article 16

Depositary

The Secretary-General of the United Nations shall be the depositary of this Convention.

Article 17

Implementation

1. Contracting Parties shall take any legislative or other measures necessary to implement this Convention.
2. Each Contracting Party shall, at appropriate times, communicate to the depositary the texts of any legislative or other measures which it has taken in order to implement this Convention.
3. The depositary shall transmit upon request to Contracting Parties the texts of the legislative or other measures which have been communicated to him pursuant to paragraph 2 of this article.

Article 18

Signature, ratification, acceptance, approval and accession

1. All States are entitled to become Contracting Parties to this Convention by:

(a) signature not subject to ratification, acceptance or approval; or

(b) signature subject to and followed by ratification, acceptance or approval; or

(c) accession.

2. This Convention shall be open for signature from 1 May 1986 to and including 30 April 1987, at the Headquarters of the United Nations in New York and shall thereafter remain open for accession.

3. Instruments of ratification, acceptance, approval or accession shall be deposited with the depositary.

Article 19

Entry into Force

1. This Convention shall enter into force 12 months after the date on which not less than 40 States, the combined tonnage of which amounts to at least 25 per cent of world tonnage, have become Contracting Parties to it in accordance with article 18. For the purpose of this article the tonnage shall be deemed to be that contained in annex III to this Convention.

2. For each State which becomes a Contracting Party to this Convention after the conditions for entry into force under paragraph 1 of this article have been met, the Convention shall enter into force for that State 12 months after that State has become a Contracting Party.

Article 20

Review and Amendments

1. After the expiry of a period of eight years from the date of entry into force of this Convention, a Contracting Party may, by written communication addressed to the Secretary-General of the United Nations, propose specific amendments to this Convention and request the convening of a review conference to consider such proposed amendments.

The Secretary-General shall circulate such communication to all Contracting Parties. If, within 12 months from the date of the circulation of the communication, not less than two-fifths of the Contracting Parties reply favourably to the request, the Secretary-General shall convene the Review Conference.

2. The Secretary-General of the United Nations shall circulate to all Contracting Parties the texts of any proposals for, or views regarding, amendments, at least six months before the opening date of the Review Conference.

Article 21

Effect of Amendments

1. The decisions of a review conference regarding amendments shall be taken by consensus or, upon request, by a vote of a two-thirds majority of the Contracting Parties present and voting. Amendments adopted by such a conference shall be communicated by the Secretary-General of the United Nations to all the Contracting Parties for ratification, acceptance, or approval and to all the States signatories of the Convention for information.
2. Ratification, acceptance or approval of amendments adopted by a review conference shall be effected by the deposit of a formal instrument to that effect with the depositary.
3. Any amendment adopted by a review conference shall enter into force only for those Contracting Parties which have ratified, accepted or approved it, on the first day of the month following one year after its ratification, acceptance or approval by two-thirds of the Contracting Parties. For any State ratifying, accepting or approving an amendment after it has been ratified, accepted or approved by two-thirds of the Contracting Parties, the amendment shall enter

into force one year after its ratification, acceptance or approval by that State.

4. Any State which becomes a Contracting Party to this Convention after the entry into force of an amendment shall, failing an expression of a different intention by that State:
   (a) Be considered as a Party to this Convention as amended; and
   (b) Be considered as a Party to the unamended Convention in relation to any Contracting Party not bound by the amendment.

***Article* 22**

Denunciation

1. Any Contracting Party may denounce this Convention at any time by means of a notification in writing to this effect addressed to the depositary.
2. Such denunciation shall take effect on the expiration of one year after the notification is received by the depositary, unless a longer period has been specified in the notification.

In Witness Whereof the undersigned, being duly authorized thereto, have affixed their signatures hereunder on the dates indicated.

Done at Geneva on 7 February 1986 in one original in the Arabic, Chinese, English, French, Russian and Spanish languages, all texts being equally authentic.

Annex I

Resolution 1

Measures to protect the interests of labour-supplying countries. The United Nations Conference on Conditions for Registration of Ships,

Having adopted the United Nations Convention on Conditions for Registration of Ships,

Recommends as follows:-

1. Labour-supplying countries should regulate the activities of the agencies within their jurisdiction that supply seafarers for ships flying the flag of another country in order to ensure that the contractual terms offered by those agencies will prevent abuses and contribute to the welfare of seafarers. For the protection of their seafarers, labour-supplying countries may require, inter alia , suitable security of the type mentioned in article 10 from the owners or operators of ships employing such seafarers or from other appropriate bodies;
2. Labour-supplying developing countries may consult each other in order to harmonize as much as possible their policies concerning the conditions upon which they will supply labour in accordance with these principles and may, if necessary, harmonize their legislation in this respect;
3. The United Nations Conference on Trade and Development, the United Nations Development Programme and other appropriate international bodies should upon request provide assistance to labour-supplying developing countries for establishing appropriate legislation for registration of ships and attracting ships to their registers, taking into account this Convention;
4. The International Labour Organisation should upon request provide assistance to labour-supplying countries for the adoption of measures in order to minimize labour displacement and consequent economic dislocation, if any, within labour-supplying countries which might result from the adoption of this Convention;
5. Appropriate international organizations within the United Nations system should upon request provide assistance to labour-supplying countries for the

education and training of their seafarers, including the provision of training and equipment facilities.

Annex II

Resolution 2

Measures to minimize adverse economic effects

The United Nations Conference on Conditions for Registration of Ships,

Having adopted the United Nations Convention on Conditions for Registration of Ships,

Recommends as follows:-

1. The United Nations Conference on Trade and Development, the United Nations Development Programme and the International Maritime Organization and other appropriate international bodies should provide, upon request, technical and financial assistance to those countries which may be affected by this Convention in order to formulate and implement modern and effective legislation for the development of their fleet in accordance with the provisions of this Convention;
2. The International Labour Organisation and other appropriate international organizations should also provide, upon request, assistance to those countries for the preparation and implementation of educational and training programmes for their seafarers as may be necessary;
3. The United Nations Development Programme, the World Bank and other appropriate international organizations should provide to those countries, upon request, technical and financial assistance for the implementation of alternative national development plans, programmes and projects to overcome economic dislocation which might result from the adoption of this Convention.

Annex III

Merchant fleets of the world

Ships of 500 grt and above as at 1 July 1985

Gross registered tons (grt)

- Albania 52,698
- Algeria 1,332,863
- Angola 71,581
- Argentina 2,227,252
- Australia 1,877,560
- Austria 134,225
- Bahamas 3,852,385
- Bahrain 26,646
- Bangladesh 300,151
- Barbados 4,034
- Belgium 2,247,571
- Benin 2,999
- Bolivia 14,913
- Brazil 5,935,899
- Bulgaria 1,191,419
- Burma 94,380
- Cameroon 67,057
- Canada 841,048
- Cape Verde 8,765
- Chile 371,468
- China 10,167,450
- Colombia 357,668
- Comoros 649
- Costa Rica 12,616
- Cote d'Ivoire 124,706
- Cuba 784,664
- Cyprus 8,134,083
- Czechoslovakia 184,299
- Democratic Kampuchea 998
- Democratic Yemen 4,229
- Denmark 4,677,360
- Djibouti 2,066
- Dominica 500
- Dominican Republic 35,667
- Ecuador 417,372
- Egypt 835,995
- Equatorial Guinea 6,412
- Ethiopia 54,499
- Faeroe Islands 39,333
- Fiji 20,145
- Finland 1,894,485
- France 7,864,931
- Gabon 92,687
- Gambia 1,597
- German Democratic Republic 1,235,840
- Germany, Federal Republic of 5,717,767
- Ghana 99,637
- Greece 30,751,092
- Guatemala 15,569
- Guinea 598
- Guyana 3,888
- Honduras 301,786

- Hungary 77,182
- Iceland 69,460
- India 6,324,145
- Indonesia 1,604,427
- Iran (Islamic Republic of) 2,172,401
- Iraq 882,715
- Ireland 161,304
- Israel 541,035
- Italy 8,530,108
- Jamaica 7,473
- Japan 37,189,376
- Jordan 47,628
- Kenya 1,168
- Kiribati 1,480
- Korea, Dem. People's Republic of 470,592
- Korea, Republic of 6,621,898
- Kuwait 2,311,813
- Lebanon 461,525
- Liberia 57,985,747
- Libyan Arab Jamahiriya 832,450
- Madagascar 63,115
- Malaysia 1,708,599
- Maldives 125,958
- Malta 1,836,948
- Mauritania 1,581
- Mauritius 32,968
- Mexico 1,282,048
- Monaco 3,268
- Morocco 377,702
- Mozambique 17,013
- Nauru 64,829
- Netherlands 3,628,871
- New Zealand 266,285
- Nicaragua 15,869
- Nigeria 396,525
- Norway 14,567,326
- Oman 10,939
- Pakistan 429,973
- Panama 39,366,187
- Papua New Guinea 10,671
- Paraguay 38,440
- Peru 640,968
- Philippines 4,462,291
- Poland 2,966,534
- Portugal 1,280,065
- Qatar 339,725
- Romania 2,769,937
- Saint Vincent and the Grenadines 220,490
- Samoa 25,644
- Saudi Arabia 2,868,689
- Senegal 19,426
- Singapore 6,385,919
- Solomon Islands 1,018
- Somalia 22,802
- South Africa 501,386
- Spain 5,650,470
- Sri Lanka 617,628
- Sudan 92,700
- Suriname 11,181
- Sweden 2,951,227

- Switzerland 341,972
- Syrian Arab Republic 40,506
- Tanzania, United Republic of 43,471
- Thailand 550,585
- Togo 52,677
- Tonga 13,381
- Trinidad and Tobago 9,370
- Tunisia 274,170
- Turkey 3,532,350
- Uganda 3,394
- Union of Soviet Socialist Republics 16,767,526
- United Arab Emirates 805,318
- United Kingdom of Great Britain and
- Northern Ireland 13,260,290
- Bermuda 969,081
- British Virgin Islands 1,939
- Cayman Islands 313,755
- Gibraltar 568,247
- Hong Kong 6,820,100
- Montserrat 711
- Saint Helena 3,150
- Turks and Caicos Islands 513
- Total 21,937,786
- United States of America 13,922,244
- Uruguay 144,907
- Vanuatu 132,979
- Venezuela 900,305
- Vietnam 277,486
- Yugoslavia 2,648,415
- Zaire 70,127
- Unallocated 4,201,669
- World total 383,533,282

Source: Compiled on the basis of data supplied by Lloyd's Shipping Information Services (London).

Notes:

(i) Types of ship included:

- Oil tankers
- Oil/chemical tankers
- Chemical tankers
- Miscellaneous tankers (trading)
- Liquified gas carriers
- Bulk/oil carriers (including ore/oil)

- Ore and bulk carriers
- General cargo ships
- Containerships (fully cellular and lighter carriers)
- Vehicle carriers
- Ferries and passenger ships and passenger/cargo ships
- Livestock carriers

(ii) Excluding the reserve fleet of the United States of America and the United States and Canadian Great Lakes Fleets.

SHIP PREFIX

A ship prefix is a combination of letters, usually abbreviations, used in front of the name of a civilian or naval ship.

Prefixes for civilian vessels may either identify the type of propulsion, such as "SS" for steamship, or purpose, such as "RV" for research vessel. Civilian prefixes are often used inconsistently, and frequently not at all. Sometimes a slash is used to separate the letters, as in "M/S".

Naval prefixes came into use as abbreviations for longer titles, such as "His/Her Majesty's Ship" in the Royal Navy, abbreviated "H.M.S" and then "HMS". Earlier uses often included the type of vessel, as for instance "U.S.F." ("United States Frigate") for frigates of the United States Navy. Today the common practice is to use a single prefix for all warships of a nation's navy, and other prefixes for auxiliaries and ships of allied services, such as coast guards.

The use of ship prefixes is not universal; in particular neither the Third Reich's Kriegsmarine nor the Imperial Japanese Navy used ship prefixes. Some English-language writers use prefixes like "DKM" (for "Deutsche Kriegsmarine") and "HIJMS" (for "His Imperial Japanese Majesty's Ship") or "IJN" (for "Imperial Japanese Navy", a translation of dai-nippon teikoku kaigun) for consistency with "HMS" and

"USS". Other writers follow the practice of the navy and omit any prefix.

From the 20th century onwards, most navies identify ships by hull numbers – identification codes typically painted on the side of the ship. Each navy has its own system: the United States Navy uses hull classification symbols, and the Royal Navy and other navies of Europe and the Commonwealth use pennant numbers.

Civilian Ships

If a ship is best known in combination with a ship prefix, use the prefix as part of the name:

- SS John W. Brown (compare John W. Brown)
- PS Waverley (compare Waverley)

  If more than one prefix was used, choose the best-known and create a redirect from the other:

- RMS Titanic should have a redirect from SS Titanic

  A ship not known by a prefix should appear under its name only, if that is unambiguous:

- Nina and Pinta

But when the name is ambiguous, append disambiguation information in parentheses as usual. The date of launching can be used if there are several ships with the same name:

- Santa Maria (ship) (compare Santa Maria)
- Nautilus (1800 submarine) (compare Nautilus (submarine))

Military ships

For ships of navies that have standard ship prefixes, use the prefix in the name of the article:

- USS Monitor (compare monitor)
- HMS Queen Mary (compare Queen Mary)
- SMS Seydlitz (compare Seydlitz)

Do not use periods after each letter:

- USS Monitor (not "U.S.S. Monitor")

Do not use the hull classification symbol as a prefix:

- USS Nimitz (CVN-68) (not "CVN Nimitz")

For ships of navies or nations that don't have a standard ship prefix, name the article (Nationality) (type) (Name):

- Soviet aircraft carrier Kuznetsov (compare Kuznetsov)
- German battleship Bismarck (compare Bismarck)

Do not be over-specific about the ship type:

- German battleship Admiral Graf Spee (not "German pocket battleship Admiral Graf Spee")

Do not make up a ship prefix for a navy that did not use one. Thus:

- German battleship Bismarck (not "DKM Bismarck")
- Japanese battleship Yamato (not "HIJMS Yamato" or "IJN Yamato")
- Italian battleship Giulio Cesare (not "RN Giulio Cesare")
- Soviet aircraft carrier Kuznetsov (not "USSRS Kuznetsov")

However, it is common practice to backdate the use of a prefix so that it applies to ships of that navy that historically would not have been referred to with that prefix;

HMS Royal Charles (not "English ship Royal Charles")

- USS Constellation (not "United States ship Constellation")

Ships with Hull Number Only

Many types of ship, such as American PT boats and German U-boats, are officially known only by a hull number. In these cases, it can be best to spell out the ship type (e.g. Unterseeboot 238), but be sure the ship type name is correct. In many cases, the designation is not an abbreviation and may not relate directly to a ship's class or even type. For the main article, create a redirect or a disambiguation page at the short form. For example, PT-109 can be a redirect to Motor Torpedo

Boat PT-109, but U-238 must be a disambiguation page, because of its alternative meaning of Uranium 238.

Articles about vessels with a numerical name should be titled like HMS A1, HMS E11, HMS M1 etc.

Disambiguating Ships with the Same Name

It is extremely common for many ships to share a name. Therefore disambiguation needs special attention.

Use ships' hull numbers (hull classification symbols for the United States Navy, and pennant numbers for the Royal Navy and many European and Commonwealth navies) for disambiguation, if available:

- USS Enterprise (CV-6) and USS Enterprise (CVN-65)
- HMS Illustrious (R87) and HMS Illustrious (R06)

Write USN hull numbers with a hyphen (the USN itself is not consistent in this respect). Write pennant numbers with neither hyphen nor space (this matches the number as it typically appears on the side of the ship). Note that not all pennant numbers have an initial letter ("flag superior"), for example HMS Ark Royal (91). Also note that in recent decades the Australian and Canadian navies have moved towards American-style three letter pennant number prefixes. These should be written with a space, for example HMCS Vancouver (FFH 331).

In a few cases, one ship is so much better-known than her namesakes that she need not be disambiguated:

- Horatio Nelson's flagship is at HMS Victory; other Victorys are disambiguated at HMS Victory (disambiguation).
- Charles Darwin's vessel of exploration is at HMS Beagle; other Beagles are disambiguated at HMS Beagle (disambiguation).

If a ship had several hull numbers in her career, use the best-known (but give all her hull numbers in the lead section, and make redirects from the others):

- USS Bogue (CVE-9), not ACV-9, or CVHP-9. (She is best known for her actions in the Second Battle of the Atlantic, when she was CVE-9.)

If none of several hull numbers is clearly the best-known, use the first:

- USS Goldsborough (DD-188), not AVP-18, AVD-5, or APD-32.

If an entire class of ships was reclassified, be consistent and make the deicision once for all the ships of the class:

- The Knox-class frigates are named with the FF (frigate) classification, not DE (destroyer escort). (Justification: known as frigates for the majority of their service.)
- The Castle-class corvettes are named with pennant numbers starting K, not F. (Justification: best known for service during World War II.)

If no hull number is available, use the ship's year of launching if known — like human birthdays, every ship has one — otherwise some other appropriate initial date, such as commissioning, or the date she is first mentioned in the historical record:

- HMS Vanguard (1748), HMS Vanguard (1787), HMS Vanguard (1835), etc.

It should be noted that European navies reuse pennant numbers, so ships of the same name may have the same pennant numbers; the second and third Sir Galahad, for example. So you may need to use the launch date to disambiguate these.

If there is only one article for a given ship name, you should still pre-emptively disambiguate it, creating a redirect from the plain name:

- There was only one Wilkes-Barre in the US Navy, so USS Wilkes-Barre redirects to USS Wilkes-Barre (CL-103)

This means that when a second article is written about another ship with that name (and so the plain name becomes a disambiguation page), you do not have to go round fixing all the links. It also means that you do not have to check each time you link to a ship whether or not to disambiguate.

Make an index page that lists all the ships in a navy with the same name:

- USS Enterprise lists eight USS Enterprises
- HMS Vanguard lists 10 HMS Vanguards
- Nautilus (disambiguation) refers to ships named Nautilus.
- Discovery refers to ships named Discovery.

Referring to ships

Put the ship's name in italics, but not the prefix or hull number:

- USS Nimitz (not "USS Nimitz" or "USS Nimitz")

"The" is not needed before the name of a ship (but neither is it wrong):

Ships named Enterprise"

- HMS Enterprise

E

- Enterprise (1776)
- Enterprise (1814)
- Enterprize (1829)

F

- French frigate L'Entreprise

H

- HMS Enterprise (1705)
- HMS Enterprise (1848)

H cont.

- HMS Enterprise (1864)
- HMS Enterprise (A71)
- HMS Enterprise (D52)
- HMS Enterprise (H88)
- HMS Enterprize (1718)
- HMS Enterprize (1774)

S

- Space Shuttle Enterprise

U

- USS Enterprise

U cont.

- USS Enterprise (1775)
- USS Enterprise (1799)
- USS Enterprise (1831)
- USS Enterprise (1874)
- USS Enterprise (CV-6)
- USS Enterprise (CVN-65)

V

- Virgin Galactic

Ships named Nautilus

- USS Nautilus

N

- Nautilus (1800 submarine)
- Nautilus (Verne)

S

- Ships named Nautilus

U

- USS Nautilus (1799)
- USS Nautilus (1838)
- USS Nautilus (SP-559)

U cont.

- USS Nautilus (SS-168)
- USS Nautilus (SSN-571)
- USS O-12 (SS-73)

Ships named Valiant

- HMS Valiant (1914)
- HMS Valiant (S102)

Auguste (Ship)

The Auguste was a full rigged sailing ship and, in September 1761, she was made ready to transport French exiles and prisoners of war from Montreal to France. For this sailing, she was under the command of Joseph Knowles, an English sea captain. The ship was unarmed and had 121 passengers and crew on board. More importantly, she carried only charts of the French coast. Almost immediately upon clearing the mouth of the St. Lawrence on October 28, it encountered a nor'west gale and heavy seas. It struck land on the northeastern side of Cape Breton Island near an inlet known as Aspy Bay. Only seven of the 121 made it to shore. This included the captain, Luc de la Corne, two soldiers, two servants, and one discharged soldier.

Many notable Canadians died during the sinking including Charles-Rene Dejordy de Villebon, Louis-Joseph Gaultier de La Vérendrye, François-Josué de la Corne Dubreuil and Louis de la Corne, Chevalier de la Corne.

The ship carried a valuable cargo of gold and silver which has been located by underwater explorer, Joe Amaral.

SHIP REGISTRATION

Ship registration provides nationality. For some ships it is compulsory to be registered. For others it is voluntary.

When a registered New Zealand ship travels overseas, its New Zealand registration gives it the protection of the New Zealand Government in much the same way as a New Zealand citizen is protected while travelling overseas.

The registration papers provide proof of identity much the same as a passport does for a person.

Register of Ships is a list of all vessels registered in under the Ship Registration Act 1992. The Register has two parts (Part A and Part B) and includes details of those ships which must be registered under the Ship Registration Act 1992 and those ships whose owners have voluntarily chosen to register them.

The Registrar of Ships is responsible for maintaining the Register.

To search the Register you must know

- The ship's name

  OR

- The ship's official/registration number

Ships registered in Part A have an official number which is usually a six digit number, e.g. 123456.

Ships registered in Part B have a registration number which is always "NZ" followed by a number.

There are four ways to obtain details of a particular ship:

- You may call the Registrar who will give you verbal information about the ship at no cost;
- You may inspect the ship's Register entry during normal business hours. The cost is $23;
- A certified transcript of the ship's Register entry (including ownership and any mortgages) can be issued upon payment of $61;
- A computer printout of the ship's Register entries (including ownership and any mortgages) can be issued upon payment of $43. The Registrar does not certify printouts as being correct.

Shipping Registration Act 1981 - Sect 3

Interpretation

(1) In this Act, unless the contrary intention appears:

"Australia" includes the external Territories.

"Australian national" means:

(a) an Australian citizen;

(b) a body corporate established by or under a law of the Commonwealth or of a State or Territory; or

(c) the Commonwealth or a State or Territory.

"Australian-owned ship" has the meaning given by section 8.

"Australian ship" means a ship having Australian nationality by virtue of section 29.

"Authority" means the Australian Maritime Safety Authority established by the Australian Maritime Safety Authority Act 1990.

"Beneficial interests" includes interests arising under contract and other equitable interests.

"Bill of sale" means a bill of sale referred to in section 36.

"Branch office" means a branch office of the Registration Office.

"Certificate of Clearance" has the same meaning as in the Customs Act 1901.

"Collector of Customs" means a person who is a Collector for the purposes of the Customs Act 1901.

"Customs officer" means a person who is an officer for the purposes of the Customs Act 1901.

"Demise charter" , in relation to a ship, means the demise, letting, hire or delivery of the ship to the charterer under a charterparty, by virtue of which the charterer has whole possession and control of the ship (including the right to appoint the master and crew of the ship).

"Deputy Registrar" means a Deputy Registrar of Ships referred to in subsection 48(2).

"Fish" includes turtles, dugong, crustacea, molluscs and any other living resources of the sea or of the seabed.

"Fishing vessel" means a ship that is used, or is intended to be used, wholly or principally for the taking, catching or capturing of fish for trading or manufacturing purposes.

"Foreign country" means a country other than Australia.

"Foreign port" means a port in a foreign country.

"Foreign resident" means a person other than an Australian national or a resident of Australia.

"Government authority" means:

(a) The Commonwealth or a State or Territory; or

(b) A body corporate established for a public purpose by or under a law of the Commonwealth or of a State or Territory, other than:

   (ii) The Western Australian Coastal Shipping Commission; or

   (iii) A body corporate that is declared by the regulations not to be a Government authority for the purposes of this definition.

Government ship means a ship 12 metres or more in length:

(a) That belongs to a Government authority or Government authorities, and to no other person;

(b) The beneficial interest in which is vested in a Government authority or Government authorities, and in no other person; or

(c) That is for the time being on demise charter to a Government authority or Government authorities, and to no other person.

"Lodged" means lodged with the Registrar in accordance with this Act.

"Master" includes a person having command or charge of a ship, but does not include a pilot.

"Mortgage" means a mortgage registered under section 38.

"National flag" means the Australian National Flag within the meaning of the Flags Act 1953.

"Offence based on" a particular provision of this Act, being a provision in respect of which section 74 creates an offence, means an offence against section 74 that relates to that provision (unless the contrary intention appears).

"Officer" means a person (who may include the Minister) exercising powers, or performing duties or functions, under this Act.

"Owner" , except in sections 8, 12, 30 and 58 and in Part VI, means a person registered as owner in accordance with the regulations.

"Pilot" means a person who has the lawful conduct of a ship, but does not belong to the ship.

"Pleasure craft" means a ship that is used, or is intended to be used, wholly for recreational or sporting activities, whether or not let, or intended to be let, for hire or reward or consideration of any kind.

"Previous law" means Part I of the Imperial Act known as the Merchant Shipping Act, 1894, as amended, or otherwise affected in its operation, by the provisions of any other Imperial Act or of any Act, in so far as that Part as so amended, or otherwise affected in its operation, is part of the law of the Commonwealth.

"Proper officer" means a person holding, or performing the duties of, any of the following offices (being an office of the Commonwealth) in a country or place outside Australia, namely:

(a) Ambassador;

(b) Minister;

(c) Head of a Mission;

(d) Chargo Affaires;

(e) Counsellor, Secretary or AttachÃ© of an Embassy, Legation or other post;

(f) Consul General;

(g) Consul; or

(h) Vice Consul.

"Provisional registration certificate" means a provisional registration certificate granted under section 21, 22 or 65.

"Red ensign" means the Australian Red Ensign within the meaning of the Flags Act 1953.

"Register" means the Australian Register of Ships referred to in section 56.

"Registered" means registered under this Act.

"Registered agent" , in relation to a ship, means the person whose name and address are entered in the Register in respect of that ship in pursuance of section 64.

"Registrar" means the Registrar of Ships referred to in subsection 48(1).

"Registration certificate" means a registration certificate, other than a provisional registration certificate, granted under this Act.

"Registration Office" means the Australian Shipping Registration Office referred to in section 54.

"Share" , in relation to a ship, means one of the shares into which the property in a ship is divided as provided by section 11.

"Ship" means any kind of vessel capable of navigating the high seas and includes:

(a) A barge, lighter or other floating vessel;

(b) A structure that is able to float or be floated and is able to move or be moved as an entity from one place to another; and

(c) An air cushion vehicle, or other similar craft, used wholly or primarily in navigation by water;

but does not include a vessel, structure, vehicle or craft declared by the regulations not to be a ship for the purposes of this definition.

"Ship on demise charter to an Australian-based operator" has the meaning given by section 9.

"Ship permitted to be registered" means a ship permitted to be registered by virtue of section 14.

"Ship required to be registered" means a ship required to be registered by virtue of section 12.

"Small craft" means a ship less than 12 metres in overall length.

"Temporary pass" means a temporary pass granted under section 23.

"This Act" includes the regulations.

"Unregistered ship" means a ship entitled to be registered that is not registered.

(2) In this Act, unless the contrary intention appears, a reference to the owner of a ship shall, if there is more than one owner of the ship, be read as a reference to each of the owners.

(3) A reference in this Act to a resident of Australia shall be read as a reference to:

(a) A person, other than a body corporate, whose permanent place of abode is in Australia, whether or not he or she is from time to time temporarily absent from Australia;

(b) A person, other than a body corporate, whose domicile is in Australia, unless his or her permanent place of abode is outside Australia; or

(c) A body corporate, wherever incorporated, that has its principal place of business in Australia.

(4) In this Act, unless the contrary intention appears, a reference to a ship entitled to be registered shall be read as a reference to a ship that is required to be registered by virtue of section 12 or permitted to be registered by virtue of section 14.

(5) A reference in this Act to failing to do an act or thing shall be read as including a reference to refusing to do that act or thing.

(6) For the purposes of this Act, strict compliance with a prescribed form is not required and substantial compliance is sufficient.

(7) A reference in this Act to an offence against this Act, to an offence against a provision of this Act or to a contravention of, or failure to comply with, a provision of this Act shall be read as including a reference to an offence created by section 6, 7 or 7A of the Crimes Act 1914 in relation to this Act.

(8) In this Act, a reference to a ship includes a reference to every thing or article belonging to or to be used in connection with, or necessary for the operation and safety of, the ship.

Chapter 3

Carriage of Goods by Seas

AFFREIGHTMENT

Contract of Affreightment is the expression usually employed to describe the contract between a shipowner and some other person called the freighter, by which the shipowner agrees to carry goods of the freighter in his ship, or to give to the freighter the use of the whole or part of the cargo-carrying space of the ship for the carriage of his goods on a specified voyage or voyages or for a specified time; the freighter on his part agreeing to pay a specified price, called freight, for the carriage of the goods or the use of the ship.

A ship may be let like a house to some person who takes possession and control of it for a specified term. The person who hires a ship in this way occupies during the currency of his term the position of shipowner. The contract by which a ship is so let may be called a charter-party; but it is not, properly speaking, a contract of affreightment, and is mentioned here only because it is necessary to remember the distinction between a charter-party of this kind, which is sometimes called a demise of the ship, and a charter-party which is a form of contract of affreightment, as will hereinafter appear.

Rules of Law

The law with regard to the contract of affreightment is, of course, a branch of the general law of contract. The rights and obligations of the shipowner and the freighter depend, as in the case of all parties to contracts, upon the terms of the agreement entered into between them. The law, however, interferes to some extent in regulating the effect to be given to contracts. Certain contracts are forbidden by the law, and being illegal are, therefore, incapable of enforcement. The most important example of illegality in the case of contracts of affreightment is when the contract involves trading with an enemy. The law interferes again with regard to the interpretation of the contract. The meaning to be given to the words of the contract, or, in other words, its construction, when a dispute arises about it, must be determined by the judge or court.

The result is, that certain more or less common clauses in contracts of affreightment have come before the courts for construction, and the decisions in these cases are treated practically, though not perhaps quite logically, as rules of law determining the sense to be put upon certain forms of expression in common use in shipping contracts. A third way in which the law interferes is by laying down certain rules by which the rights of the parties are to be regulated in the absence of any express stipulation with regard to the matter dealt with by such rules. This is done either by statutory enactment, as by that part (Part VIII) of the Merchant Shipping Act 1804 which deals with the liability of shipowners; or by established rules of the unwritten law, the common law as it is called, as, for instance, the rule that the common carrier is absolutely responsible for the safe delivery of the goods carried, unless it is prevented by the act of God or the king's enemies.

These rules of law, whether common law or statute law, regulating the obligations of carriers of goods by sea, are of most importance in cases which are uncommon though not unknown at the present day, in which there is an affreightment without any written agreement of any kind. It will, therefore, be convenient to consider first cases of this kind where there is no express agreement, oral or written, except as to the freight and destination of the goods, and where, consequently, the rights and obligations of the parties as to all other terms of carriage depend wholly upon the rules of law, remembering always that these same rules apply when there is a written contract, except in so far as they are qualified or negatived by the terms of such contract.

In Defaults of Express Contract

The rules of the common or ancient customary law of England with regard to the carriage of goods were no doubt first considered by the courts and established with regard to the carriage of goods by common carriers on land. These rules were applied to common carriers by water, and it may now be taken to be the general rule that shipowners who carry goods by sea are by the English law subject to the liabilities of common carriers. (See, as to the grounds and precise extent of this doctrine, the judgments in Liver Alkali Company v. Johnson (1874), L.R., 9 Ex. 338, and Nugent v. Smith (1876) 1 C.P.D. 423.) In practice goods are not often shipped without a written contract or acknowledgment of the terms upon which they are to be carried. For each separate consignment or parcel of goods shipped a bill of lading is almost invariably given, and when a whole cargo is agreed to be carried the terms are set out in a document called a charter-party, signed by or on behalf of the shipowner on the one part, and the shipper, who is called the charterer, on the other part. But at present we are considering the relations of shipowner and shipper independently of any express contract, as in a case when goods are shipped and received to be carried to the place to which the ship is bound for a certain freight, but without any further agreement as to the terms of carriage.

In such a case the rights of the parties depend on the rules of law, or, which is much the same thing, upon the warranties or promises which though not expressed must, as the courts have held, be implied as arising from the relation between the parties as shipper and carrier. The obligations on the one side and the other may be defined shortly to be as follows:—The shipper must not ship goods of a nature or in a condition which he knows, or ought, if he used reasonable care, to know to be dangerous to the ship, or to other goods, unless the shipowner has notice of or has sufficient opportunity to observe their dangerous character. The shipper must be prepared, without notice from the shipowner, to take delivery of his goods with reasonable despatch on the arrival of the ship at the place of destination, being ready there to discharge in some usual discharging place. The shipper must pay the agreed freight, and will not be entitled to claim delivery until the freight has been paid. In other words, the shipowner has a lien on the goods carried for the freight payable in respect of the carriage.

On the other hand, the obligation upon the shipowner is first and foremost to deliver safely at their destination the goods shipped, and this obligation is, by the common law, subject to this exception only that the shipowner is not liable for loss or damage caused by the act of God or the king's enemies; but by statute (Merchant Shipping Act 1894, Part Viii.) it is further qualified to this extent that the shipowner is not liable for loss, happening without his actual fault or privity, by fire on board the ship, or by the robbery or embezzlement of or making away with gold or silver or jewellery, the true nature and value of which have not been declared in writing at the time of shipment; and, further, the shipowner is not liable for damage to or loss of goods or merchandise beyond an aggregate amount, not exceeding eight pounds per ton for each ton of the ship's tonnage. The shipowner is bound by an implied undertaking, or, in other words, is made responsible by the law as if he had entered into an express undertaking: (1) that the ship is seaworthy; (2) that she shall proceed upon the voyage with reasonable despatch, and shall not deviate without necessity from the usual course of the voyage.

It is not our purpose in this article to discuss minute or doubtful questions; but in their general outline the obligations of shipper and shipowner, where no terms of carriage have been agreed, except as to the freight and destination of the goods, are such as have been described above. The importance of appreciating clearly this view of the relations of shipper and shipowner arises from the fact that these fundamental rules apply to all contracts of affreightment, whether by bill of lading, charter-party or otherwise, except in so far as they are modified or negatived by the express terms of the contract.

Bills of Lading

The document signed by the master or agent for the shipowner, by which are acknowledged the shipment of a parcel of goods and the terms upon which it is to be carried, is called a Bill of Lading. Very many different forms of bills of lading are used. For the purpose of illustration the following form (from Mr Scrutton's book on Charter-parties and Bills of Lading) has been selected as a sample:—

Shipped, in apparent good order and condition by _________ in and upon the good Vessel called the _________ now lying in the port of ________ and bound for ________, with liberty to call at any ports in any order, to sail without Pilots, and to tow and assist Vessels in distress, and to deviate for the purpose of saving life or property; and to be delivered in the like good order and condition at the aforesaid port of _________ unto _______ or to his or their assigns, freight and all other conditions as per Charter Party. The act of God, perils of the sea, fire, barratry of the Master and Crew, enemies, pirates, and thieves, arrests, and restraints of princes, rulers, and people, collisions, stranding, and other accidents of navigation excepted, even when occasioned by negligence, default, or error in judgment of the Pilot, Master, Mariners, or other servants of the Shipowners.

Ship not answerable for losses through explosion, bursting of boilers, breakage of shafts, or any latent defect in the machinery or hull, not resulting from want of due diligence by the Owners of the Ship, or any of them, or by the Ship's Husband or Manager.

General Average payable according to York-Antwerp Rules.

In Witness whereof, the Master or Agent of the said Ship hath affirmed to three Bills of Lading, all of this tenor and date, drawn as first, second and third, one of which Bills being accomplished, the others to stand void.

Dated in _______ this _______ day of ______ 188_.

The bill of lading is an acknowledgment of the shipment of goods in a named vessel for carriage to a specified destination on terms set forth in the document. It is usually signed by the master of the vessel, but very commonly by the agents of the shipowner or sometimes of the charterers of the vessel. A vessel may be employed by its owners to earn freight in various ways: (1) It may be placed, as it is said, on the berth as a general ship, to receive cargo from any shippers who may desire to send goods to the port, or one of the ports, to which the vessel is bound. The mate or chief officer usually superintends the loading, and, as goods are shipped, a mate's receipt is given as an acknowledgment of the shipment. The mate's receipt is afterwards exchanged for the bill of lading. In the case of a shipment by a general ship the bill of lading is the evidence and memorandum of the contract between the shipowner and the shipper. (2) A shipper may, however, require the whole cargo space of the vessel to carry, for example, a full cargo of grain. In such a case the vessel will be chartered by the shipowner to the shipper. and the contract will be the charter-party. Even in such a case a bill or bills of lading will usually be given to enable the shipper to deal more conveniently with the goods by way of sale or otherwise. By the ancient custom of merchants recognized and incorporated in the law, the bill of lading is a document of title, representing the goods themselves, by the transfer of which symbolical delivery of the goods may be made.

But when a cargo is shipped under a charter party, although bills of lading may be given to the charterer, it is the charter-party, and not the bills of lading, which constitutes the record of the contract between the parties—of charter-parties. (3) There is a third class of case which is a combination of the two with which we have dealt above. A vessel is very commonly chartered by her owner to a charterer who has no intention to ship and does not ship any cargo on his own account, but places the vessel on the berth to receive cargo from shippers who ship under bills of lading. The charterer receives the bill of lading freight and pays the charter-party freight, his object being of course to obtain a total bill of lading freight in excess of the chartered freight, and so make a profit. The master, although he usually, remains the servant of the shipowner during the term of the charter-party, acts nevertheless under the directions and on behalf of the charterer in signing bills of lading.

The legal effect of this situation is that shippers who ship goods under bills of lading without knowledge of the terms of the charter-party are entitled to look to the shipowner as the person responsible to them for the safe carriage of their goods. This right depends essentially on the fact that the master who signs the bills of lading, although in doing so he is acting for the charterer, remains nevertheless the servant of the shipowner, who is not allowed to deny as against third persons, who do not know the relations between the charterer and the shipowner, that his servant, the master of the ship, has the ordinary authority of a master to bind his owner by signing bills of lading.

The forms of bills of lading vary very much, and their clauses have been the subject of judicial consideration and decision in a vast number of reported cases. The essential particulars, or at all events those common to all bihs of lading, may be stated as follows:

1. The name of the shipper.
2. The name of the ship.
3. The place of loading and destination of the ship.
4. A description of the goods shipped.
5. The place of delivery.
6. The persons to whom delivery is to be made.
7. The freight to be paid.
8. The excepted perils.
9. The shipowner's lien.

The description of (1) the shipper and (2) the ship calls for no remark. The (3) description of the voyage is important, because there is, as we have already explained, an implied undertaking by the shipowner in every contract of carriage not unnecessarily to deviate from the ordinary route of the voyage upon which the goods are received to be carried. The consequences of a deviation are serious, inasmuch as the shipowner is liable, not only for any loss or damage which the shipper suffers in consequence of the deviation, but for any loss of goods which occurs after the deviation, even though such loss is caused by one of the excepted perils. The only exception to this rule is that a deviation may be made to save life, but not to save property.

It is, however, very usual to qualify the strictness of this implied undertaking by introducing in the bill of lading certain liberties to deviate, as, for example, in the form given above, liberty to call at any ports in any order, to tow and assist vessels in distress, and to deviate for the purpose of saving life and property. The nature and extent of the liberty will depend on the words of the contract. The inclination of English courts has been to construe clauses giving a liberty to deviate somewhat strictly against the shipowner.

The (4) importance of the description of the goods shipped and their condition is obvious, as the contract is to deliver them as described and in the like good condition, subject, of course, to the exceptions. It must, moreover, be noted that, as against the master or person who has himself signed the bill of lading, the statement therein of the goods shipped is absolutely conclusive. But as against the shipowner, unless he has himself signed the bill of lading, the statement of the goods shipped is not conclusive. It is evidence as against him that the goods described were shipped, but he is allowed to rebut this evidence by proving, if he can, that the goods mentioned, or some of them, were not in fact shipped.

As to (5) the place of delivery, very serious questions frequently arise. Primarily, of course, the shipowner is bound to deliver at the place named. Should he be prevented by some obstacle or difficulty which is of a temporary nature, the vessel must wait, and delivery must be made as soon as possible.

Where, however, the obstacle is permanent, or at all events such as must cause unreasonable delay, having regard to the nature of the adventure, the shipowner is excused from delivery at the place named in the bill of lading, provided the difficulty arises from an excepted peril, or in consequence of delivery at the place named being forbidden by the law of England, as may happen, for example, in the case of a declaration of war between the United Kingdom and the state in which the port named in the bill of lading is situate. A party to a contract cannot be held liable for breaking his contract if its performance has become illegal.

There may be other cases in which, from the circumstances of the voyage and adventure, it must be inferred that the parties intended the performance of the contract to be conditional on the existence at the time of performance of a certain state of things, the non-existence of which would render performance impossible. For instance, if the port named in the bill of lading became permanently closed and inaccessible to shipping in consequence of an earthquake, it would probably be held that the continued existence of the place named as a port was an implied condition of the contract, and that the shipowner was excused.

Where, however, the performance of the contract remains lawful, and is not excused by the express terms of the contract, or by some implied condition, the shipowner is liable for any loss or damage suffered by the shipper by reason of his goods not being delivered at the named place, even though such delivery has become impossible. There is another reason why the precise description of the place of delivery often becomes important. It is only on the arrival of the ship at the place described as the place of delivery that the obligation of the consignee of the goods to take delivery commences. Delay involves considerable loss and expense to the shipowner. The shipper or consignee is not responsible for any delay which occurs before the ship has arrived at the place of delivery described in the bill of lading.

(6) The goods may be deliverable by the terms of the bill of lading to a named consignee, and to him only, but more

usually they are made deliverable to the order or assigns of the named consignee or of the shipper. If the goods are made deliverable to order or assigns the bill of lading is a negotiable instrument, or, in other words, the right to the goods, and the rights and liabilities under the contract contained in the bill of lading, may be transferred by indorsement and delivery of the document.

When an indorsement has once been made by the shipper or consignee writing his name and nothing more on the back of the bill of lading, the rights in and under it may be transferred from hand to hand by mere delivery. A bill of lading so indorsed is said to be indorsed in blank. But the shipper or consignee may restrict the negotiability of the bill of lading by indorsing it not in blank, but with a direction requiring delivery to be made to a particular person or indorsee, or to his order. This is called an indorsement in full. When an indorsement has been made in full to a named indorsee or order, such indorsee must again indorse in blank or in full to effect a new transfer of the rights in the bill of lading.

(7) The amount or rate of freight payable is stated in the bill of lading, either expressly, or, not uncommonly when the freight under the bill of lading is the same as under the charter-party, by reference to the charter-party. A common form of such reference is freight and other conditions, as per charter-party. It may here be mentioned that this form of words does not incorporate in the contract under the bill of lading all the terms and conditions of the charter-party, but only those which apply to the person who is to take delivery, and relate to matters ejusdem generis, or similar to the payment of freight, such as demurrage and the like.

The conditions of the charter-party thus incorporated do not include, for instance, the exceptions in the charter-party so as to add them to the exceptions in the bill of lading. Freight, unless it is otherwise provided by the contract, is payable only on delivery of the goods at their destination. If the voyage is interrupted and its completion becomes impossible, the shipowner cannot claim payment of freight even pro rata itineris. He loses his freight altogether.

This is so even when the completion of the voyage is prevented by causes for which the shipowner is not responsible, such as the act of God or the king's enemies, or perils which are within the express exceptions in the bill of lading. When the voyage is interrupted by accident, and indeed in any case, the goods may, by agreement between the shipowner and the consignee, be delivered at some place short of their destination upon payment of a freight pro rata; that is to say, proportional to the length of voyage accomplished, and such an agreement may be implied in certain circumstances from the conduct of the consignee in taking delivery before they arrive at their destination. In all such cases it will be a question of fact whether the goods were in fact delivered upon the terms, express or implied, that freight pro rata should be paid. As a rule such an agreement would not be implied where the shipowner is unable or unwilling to forward the goods to their destination, and the owner of the goods, therefore, has no option but to take delivery where offered.

When the ship is disabled and cannot proceed, or she is prevented by some obstacle from proceeding to the place of delivery named in the bill of lading, and the shipowner is unwilling or unable to forward the goods by another ship, even though he may be excused for his failure to carry the goods to their destination, he is not entitled to be paid any part of the freight; and the consignee is entitled to have the goods delivered to him either at the place where the vessel has taken refuge in her disabled condition, or, if the obstacle arises without disablement of the vessel, at the place which is nearest and most reasonably convenient at the time and in the circumstances when the further prosecution of the voyage has to be abandoned.

On the other hand, after the goods have been shipped, so long as the shipowner is ready and willing to carry the goods to their destination, or, if the ship is disabled, to forward them to their destination by some other ship without unreasonable delay, the owner of the goods cannot require the goods to be delivered to him at any place short of their destination without payment of the full freight. Sometimes the freight, either wholly or in part, is made payable in advance. If freight payable in advance has become due, even though the ship is lost before it is paid, it must, in the absence of some special provision to the contrary, still be paid, and freight already paid in advance does not become repayable because the goods do not reach their destination. If, however, goods upon which freight has been paid in advance are lost, and the shipowner is liable for their loss, the amount of freight paid in advance must be taken into account in assessing the damage recoverable from the shipowner.

(8) There is no part of the bill of lading which is of greater practical importance or which demands more careful consideration by shipowner and shipper alike than that which sets forth the excepted perils: those perils, or in other words causes of loss, for which the shipowner is to be exempt from liability. By the common law, as we have seen, the exemption of the carrier, apart from express contract, extended only to loss by the act of God or the king's enemies. The expression act of God requires a word of explanation. It will be sufficient to say that it is not synonymous with force majeure; but it includes every loss by force majeure in which human agency, by act or negligence, has had no part.

The list of excepted perils varies much in different forms of bills of lading. In the older forms it usually included perils of the seas, robbers and pirates, restraint of princes and rulers, fire and barratry (that is, wilful wrongdoing) of the master and crew. The list, however, has grown in modern times, and is still growing; the tendency being to exempt the shipowner from liability for all loss which does not arise from his own personal default, or from the negligence of his managers or agents in failing to provide a vessel seaworthy and fit for the voyage at its commencement.

It is important to point out in this connection that there are two duties which the shipowner is always presumed to undertake, and which are assumed to be unaffected and unqualified by the exceptions, unless a contrary intention is very clearly expressed by the terms of the contract. In the first place, he undertakes absolutely that the ship in which the goods are shipped is fit at the commencement of the voyage for the service to be performed. If during the voyage loss arises even from dangers of the seas or other excepted peril which would not have occurred if the vessel had been seaworthy and fit for the voyage at its commencement, the shipowner is not protected by the exceptions, and is liable for the loss. In the second place, there is an implied undertaking by the shipowner that all reasonable care will be taken by himself, his servants and agents, safely to carry and deliver at their destination the goods received by him for carriage. Should loss or damage occur during the voyage, though the direct cause of such loss or damage be perils of the seas or other excepted peril, still the shipowner cannot claim exemption under the exceptions, if the shipper can prove that the loss or damage would not have occurred but for the negligence of the master or crew, or other servants of the shipowner. The shipowner, in other words, is bound, with his servants, to use all reasonable care to prevent loss by excepted perils and by any other cause.

Express Stipulations

- It must not be supposed that even these primary obligations, which are introduced into every contract of affreightment not by express terms of the contract.
- It has now become common form to stipulate that the shipowner shall not be liable for any loss arising from the negligence of his servants, or that he shall not be liable for loss by the excepted perils even when brought about by the negligence of his servants.
- And with regard to seaworthiness, it is not uncommon for the shipowner to stipulate that he shall not be responsible for loss arising even from the unseaworthiness of the ship on sailing, provided that due care has Been taken by the owner and his agents

and servants to make the ship seaworthy at the commencement of the voyage.

- There is indeed no rule of English law which prevents a shipowner from exempting himself by the terms of the bill of lading from liability for damage and loss of every kind, whether arising from unseaworthiness or any other cause whatsoever.
- In such a case the goods are carried at their owner's risk, and if he desires protection he must obtain it by insurance.
- In this respect the law of England permits greater freedom of contract than is allowed by the law of some other states.
- The owners, agents and masters of vessels loading in the United States of America are forbidden by an act of Congress, commonly called the Harter Act, passed in the year 1893, to insert in their contracts of affreightment any clause exempting the shipowner from liability for the negligence of his servants; but it is at the rame time enacted that, provided all reasonable skill and care has been exercised by the shipowner to make the vessel seaworthy and fit for the voyage at its commencement, the shipowner shall not be liable for any loss caused by the negligence of the master or crew in the navigation of the vessel, or by perils of the sea or certain other causes set forth in the act.
- It is now very usual to insert in the bills of lading of British vessels loading in the United States a reference to the Harter Act, incorporating its provisions so as to make them terms and conditions of the bill of lading.

The difficulty of construing the terms of bills of lading with regard to the excepted perils, often expressed in obscure and inexact language, has given rise to much litigation, the results of which are recorded in the law reports. Where such difficulties arise the question must be, What is the true and natural meaning of the language used by the parties? This question is not governed by the general rules which we have endeavouted to explain: but the words of the contract must always be considered with reference to these rules, which are founded upon the well-established customs of merchants recognized and formulated by the courts of law.

(9) The bill of lading sometimes contains a clause as to the shipowner's lien. Without any express provision for it the shipowner has by the common law a lien for freight. If it is desired to give the shipowner a lien for demurrage or other charges, it must be expressly provided for. The lien is the right of the shipowner to retain the goods carried until payment has been made of the freight or the demurrage, or other charge for which a lien has been given. The lien may be waived, and is lost by delivery of the goods, or by any dealing with the consignee which is inconsistent with a right of the shipowner to retain possession of the goods until payment has been made. The shipowner may preserve his lien by landing the goods and retaining them in his own warehouse, or by storing them in a public warehouse, subject to the conditions required by the Merchant Shipping Act 1894.

Charter-parties

Charter-parties are, as we have already explained, either for a voyage or for a period of time. (1) A charter-party for a voyage is a formal agreement made between the owner of the vessel and the charterers by which it is agreed that the vessel being tight, staunch and strong, and every way fitted for the voyage, shall load at a certain named place a full cargo either of goods of a specified description or of general merchandise, and being so loaded shall proceed with all possible despatch either to a specified place or to a place to be named at a specified port of call, and there deliver the cargo to the charterers or their assigns. There are clauses which provide for the amount of freight to be paid and the manner and time of payment; for the time, usually described as lay days, to be allowed for loading and discharging, and for the demurrage to be paid if the vessel is detained beyond the lay days; usually also a clause requiring the cargo to be brought to and taken from alongside at merchant's risk and expense; a clause that the master shall sign bills of lading for the cargo shipped either at the same rate of freight as is payable under the charter-party or very commonly at any rate of freight (but in this case with a stipulation that, if the total bill of lading freight is less than the total freight payable under the charter-party, the difference is to be paid by the charterers to the master before the sailing of the vessel); and there is usually vhat is called the cesser clause, by which the charterer's liability under the charter-party is to cease on shipment of the cargo, the shipowner taking a lien on the cargo for freight, dead freight and demurrage. The charter-party is made subject to exceptions similar to those which are found in bills of lading. There are also usually clauses providing for the commissions to be paid to the brokers on signing the charter-party, the address commission to be paid to the agents for the Vessel at the port of discharge, and other matters of detail. The clauses in charter-parties vary, of course, indefinitely, but the above is probably a sufficient outline of the ordinary form of a charter-party for a voyage.

What has been said with regard to bills of lading as to the voyage, the place of delivery, the exceptions and excepted perils, and the liability of the shioowner and his lien applies equally to charter-parties. It may be desirable to add a few words on demurrage, dead Freight, and on the cesser clause.

Demurrage is, properly speaking, a fixed sum per day or per hour agreed to be paid by the charterer for any time during which the vessel is detained in loading or discharging over and above the time allowed, which is, as we have said, usually described as the lay days. Sometimes the number of days during which the vessel may be kept on demurrage at the agreed rate is fixed by the charter-party. If no demurrage is provided for by the charter-party, and the vessel is not loading or discharging beyond the lay days, the shipowner is entitled to claim damages in respect of the loss which he has suffered by the detention of his ship; or, if the vessel is detained beyond the fixed number of demurrage days, damages for detention will be recoverable. Sometimes there is no time fixed by the charter-party for loading or discharging.

The obligation in such cases is to load or discharge with all despatch that is possible and reasonable in the circumstances; and if the loading or discharging is not done with such reasonable despatch, the shipowner will be entitled to claim damages for detention of his ship. The rate of demurrage (if any) will generally be accepted as the measure of the damages for detention, but is not necessarily the true measure. When the claim is for detention and not demurrage the actual loss is recoverable, which may be more or may be less than the agreed rate of demurrage. The contract usually provides that Sundays and holidays shall be excepted in counting the lay days, but unless expressly stipulated this exception does not apply to the computation of the period of detention after the lay days have expired.

Dead freight is the name given to the amount of freight lost, and therefore recoverable by the shipowner from the charterer as damages if a full and complete cargo is not loaded in accordance with the terms of the charter-party.

The cesser clause has come into common use because very frequently the charterers are not personally interested in the cargo shipped. They may be agents merely, or they may have chartered the vessel as a speculation to make a profit upon the bill of lading freight. The effect of the clause is that when the charterers have shipped a full cargo they have fulfilled all their obligations, the shipowner discharging them from all further liability and taking instead a lien on the cargo for payment of all freight, demurrage or dead freight that may be payable to him. It has become an established rule for the construction of the cesser clause that, if the language used will permit it, the cesser of liability is assumed to be co-extensive only with the lien given to the shipowner; or, in other words, the charterers are released from those liabilities only for which a lien is given to the shipowner. The shipowner is further secured by the stipulation already referred to, that if the total freight payable under the bills of lading is less than the full chartered freight the difference shall be paid to the shipowner before the vessel sails.

A difficulty which sometimes arises, notwithstanding these precautions, is that although an ample lien is given by the charter-party, the terms of the bills of lading may be insufficient to preserve the same extensive lien as against the holder of the bills of lading. The shippers under the bills of lading, if they are not the charterers, are not liable for the chartered freight, but only for the bill of lading freight; and unless the bill of lading expressly reserves it, they are not subject to a lien for the chartered freight. The master may guard against this difficulty by refusing to sign bills of lading which do not preserve the shipowner's lien for his full chartered freight. But he is often put into a difficulty by a somewhat improvident clause in the charter-party requiring him to sign bills of lading as presented. See Kruger v. Moel Tryvan, 1907 A. C. 272.

(2) A time charter-party is a contract between the shipowner and charterers, by which the shipowner agrees to let and the charterers to hire the vessel for a specified term for employment, either generally in any lawful trade or upon voyages within certain limits. A place is usually named at which the vessel is to be re-delivered to the owners at the end of the term, and the freight is payable until such re-delivery; the owner almost always pays the wages of the master and crew, and the charterers provide coals and pay port charges; the freight is usually fixed at a certain rate per gross register ton per month, and made payable monthly in advance, and provision is made for suspension of hire in certain cases if the vessel is disabled; the master, though he usually is and remains the servant of the owner, is required to obey the orders of the charterers as regards the employment of the vessel, they agreeing to indemnify the owners from all liability to which they may be exposed by the master signing bills of lading or otherwise complying with the orders of the charterers; and the contract is made subject to exceptions similar to those in bills

of lading and voyage charter-parties. This is the general outline of the ordinary form of a time charter-party, but the forms and their clauses vary, of course, very much, according to the circumstances of each case.

It is apparent that under a time charter-party the shipowner to a large extent parts with the control of his ship, which is employed within certain limits according to the wish and directions, and for the purposes and profit of, the charterers. But, as we have already explained at the beginning of this article, the shipowner continues in possession of his vessel by his servant the master, who remains responsible to his owner for the safety and proper navigation of the ship. The result of this, as has been already pointed out, is that the holder of a bill of lading signed by the master, if he has taken the bill of lading without knowledge of the terms of the time charter-party, may hold the owner responsible for the due performance of the contract signed by the master in the ordinary course of his duties, and within his ostensible authority as servant of the shipowner, although in fact in signing the bill of lading the master was acting as agent for and at the direction of the time charterer, and not the shipowner. In the language of the ordinary time charter-party the ship is let to the charterers; but there is no true demise, because, as we have pointed out, the vessel remains in the possession of the shipowner, the charterer enjoying the advantages and control of its employment. Where the possession of a ship is given up to a hirer, who appoints his own master and crew, different considerations apply; but though the instrument by which the ship is let may be called a charter-party, it is not truly a contract of affreightment.

Customary Rights

There are certain rights and obligations arising out of the relationship of shipowner and cargo-owner in circumstances of extraordinary peril or urgency in the course of a voyage, which, though not strictly contractual, are well established by the customs of merchants and recognized by the law. It is obvious that, when a ship carrying a cargo is in the course of a voyage, the master to some extent represents the owners of both ship and cargo. In cases of emergency it may be necessary that the master should, without waiting for authority or instructions, incur expense or make sacrifices as agent not only of his employer, the shipowner, but also of the cargo-owner. Ship and cargo may be in peril, and it may be necessary for the safety of both to put into a port of refuge. There it may be necessary to repair the ship, and to land and warehouse, and afterwards re-ship the cargo. For these purposes the master will be obliged to incur expense, of which some part, such as the cost of repairing the ship, will be for the benefit of the shipowner; part, such as the warehousing expenses, will be for the benefit of the cargo-owner; and part, such as the port charges incurred in order to enter the port of refuge, are for the common benefit and safety of ship and cargo. Again, in a storm at sea, it may be necessary for the safety of ship and cargo to cut away a mast or to jettison, that is to say, throw overboard part of the cargo.

In such a case the master, acting for the shipowner or cargo-owner, as the case may be, makes a sacrifice of part of the ship or part of the cargo, in either case for the purpose of saving ship and cargo from a danger common to both. Voluntary sacrifices so made and extraordinary expenses incurred for the common safety are called general average sacrifices and expenses, and are made good to the person who has made the sacrifice or incurred the expense by a general average contribution, which is recoverable from the owners of the property saved in proportion to its value, or, in other words, each contributes rateably according to the benefit received. The law regulating the rights of the parties with regard to such contribution is called the law of General Average. It must, however, be remembered that the owner of the cargo is entitled under the contract of affreightment to the ordinary service of the ship and crew for the safe carriage of the cargo to its destination, and the shipowner is bound to pay all ordinary expenses incurred for the purpose of the voyage. He must also bear all losses arising from damage to the ship by accidents. But when extraordinary expense has been incurred by the shipowner for the safety of the cargo, he can recover such expense from the owner of the cargo as a special charge on cargo; or when an extraordinary expense has been incurred or a voluntary sacrifice made by the shipowner to save the ship and cargo from a peril common to both, he may require the owner of cargo to contribute in general average to make good the loss.

FREIGHT

Freight is just a description of the cargo Cargo on the shipment. Items being shipped typically fall into various categories depending on 1) what the item is, 2) how large the shipment is, both in terms of item size and in terms of how many items make up the shipment, and 3) how fast the shipment needs to get to where it is going. Shipments are typically categorized as household goods, express, parcel, and freight shipments

Furniture, art, or similar items are usually classified as "household goods" and are transported by specialized household goods (HHG) carriers like Bekins and North American Van Lines.

Very small business or personal items like envelopes are considered "overnight express" or "express letter" shipments, and are transported by carriers like UPS, FedEx Express and DHL. These shipments are rarely over a few pounds, and almost always travel in the carrier's own packaging. Service levels are variable, depending on the shipper's choice. Express shipments almost always travel some distance by air. An envelope may go coast to coast overnight or it may take several days, depending on the service options and prices chosen.

Slightly larger items like small boxes are considered "parcel" or "ground" shipments, and are transported by carriers like UPS and FedEx Ground. These shipments are rarely over 100 pounds, with no single piece of the shipment weighing more than about 70 pounds. Shipments are always boxed, sometimes in the shipper's packaging and sometimes in carrier-provided packaging. Service levels are again variable; but most "ground" shipments will move about 500-700 miles per day, going coast to coast in about four days. Parcel shipments rarely travel by air, and typically move via road and rail. Parcels represent the majority of business-to-consumer (B2C) shipments.

Beyond HHG, express, and parcel shipments, you get into the category of "freight shipments."

Less-than-Truckload (LTL) Freight

The first category of freight shipment is "less than truckload" (LTL), which represents the majority of "freight" shipments and the majority of business-to-business (B2B) shipments. LTL shipments are also often referred to as "motor freight." LTL shipments range from 100 pounds to about 17,999 pounds, and are often less than 40′ long because LTL carriers' trailers are typically 20′ to 40' long. The shipments are usually palletized and packaged for a mixed-freight environment. Unlike express or parcel, LTL shippers must provide their own packaging, as LTL carriers do not provide any packaging supplies or assistance. However, crating or other substantial packaging is required for LTL shipments due to the mixed freight environment.

LTL shipments are transported by regional carriers like AAA Cooper or Averett Express , or by multi-regional or national carriers like Roadway , Old Dominion,or Southeastern. Shipments may be booked directly with the carriers or through brokers or online marketplace service. Major brokers include CHRobinson , Twin Modal , Hub Group, and Rockwell. Leading online intermediaries are uShip.com ,Freightquote.com and Transcore DAT. Service levels are again variable; but most LTL shipments will move about 500 miles per day, going coast to coast in about five business days, traveling by road and rail.

"Air cargo" or "air freight" shipments are very similar to LTL shipments in terms of size and packaging requirements. However, air freight shipments typically need to move at much faster speeds than 500 miles per day.

Truck Load (TL) Freight

Shipments larger than about 18,000 pounds are typically classified as "truckload" (TL). Truckload shipments may be up to 40,000 pounds or 53' long. While express, parcel, and LTL shipments are always intermingled with other shipments on a single piece of equipment and are typically reloaded across multiple pieces of equipment during their transport, TL shipments usually travel as the only shipment on a trailer and TL shipments usually deliver on exactly the same trailer as they are picked up on. While very large shippers may contract directly with TL carriers like JB Hunt and Schneider , most TL shipments are arranged through freight brokers or online marketplaces. When shipping freight, it is extremely important to understand pricing, claims, and insurance.

How Freight Pricing Works

Express letter and parcel carriers typically have fairly simple pricing based on package size and service level requested; however, freight pricing is considerably more complicated. LTL carriers typically charge by freight "class." The National Motor Freight Traffic Association (NMFTA) issues a publication called the National Motor Freight Classification (NMFC). The NMFC is basically a list of every kind of item that ships via truck. Each item has a class assigned to it based on the item's density, loadability or mixability, value, and other factors. Freight classes range from 50 to 500, and generally indicate the percentage of the base rate that should apply. So class 85 freight should be charged 85% of the full rate between points A and B, theoretically. Denser items such as steel and machinery have low classifications such as Class 50 thru 85. Fragile or bulky items fall into freight classes 125 to 500, and pay higher shipment costs.

LTL rates are quoted "per 100 pounds" or "cwt" or "per hundred weight." Besides the discount off of base rate created by the freight class, there is typically a second discount applied to the calculated transportation rate. So a given LTL lane may have a rate of $50 cwt. If your shipment is class 70, then your adjusted base rate is $35 cwt (70% of 50 cwt); then the carrier applies a negotiated discount of 50% for example, to give you a rate of $17.50 cwt. So a 1,000 class 70 shipment would have a base rate of $175.

Besides class, rates, and discounts, an LTL carrier will apply a wide range of surcharges and accessorial charges that will affect the final price of the shipment. Most shipments will receive a fuel surcharge, which is always a significant proportion of the overall cost, possibly as much as 30% or more. Some common accessorial charges are:

- Liftgate: this is a service that assists the driver in loading or unloading his truck when a loading dock or forklift is not available. The trailer is equipped with a hydraulic ramp that lowers to the ground. Liftgate service is almost always billed on residential pickups or deliveries and in commercial pickup and deliveries where loading docks or forklifts are not available. Only a small percentage of most trucking companies' trailers are equipped with liftgates, so be sure to notify them of your need for one in advance.
- Residential pickup or delivery: anytime a carrier must pickup or delivers into a residential area an extra fee is charged, because in most cases the local laws restrict the size of delivery trucks, causing the carrier to utilize a smaller truck to service a residential area. These requirements equal less shipments per day picked up and delivered, so these fees are assessed to offset the carrier's costs.
- Appointments or notification before pickup or delivery: by default, carriers make pickups and deliveries in order arranged by geographic location (a route). If your shipment requires the carrier to call ahead, or schedule and appointment, the carrier will charge an additional fee for this service.
- Inside pickup or delivery: by requiring the truck driver to pickup or deliver inside a building his route takes longer to complete. The carrier will charge an additional fee for this service.

Also, charges for additional insurance or literally hundreds of other possibilities may be added to the final freight bill. It is extremely important that the LTL shipper works with the carrier or intermediary to completely understand all of the requirements of their shipment in order for an accurate price to be quoted.

Often, an LTL shipper may realize savings by utilizing a freight "broker," online marketplace, or other intermediary instead of contracting directly with a trucking company. Brokers can shop the marketplace and obtain lower rates than most smaller shippers can directly. In the Less-than-Truckload (LTL) marketplace, intermediaries typically receive 50% to 80% discounts from published rates, where a small shipper may only be offered a 5% to 30% discount by the carrier.

Truckload (TL) carriers usually charge a rate per mile. The rate varies depending on the distance, items being shipped, equipment type required, and service times required. TL shipments usually receive a variety of surcharges very similar to those described for LTL shipments above. In the TL market, there are thousands more small carriers than in the LTL market; so the use of transportation intermediaries or "brokers" is extremely common.

One other cost-saving method is facilitating pickups or deliveries at the carrier's terminals. By doing this, shippers avoid any accessorial fees that might normally be charged for liftgate, residential pickup/delivery, inside pickup/delivery or notifications/appointments. Carriers or intermediaries can provide shippers with the address and phone number for the closest shipping terminal to the origin and/or destination.

Shipping experts optimize their service and costs by sampling rates from several carriers, brokers, and online marketplaces. When obtaining rates from different providers, shippers may find quite a contrast in the pricing offered. If a shipper uses a broker, freight forwarder, or other transportation intermediary, it is common for the shipper to receive a copy of the carrier's Federal Operating Authority. Freight intermediaries are also required by Federal Law to be licensed by the Federal Highway Administration. Shippers are cautioned to avoid unlicensed brokers and forwarders; if brokers are working outside the law by not having a Federal Operating License, the shipper will have no protection in the event of a problem. Also shippers normally ask for a copy of the broker's insurance certificate and any specific insurance that applies to the shipper's shipment. The internet is full of websites operated by unlicensed and inexperienced brokers, forwarders, and other intermediaries who come and go and come again overnight. Shippers typically favor major brokers and established online marketplaces that have been in business many years and manage hundreds of thousands of shipments annually, in order to get the best service and price.

Cargo Insurance

Whether a shipper deals directly with a carrier or use an intermediary, they typically question the amount of cargo insurance coverage the carrier will be providing on the shipment. Shippers do not assume that full-coverage insurance is provided, as it almost never is. Many carriers offer minimal cargo coverage, typically pennies per pound, and intermediaries typically just pass along the carrier's coverage. In the event of a damage claim, shippers may find themselves without enough coverage and having to file a claim with the carrier directly without the assistance of the broker. Shippers typically ask the broker about the procedure the broker has in place regarding freight loss or damage claims. Responsible carriers and intermediaries will always have additional insurance available for purchase; and the will have fast and easy ways to manage claims.

About 10% of all freight shipments will experience some significant loss or damage. It is a common misconception that a freight rate includes full coverage insurance, when in fact a base freight rate typically includes only a bare minimum of cargo insurance. A shipper should always ask their carrier or intermediary what the insurance coverage is for every specific shipment. LTL shipments will often be insured for less than 25 cents per pound, and TL shipments will often be insured for only slightly more than LTL shipments. Most good TL carriers have maximum cargo insurance of $100,000 for the entire load; but for a 40,000 load, that's only about $2.50 per pound.

Furthermore, cargo insurance only covers significant loss or damage to the cargo only. Carriers' insurance does not cover "consequential" damages like lost sales or downtime on a production line. Also, carrier insurance does not cover the cost of returning damaged cargo to the shipper. Again, cargo insurance is very low and very tightly defined; so shippers must package shipments extremely well and be sure to clarify the specific insurance that will apply to each shipment.

Carriers and intermediaries do typically offer "additional insurance" though known insurance companies like Fireman's Fund. Rates vary widely depending on the item to be covered and the amount of additional insurance that the shipper would like to purchase.

Tips to Avoid Shipping Loss, Damage, and Claims

Unlike small parcel shipping via Fed EX or UPS, shipping freight has a much higher likelihood of damage. Trucking companies pack lots of different types of freight onto lots of different trailers using forklifts and other heavy equipment, creating a harsh and dirty environment for freight. Other shipments will be packed around and on top of your shipment; so all freight shipments should be packaged very carefully. All shipments should be palletized and wrapped in plastic, at a minimum. Most shipments should be fully crated in order to ensure a damage free delivery. Shippers typically ask the carrier or intermediary for the specific packaging requirements for each shipment – then exceed those requirements. Also, since shipments may be reloaded several times, it is important that the packaging has all of the shipper and consignee info clearly noted on at least two sides of the shipment. Filing claims with freight companies is a huge hassle and claims are almost always denied; so shippers typically do as much as possible to avoid freight claims.

Freight Shipping Summary

Shippers typically first ensure that they are using the best type of carrier for their specific type of shipment: using an LTL carrier for an LTL shipment, for example. While parcel carriers will accept LTL shipments, and LTL carriers will accept TL shipments, shippers will typically realize lower service at higher rates when carriers service freight that is "non-standard" for their specific company.

Once the shipper has chosen the right kind of carrier, the shipper then shops several carriers in order to find the best service and price for their shipment. Shippers search out "all-inclusive" quotes that include all surcharges and accessorial fees.

When the shipper has chosen the mode and carrier and is ready to ship, they typically over-package their freight shipment and verify insurance coverage, to minimize damage and claims.

Inexperienced shippers often use the services of a freight intermediary to help them find the best carrier, service, and price for their shipments.

SHIPPING

Shipping is basic process of transporting goods and cargo. Virtually every product ever made, bought, or sold has been affected by shipping. Despite the many variables in shipped products and locations, there are only three basic types of shipments: land, air, and sea.

Ground shipping is easily the most popular form of shipping. Even in Air and Sea shipments, ground transportation is still required to take the product from its origin to the airport or seaport and then to its destination. Ground transportation is typically more affordable than air or sea shipments, so whenever possible shippers attempt to keep their freight in trucks. Many trucks will take freight directly from the shipper to its destination in what is known as a door to door shipment. Vans and trucks of all sizes make deliveries to sea ports and air ports where freight is moved in bulk also. Many nations have built specialized naval ships to ensure the free movement of legitimate cargo; these "merchant navies" are essential to the world economy, carrying the bulk of international trade. The ships are also extremely expensive constructions themselves, being some of the largest man-made vehicles ever. The term originates with the shipping trade of wind power ships, and has come to refer to the delivery of cargo and parcels of any size above the common mail of letters and postcards.

Most cargo transport is by ground shipping rather than by air transport because ground shipping can be cheaper and less restrictive to size, quantity, weight, and type of freight. Air transport is usually reserved for products which must be sent within a certain time frame.

Shipping can more generally refer to the transport of freight ("shipments"), independent of the mode of transport.

Types of Ships Involved

- Container ships / box boats
- Bulk carriers (wet and dry)
  - Tankers
    - chemical
    - crude oil
    - gas carriers
    - LNG, LPG
    - product
- General cargo ships
- Cable layers
- Offshore supply vessels
- Dynamically Positioned ships
- Ferries / RORO (roll on-roll off)
- Car carriers
- Tugboats
- Dredgers
- Barges

BILL OF LADING

The Bill of Lading is a document that establishes the terms of a contract between a shipper and a transportation company. Lading is another word for cargo or freight. The Bill of Lading (BL) has evolved from a simple ship captain's receipt into a multi-purpose financial and legal record for modern international trade.

The BL is a legally binding agreement between the shipper and the carrier (APL) for the movement of cargo between point A and point B. This agreement is called a contract of carriage. This contract of carriage specifies what and how much is being shipped, how and when it will be shipped and to whom APL will release the cargo.

A Bill of Lading may be negotiable or non-negotiable. A negotiable BL is made "to the order of," just like a check. It may be made to the order of the consignee, shipper, foreign bank, a third party in the consignee's country, or blank endorsed. A negotiable BL may be bought or sold, and the buyer must present at least one original Bill of Lading, properly endorsed, in order to get delivery of the goods.

A non-negotiable BL provides for delivery to the party named in the BL and no one else. The buyer must present proper identification that he or she is the named party on the BL and the owner of the cargo. He or she does not need the BL to get delivery of the goods.

The BL serves several functions:

1. As a final receipt for the goods issued by the carrier
2. As evidence of the contract of carriage between shipper and carrier
3. As a negotiable financial instrument which confers title/ownership to the goods, which therefore can be bought and sold
4. As legal evidence in cases of dispute
5. As source of cargo and shipment information for APL

Functions of Bills of Lading

A bill of lading is a document issued by a carrier, e.g. a ship's master or by a company's shipping department, acknowledging that specified goods have been received on board as cargo for conveyance to a named place for delivery to the consignee who is usually identified. A through bill of lading involves the use of at least two different modes of transport from road, rail, air, and sea. The term derives from the noun "bill", a schedule of costs for services supplied or to be supplied, and from the verb "to lade" which means to load a cargo onto a ship or other form of transport.

Short Statement of Principles

The standard short form bill of lading is a part of the contract of carriage of goods and it serves a number of purposes:

- It is evidence that a valid contract of carriage exists and it incorporates the full terms of the contract between the consignor and the carrier by reference (i.e. the short form simply refers to the main contract as an existing document, whereas the long form of a bill of lading (connaissement intégral) issued by the carrier sets out all the terms of the contract of carriage);
- It is a receipt signed by the carrier confirming whether goods matching the contract description have been received in good condition (a bill will be described as clean if the goods have been received on board in apparent good condition and stowed ready for transport); and
- It is also a document of transfer, but not a negotiable instrument, i.e. it governs all the legal aspects of physical carriage but, unlike a cheque or other negotiable instrument, it does not affect ownership of the goods actually being carried. This matches everyday experience in that the contract a person might make with a commercial carrier like FedEx is separate from any contract for the sale of the goods to be carried.

Main types of Bill

Straight Bill of Lading

This bill states that the goods are consigned to a specified person and it is not negotiable free from existing equities, i.e. any endorsee acquires no better rights than those held by the endorsor. So, for example, if the carrier or another holds a lien over the goods as security for unpaid debts, the endorsee is bound by the lien although, if the endorsor wrongfully failed to disclose the charge, the endorsee will have a right to claim damages for failing to transfer an unencumbered title.

Order Bill of Lading

This bill uses express words to make the bill negotiable, e.g. it states that delivery is to be made to the further order of the consignee using words such as "delivery to A Ltd. or to order or assigns". Consequently, it can be endorsed by A Ltd. or the right to take delivery can be transferred by physical delivery of the bill accompanied by adequate evidence of A Ltd.'s intention to transfer.

Bearer Bill of Lading

This bill states that delivery shall be made to whosoever holds the bill. Such bill may be created explicitly or it is an order bill that fails to nominate the consignee whether in its original form or through an endorsement in blank. A bearer bill can be negotiated by physical delivery.

Other Terminology

A waybill is a non-negotiable receipt issued by the carrier. It is most common in the container trade either where the cargo is likely to arrive before the formal documents or where the shipper does not insist on separate bills for every item of cargo carried (e.g. because this is one of a series of loads being delivered to the same consignee). Delivery is made to the consignee who identifies himself. It is customary in transactions where the shipper and consignee are the same person in law making the rigid production of documents unnecessary.

The UK's Carriage of Goods by Sea Act 1992 creates a further class of document known as a ship's delivery order which contains an undertaking to carry goods by sea but is neither a bill nor a waybill.

A Sample of the Issues

In most national and international systems, a bill of lading is not a document of title, but does no more than identify that a particular individual has a right to possession at the time when delivery is to be made. Problems arise when goods are found to have been lost or damaged in transit, or delivery is delayed or refused. Because the consignee is not a party to the contract of carriage, the doctrine of privity of contract states that a third party has no right to enforce the agreement. However, whether this is a problem to the consignee depends on who owns the goods and who holds the risks associated with the carriage. This will be answered by examining the terms of all the relevant contracts.

If the consignor has reserved title until payment is made, the consignor can sue to recover his or her loss. But if ownership and/or the risk of loss has transferred to the consignee, the right to sue may not be clear in contract, although there could be remedies in tort/delict (the issue of risk will have been most carefully considered to decide who should insure the goods during transit). Hence, a number of international Conventions and domestic laws specifically address when a consignee has the right to sue. The legal solution most often adopted is to apply the principle of subrogation, i.e. to give the consignee the same rights of action held by the consignor. This enables most of the more obvious cases of injustice to be avoided.

In the municipal law of the U.S., the issue and enforcement of bills which may be documents of title, is governed by Article 7 of the Uniform Commercial Code. However, since bills of lading are most frequently used in transborder, overseas or airborne shipping, the laws of whatever other countries are involved in the transaction covered by a particular bill may also be applicable including The Hague Rules, The Hague/

Visby Rules and The Hamburg Rules at international level for shipping, The Warsaw Convention for the Unification of Certain Rules for International Carriage by Air 1929 and The Montreal Convention for the Unification of Certain Rules for International Carriage by Air 1999 for air waybills, etc.

It is customary for parties to the bill to agree both which country's courts shall have the jurisdiction to hear any case in a forum selection clause, and the municipal system of law to be applied in that case choice of law clause. The law selected is termed the proper law in private international law and it gives a form of extraterritorial effect to an otherwise sovereign law, e.g. a Chinese consignor contracts with a Greek carrier for delivery to a consignee based in New York: they agree that any dispute will be referred to the courts in New York (since that is the most convenient place — the forum conveniens) but that the New York courts will apply Greek law as the lex causae to determine the extent of the carrier's liability.

Shipped Bill of Lading

After the goods are loaded the bill of lading to be issued by the carrier, master, or agent of the carrier to the shipper shall, if the shipper so demands, be a "shipped" bill of lading: Provided, That if the shipper shall have previously taken up any document of title to such goods, he shall surrender the same as against the issue of the "shipped" bill of lading, but at the option of the carrier such document of title may be noted at the port of shipment by the carrier, master, or agent with the name or names of the ship or ships upon which the goods have been shipped and the date or dates of shipment, and when so noted the same shall for the purpose of this section be deemed to constitute a "shipped" bill of lading.

Bill of Lading, Received for Shipment

A bill of lading acknowledging the receipt of goods by a carrier for shipment on a specified vessel. This type of bill of lading is not acceptable under a letter of credit unless it is specially authorized. English law does not regard these bills as a valid tender under CIF contracts because the CIF seller is obligated to ship the goods, and a Received for Shipment Bill of Lading is not considered proof of shipment.

Letter of Indemnity

In order to obtain the clean bill of lading, the shipper signs a letter of indemnity to the carrier on the basis of which may be obtained the clean bill of lading, although the dock or mate's receipt showed that the shipment was damaged or in bad condition.

Freight Surcharges

Levy of additional charges include:

1. Currency Exchange surcharge to allow for charges in foreign exchange rates after publication of freight rates.
2. Bunkers Surcharge to allow for higher world oil prices, as determined by OPEC.
3. Basic Rate Services Additional for Containers.

This is a "stuffing" charge for containers to cover stuffing and "un-stuffing" the container, even though you may have stuffed it yourself.

4. Equipment Handling Charge for Containers. This is heavy lift charge for goods shipped in containers.5. Port Surcharge this is an extra charge to cover extra port fees e.g. for shallow draft vessels.
6. Congestion Surcharge this is to help offset the extra cost of shipping shipping delays caused by port congestion.

Shipping Stowage

"Which part of the ship" the exporter's goods may be placed or "stowed" in different parts of the ship according to arrangements made.

Regular Stowage

If no special request is made, the exporter's goods are placed anywhere in the regular holds, below deck, with other goods probably stacked on top. To avoid damage from crushing, etc., the exporter's goods need to be well packed in a strong box.

Special Stowage

The exporter may request, at extra cost, that his goods be placed in the freezer hold or for certain perishable goods, he may request that they be stowed away from the heat, but not refrigerated or refrigerated, but not frozen.

On Deck Stowage

The cheapest way of shipping goods by sea is to have them carried on deck. However, such goods are then exposed to the weather with no liability of the shipping company for such damage.

Also, of course, such goods would be the first to be thrown overboard or jettisoned should the ship run into trouble and need to be lightened. Because of the above factors, marine insurance rates for such goods are higher than for goods stowed below deck.

Liquid Cargo

Most ocean cargo vessels have liquid cargo tanks on board with capacities ranging from 20,000 to 40,000 gallons.

Many of these are located in the lowest part of the vessel and are often filled with seawater, if no liquid cargo is available. Other such tanks are between the decks. For very large liquid cargo, specialized tanker ships are used.

Containers

These are metal rectangular boxes of various sizes that can be leased for one voyage or on a round-trip basis. Goods shipped in containers are levied a special charge additional to the regular freight rate.

Ocean Shipping Procedure

Bigger export firm have a traffic department will take care of overseas shipping. With smaller firm, this task is usually delegated on a fee basis, to freight forwarder. The following steps are involved in a typical overseas shipping procedure.

1. The Freight Forwarder is advised of the export order.
2. The terms of sale are examined to determine the exporter's shipping responsibility and ability to fill the order.
3. If letter of credit is involved, it must also be carefully examined to insure that any shipping conditions (such as shipping date, no partial shipments, discharge port, transshipment restrictions, etc.) are met or, if impossible to meet, arrangements be made for the letter of credit to be amended.
4. Quotations on freight rates sought from different shipping agents.
5. A shipping line and vessel are selected.
6. Space is booked as early as possible (as shipping space is not easily available to all destinations) through a shipping agent. The space should be on a ship with an acceptable loading port and acceptable estimated time of arrival (or ETA) at the required port of destination.

   The choice of loading port must be balanced against the preferred date of sailing. Information about sailing schedules is available in specialized shipping publications and in the business sections of the major newspapers.

   The agent that represents the shipping line will, in booking the space, requires full details of the shipment, including weight, size, contents value, ports of shipment and destination. This is recorded by the exporter onto a shipping note that is sent to the steamship office.

   The shipping agent then sends the exporter a contract number and an engagement note showing the details of the shipment, including name of the ship, destination, loading port, loading date, arrival date, and the shipping rate.

The exporter may cancel the space that has been reserved if the export order falls through. However, it should let the shipping company know as soon as possible so that the space can be allocated to someone else. Otherwise the shipping company will invoice the exporter for the unused space.

7. Customs forms are filled out for the country of destination.
8. The shipment is appropriately packaged and marked.
9. Wait for the "calling forward" notice from the shipping company.
10. The shipment is dispatched to the port with a consignment note.
11. A bill of lading is obtained from the shipping company and freight charges are paid.
12. The bill of lading and other required documents are delivered to the bank for collection.

Loading the Goods aboard Ship

When the exporter's goods have been unloaded at the dockside, it is the shipping company's responsibility to ensure that they are properly loaded aboard the correct ship.

Usually, a stevedoring firm does this on behalf of the shipping company and the cost involved is already included in the freight rate paid by the exporter.

With the goods safely loaded aboard the ship, the shipping agent issues a "clean" ocean bill of lading to the exporter so long as no shortages or damaged crates, boxes, etc. have been discovered.

If damage had been noted, the exporter can still obtain a clean bill of lading by signing a letter of indemnity that absolves the shipping line of any responsibility for the damage should insurance claim be made.

The bill of lading, in the required number of copies, is evidence of ownership and is negotiable - it is the key document that is surrendered to the foreign importer upon payment for the goods or acceptance of a time draft as specified in a letter of credit

Transportation Strategy

Careful thought should be given as to the best way to ship the goods to market.

In some cases, ocean shipping is the only alternative. But, often, there are different possibilities at the most reasonable cost. In choosing the method or methods of shipment, the exporter must keep in mind:

1. The delivery time, to be as fast as possible to achieve better customer satisfaction.
2. The cost, trying to keep transportation costs to a minimum.
3. The hidden cost, of working capital tied up in goods in transit.
4. Effect on cash flow, on the exporter's business.
5. The cost of packing and insurance, for different modes of international transportation.

   In making an export price quotation, the exporter must indicate which method of transportation he plans to use.

CHARTER PARTIES

Charter-Party a legal paper or instrument, divided, i.e. written in duplicate so that each party retains half, a written, or partly written and partly printed, contract between merchant and Shipowner, by which a ship is let or hired for the conveyance of goods on a specified voyage, or for a definite period. Also, a written contract between Shipowner and Charterer whereby a ship is hired; all terms, conditions and exceptions are stated in the contract.

Charter Parties the term "charter party" stands for the contract between the owner of a vessel and the charterer, that is the one that takes over the vessel for a certain amount of time or voyage.

Three are the main types of charter:

1) The Voyage Charter. The charterer hires the vessel for a single voyage. The owner and his crew manage the vessel; 2) The Time Charter. Here the vessel is hired for a specific amount of time. The owner still manages the vessel but the charterer selects the ports of destination and controls the operation of the ship. It is a more permanent arrangement than the voyage charter and more representations are made about the ship to the charterer; 3) Demise or Bareboat Charters. This arrangement is completely different from the previous two. The charterer takes full control of the vessel along with the legal and financial responsibility for it. The demise shifts the control and possession of the vessel.

Charters are not in themselves subject to Cogsa but bills of lading issued in conjunction with a charter are. As a practical matter, many charter party forms stipulate the applicability of Cogsa or the Harter Act to the relations between owner and charterer. Such stipulation is valid and enforceable even without the issuance of a bill of lading. Suits brought for the breach of an obligation under a charter party are generally within the admiralty jurisdiction. As long as the agreement is executory, for inadequate performance the remedy is in personam which allows the plaintiff to go to state court under the saving clause. If, however, a charter breach creates a maritime lien, the suit is in rem with exclusive admiralty jurisdiction.

What has been said above mostly applies to commercial operations and voyages. In pleasure boating, the most frequent charter arrangement is the bareboat charter. The voyage or time charter is only used for larger yachts and is more the exception than the rule. Charter fleets are mostly made up of boats belonging to individuals or companies who only use their boats on a part time basis or as an investment. a recent arrangement in recreational boating is the time-share chartering in which several charterers are assigned a certain number of days per month or season in a manner which resembles time-share for residential resorts.

The term "charter party" stands for the contract between the owner of a vessel and the charterer, that is the one that takes over the vessel for a certain amount of time or voyage. Three are the main types of charter:

The Voyage Charter

A voyage charter, the third type, is essentially a contract of carriage. The voyage charter is a contract to rent all or part of the cargo space of a vessel on one or a series of voyages. When a charterer contracts for only a portion of the cargo space, it is called a space charter. Even though the voyage charter is the governing contract, it is customary for master to issue a bill of lading to the charterer.The charterer hires the vessel for a single voyage. The owner and his crew manage the vessel;

The Time Charter

Another common arrangement is a time charter, where shipowner employs a master and crew, and charterer acquires only a contractual right, to direct the movement of the ship, and the cargoes to be transported during the charter period. Under both demise and time charters, charterer pays a "charter hire" for use of ship at daily, monthly or other periodic rate.

Here the vessel is hired for a specific amount of time. The owner still manages the vessel but the charterer selects the ports of destination and controls the operation of the ship. It is a more permanent arrangement than the voyage charter and more representations are made about the ship to the charterer.

Demise or Bareboat Charters

A charter party is a significant device for international commerce and transportation by water. Many shipping companies lease ships from shipowners. The relationship and division of responsibilities between the shipowner and ship user is often defined by the charter party. Many contracts governing the transportation of goods by ship involve bills of lading or charter parties. The term charter party is used to describe three types of contracts dealing with the use of ships owned or controlled by others. With a demise charter, possession of the vessel is given to a charterer, who engages a master and crew, arranges supplies, repairs, and cargo, and acts like an owner during the period of the charter.

This arrangement is completely different from the previous two. The charterer takes full control of the vessel along with the legal and financial responsibility for it. The demise shifts the control and possession of the vessel.

Charters are not in themselves subject to Cogsa but bills of lading issued in conjunction with a charter are. As a practical matter, many charter party forms stipulate the applicability of Cogsa or the Harter Act to the relations between owner and charterer. Such stipulation is valid and enforceable even without the issuance of a bill of lading. Suits brought for the breach of an obligation under a charter party are generally within the admiralty jurisdiction. As long as the agreement is executory, for inadequate performance the remedy is in personam which allows the plaintiff to go to state court under the saving clause. If, however, a charter breach creates a maritime lien, the suit is in rem with exclusive admiralty jurisdiction.

What has been said above mostly applies to commercial operations and voyages. In pleasure boating, the most frequent charter arrangement is the bareboat charter. The voyage or time charter is only used for larger yachts and is more the exception than the rule. Charter fleets are mostly made up of boats belonging to individuals or companies who only use their boats on a part time basis or as an investment. a recent arrangement in recreational boating is the time-share chartering in which several charterers are assigned a certain number of days per month or season in a manner which resembles time-share for residential resorts.

TEXT OF THE CHARTER PARTY

Tanker Voyage Charter Party

1. *Warranty - Voyage - Cargo*

The vessel, classed as specified in Part I hereof,and to be so maintained during the currency of this Charter, shall,with all convenient dispatch, proceed as ordered to Loading Port(s) named in accordance with Clause 4 hereof, or so near thereunto as she may safely get (always afloat), and being seaworthy, and having all pipes, pumps and heater coil's in good working order, and being in every respect fitted for the voyage, so far as the foregoing conditions can be attained by the exercise of due diligence, perils of the sea and any other cause of whatsoever kind beyond the Owner's and / or Master's control excepted, shall load (always afloat) from the factors of the Charterer a full and complete cargo of petroleum and / or its products in bulk, not exceeding what she can reasonably stow and carry over and above her bunker fuel, consumable stores, boiler feed, culinary and drinking water, and complement and their effects (sufficient space to be left in the tanks to provide for the expansion of the cargo), and being so loaded shall forthwith proceed, as ordered on signing Bills of Lading, direct to the Discharging Port(s), or so near thereunto as she may safely get (always afloat), and deliver said cargo. If heating of the cargo is requested by the Charterer, the Owner shall exercise due diligence to maintain the temperatures requested.

2. *Freight*

Freight shall be at the rate stipulated in Part I and shall be computed on intake quantity (except deadfreight as per Clause3) as shown on the Inspector's Certificate of Inspection. Payment offreight shall be made by Charterer without discount upon delivery of cargo at destination, less any disbursements or advances made to theMaster or Owner's agent at ports of loading and / or discharge and cost of insurance thereon. No deduction of freight shall be made for waterand / or sediment contained in the cargo. The services of the Petroleum Inspector shall be arranged and paid for by the Charterer who shall furnish the Owner with a copy of the Inspector's Certificate.

3. *Deadfreight*

Should the Charterer fail to supply a full cargo, the Vessel may, at the Master's option, and shall, upon request of the Charterer, proceed on her voyage, provided that the tanks in which cargo is loaded are sufficiently filled to put her in seaworthycondition. In that event, however, deadfreight shall be paid at the rate specified in Part I hereof on the difference between the intake quantity and the quantity the Vessel would have carried if loaded to her minimum permissible freeboard for her voyage.

4. *Naming Loading and Discharge Ports*

The Charterer shall name the loading port or ports at least twenty-four (24) hours prior to the Vessel's readiness to sail from the last previous port of discharge, or from bunkering port for the voyage, or upon signing this Charter if the Vessel has already sailed.

Any extra expense incurred in connection with anychange in loading or discharging ports (so named) shall be paid for bythe Charterer and any time thereby lost to the Vessel shall count asused laytime.

5. *Laydays*

Laytime shall not commence before the date stipulatedin Part I, except with the Charterer's sanction. Should the Vessel not be ready to load by 4:00 o'clock P.M. (local time) on the cancelling date stipulated in Part I, the Charterer shall have the option of cancelling this Charter by giving the Owner notice of such cancellation within twenty-four (24) hours after such cancellation date; otherwise this Charter to remain in full force and effect.

6. *Notice of Readiness*

Upon arrival at customary anchorage at each port of loading or discharge, the Master or his agent shall give the Charterer or his agent notice by letter, telegraph, wireless or telephone that the Vessel is ready to load or discharge cargo, berth or no berth, and laytime, as hereinafter provided, shall commence upon the expiration of six (6) hours after receipt of such notice, or upon the Vessel's arrival in berth (i.e. finished mooring when at a sea loading or discharging terminal and all fast when.loading or discharging alongsidea wharf), whichever first occur. However, where delay is caused to Vessel getting into berth after giving notice of readiness for any reason over which Charterer has no control, such delay shall not count as used laytime.

7. Hours for Loading and Discharging

The number of running hours specified as laytime inPart I shall be permitted the Charterer as laytime for loading and discharging cargo; but any delay due to the Vessel's condition orbreakdown or inability of the Vessel's facilities to load or discharge cargo within the time allowed shall not count as used laytime. If regulations of the Owner or port authorities prohibit loading or discharging of the cargo at night, time so lost shall not count as used laytime; if the Charterer, shipper or consignee prohibits loading or discharging at night, time so lost shall count as used laytime. Time consumed by the vessel in moving from loading or discharge port anchorage to her loading or discharging berth, discharging ballastwater or slops, will not count as used laytime.

8. Demurrage

Charterer shall pay demurrage per running hour and pro rata for a part thereof at the rate specified in Part I for all time that loading and discharging and used laytime as elsewhere herein provided exceeds the allowed laytime elsewhere herein specified. If,however, demurrage shall be incurred at ports of loading and / or discharge by reason of fire, explosion, storm or by a strike, lockout, stoppage or restraint of labor or by breakdown of machinery or equipment in or about the plant of the Charterer, supplier, shipper or consignee of the cargo, the rate of demurrage shall be reduced one-half of the amount stated in Part I per running hour or pro rata for part of an hour for demurrage so incurred. The Charterer shall not be liablefor any demurrage for delay caused by strike, lockout, stoppage or restraint of labor for Master, officers and crew of the Vessel ortugboat or pilots.

9. Safe Berthing - Shifting

The Vessel shall load and discharge at any safe placeor wharf, or alongside vessels or lighters reachable on her arrival,which shall be designated and procured by the Charterer, provided theVessel can proceed thereto, lie at, and depart therefrom always safelyafloat, any ligtherage being at the expense, risk and peril of the Charterer. The Charterer shall have the right of shifting the Vessel at ports of loading and / or discharge from one safe berth to another on payment of all towage and pilotage shifting to next berth, charges for running lines on arrival at and leaving that berth, additional agency charges and expenses, customs overtime and fees, and any other extraport charges or port expenses incurred by reason of using more than oneberth. Time consumed on account of shifting shall count as used laytime except as otherwise provided in Clause 15.

10. Pumping in and Out

The cargo shall be pumped into the Vessel at the expense, risk and peril of the Charterer, and shall be pumped out of the Vessel at the expense of the Vessel, but at the risk and peril only so far as the Vessel's permanent hose connections, where delivery of the cargo shall be taken by the Charterer or its consignee. If required by Charterer, Vessel after discharging is to clear shore pipe lines of cargo by pumping water through them and time consumed for this purpose shall apply against allowed laytime. The Vessel shall supply her pumps and the necessary power for discharging in all ports, as well as necessary hands. However, should the Vessel be prevented from supplying such power by reason of regulations prohibiting fires on board, the Charterer or consignee shall supply, at its expense, all power necessary for discharging as well as loading, but the Owner shall pay for power supplied to the Vessel for other purposes. If cargo is loaded from lighters, the Vessel shall furnish steam at Charterer's expense for pumping cargo into the Vessel, if requested by the Charterer,providing the Vessel has facilities for generating steam and is permitted to have fires on board. All overtime of officers and crew incurred in loading and / or discharging shall be for account of the Vessel.

11. Hoses: Mooring at Sea Terminals

Hoses for loading and discharging shall be furnishedby the Charterer and shall be connected and disconnected by the Charterer, or, at the option of the Owner, by the Owner at the Charterer's risk and expense. Laytime shall continue until the hoses have been disconnected. When Vessel loads or discharges at a sea terminal, the Vessel shall be properly equipped at Owner's expense for loading or discharging at such place, including suitable ground tackle,mooring lines and equipment for handling submarine hoses.

12. Dues - Taxes - Wharfage

The Charterer shall pay all taxes, dues and other charges on the cargo, including but not limited to Customs overtime on the cargo, Venezuelan Habilitation Tax, C.I.M. Taxes at Le Havre and Portuguese Imposto de Commercio Maritime. The Charterer shall also payall taxes on freight at loading or discharging ports and any unusual taxes, assessments and governmental charges which are not presently ineffect but which may be imposed in the future on the Vessel or freight.The Owner shall pay all dues and other charges on the Vessel (whetheror not such dues or charges are assessed on the basis of quantity of cargo), including but not limited to French droits de quai and Spanish derramas taxes. The Vessel shall be free of charges for the use of anywharf, dock, place or mooring facility arranged by the Charterer for the purpose of loading or discharging cargo; however, the Owner shall be responsible for charges for such berth when used solely for Vessel's purposes, such as awaiting Owner's orders, tank cleaning, repairs,etc., before, during or after loading or discharging.

13. (a) Cargoes Excluded Vapour Pressure

Cargo shall not be shipped which has a vapor pressure at one hundred degrees Fahrenheit (100 degree F.) in excess of thirteenand one-half pounds (13.5 lbs.) as determined by the current A.S.T.M.Method (Reid) D-323.

13. (b) Flash Point

Cargo having a flash point under one hundred and fifteen degrees Fahrenheit (115 degree F.) (closed cup) A.S.T.M. MethodD056 shall not be loaded from lighters but this clause shall not restrict the Charterer from loading or topping off Crude Oil from vessels or barges inside or outside the bar at any port or place wherebar conditions exist.

14. (a) Ice

In case port of loading or discharge should be inaccessible owing to ice, the Vessel shall direct her course accordingto Master's judgement, notifying by telegraph or radio, if available,the Charterers, shipper or consignee, who is bound to telegraph or radio orders for another port, which is free from ice and where thereare facilities for the loading or reception of the cargo in bulk. The whole of the time occupied from the time the Vessel is diverted by reason of the ice until her arrival at an ice-free port of loading or discharge, as the case may be, shall be paid for by the Charterer at the demurrage rate stipulatcd in Part I.

14. (b)

If on account of ice the Master considers it dangerous to enter or remain at any loading or discharging place for fear of the Vessel being frozen in or damaged, the Master shall communicate by telegraph or radio, if available, with the Charterer, shipper or consignee of the cargo, who shall telegraph or radio him in reply, giving orders to proceed to another port as per Clause 14 (a)where there is no danger of ice and where there are the necessary facilities for the loading or reception of the cargo in bulk, or to remain at the original port at their risk, in either case Charterer to pay for the time that the Vessel may be delayed, at the demurrage rate stipulated in Part I.

15. Two or More Ports Counting as One

To the extent that the freight rate standard ofreference specified in Part I F hereof provides for special groupings or combinations of ports or terminals, any two or more ports or terminals within each such grouping or combination shall count as one port for purposes of calculating freight and demurrage only, subject to the following conditions:

a) Charterer shall pay freight at the highest rate payable under Part I F hereof for a voyage between the loading and discharge ports used by Charterer.

b) All charges normally incurred by reason of using more than one berth shall be for Charterer's account as provided inClause 9 hereof.

c) Time consumed shifting between the ports or terminals within the particular grouping or combination shall not count as used laytime.

d) Time consumed shifting between births within one of the ports or terminals of the particular grouping or combination shall count as used laytime.

16. General Cargo

The Charterer shall not be permitted to ship any packaged goods or non-liquid bulk cargo of any description; the cargot he Vessel is to load under this Charter is to consist only of bulkliquid cargo as specified in Clause I.

17. (a) Quarantine

Should the Charterer send the Vessel to any port orplace where a quarantine exists, any delay thereby caused to the Vessel shall count as used laytime; but should the quarantine not be declared until the Vessel is on passage to such port, the Charterer shall not be liable for any resulting delay.

17. (b) Fumigation

If the Vessel, prior to or after entering upon thisCharter, has docked or docks at any wharf which is not rat-free orstegomyia-free, she shall, before proceeding to a rat-free orstegomyia-free wharf, be fumigated by the Owner at his expense, except that if the Charterer ordered the Vessel to an infected wharf the Charterer shall bear the expense of fumigation.

18. Cleaning

The Owner shall clean the tanks, pipes and pumps ofthe Vessel to the satisfaction of the Charterer's Inspector. The Vessel shall not be responsible for any admixture if more than one quality of oil is shipped, nor for leakage, contamination or deterioration in quality of the cargo unless the admixture, leakage, contamination or deterioration results from

a) unseaworthiness existing at the time of loading or at the inception of the voyage which was discoverable by the exerciseof due diligence, or

b) error or fault of the servants of the Owner in the loading, care or discharge of the cargo.

19. General Exceptions Clause

The Vessel, her Master and Owner shall not, unless otherwise in this Charter expressly provided, be responsible for anyloss or damage, or delay or failure in performing hereunder, arising from:

- Any act, neglect, default or barratry of theMaster, pilots, mariners or other servants of the Owner in the navigation or management of the Vessel;
- Fire, unless caused by the personal design orneglect of the Owner; - collision, stranding or peril, danger or accident of the sea or other navigable waters;
- Saving or attempting to save life or property;
- Wastage in weight or bulk, or any other loss or damage arising from inherent defect, quality or vice of the cargo;
- Any act or omission of the Charterer or Owner, shipper or consignee of the cargo, their agents or representatives;

- Insufficiency of packaging;
- Insufficiency or inadequacy of marks;
- Explosion, bursting of boilers, breakage of shafts, or any latent defect in hull, equipment or machinery;
- Unseaworthiness of the Vessel unless caused by wantof due diligence on the part of the Owner to make the Vessel seaworthyor to have her properly manned, equipped and supplied; or
- From any other cause of whatsoever kind arising without the actual fault or privity of the Owner.

And neither the Vessel nor Master or Owner, nor the Charterer, shall, unless otherwise in this Charter expressly provided,be responsible for any loss or damage or delay or failure in performing hereunder, arising or resulting from:

- Act of God;
- Act of war;
- Perils of the seas;
- act of public enemies, pirates or assailing thieves;
- Arrest or restraint of princes, rulers or people; or
- Seizure under legal process provided bond is promptly furnished to release the Vessel or cargo;
- Strike or lockout or stoppage or restraint of labor from whatever cause, either partial or general; or
- Riot or civil commotion.

20. Issuance and Terms of Bills of Lading

a) The Master shall, upon request, sign Bills ofLading in the form appearing below for all cargo shipped but without prejudice to the rights of the Owner and Charterer under the terms ofthis Charter. The Master shall not be required to sign Bills of Lading for any port which, the Vessel cannot enter, remain at and leave insafety and always afloat nor for any blockaded port.

b) The carriage of cargo under this Charter Party and under all Bills of Lading issued for the cargo shall be subject to the statutory provisions and other terms set forth or specified insub-paragraphs (i) through (vii) of this clause and such terms shall be incorporated verbatim or be deemed incorporated by the reference in any such Bill of Lading. In such sub-paragraphs and in any Act referred totherein, the word "carrier" shall include the Owner and the Chartered Owner of the Vessel.

(i) Clause Paramount

This Bill of Lading shall have effect subject to the provisions of the Carriage of Goods by Sea Acts of the United States,approved April 16, 1936, except that if this Bill of Lading is issued at a place where any other Act, ordinance or legislation gives statutory effect to the International Convention for the Unification ofCertain Rules relating to Bills of Lading at Brussels, August 1924,then this Bill of Lading shall have effect, subject to the provisionsof such Act, ordinance or legislation. The applicable Act, ordinance or legislation (hereinafter called the "Act") shall be deemed to be incorporated herein and nothing herein contained shall be deemed asurrender by the Owner of any of its rights or immunities or anincrease of any of its responsibilities or liabilities under the Act.If any term of this Bill of Lading be repugnant to the Act to anyextent, such term shall be void to that extent but no further.

(ii) Jason Clause

In the event of accident, danger, damage or disaster before or after the commencement of the voyage, resulting from anycause whatsoever, whether due to negligence or not, for which, or for the consequence of which, the Owner is not responsible by statute, contract or otherwise, the cargo shippers, consignees or owners of the cargo shall contribute with the Owner in General Average to the payment of any sacrifices, losses or expenses at General Average nature that may be made or incurred and shall pay salvage and special charges incurred in respect of the cargo. If a salving ship is owned oroperated by the Owner, salvage shall be paid for as if the said salving ship or ships belong to strangers. Such deposit as the Owner or his agents may deem sufficient to cover the estimated contribution of the cargo and any salvage and special charges thereon shall, if required, be made by the cargo, shippers, consignees or owners of the cargo to the carrier before delivery.

(iii) General Average

General Average shall be adjusted, stated and settled according to York / Antwerp Rules 1950 and, as to matters not provided for by those rules, according to the laws and usages at the port of NewYork or at the port of London, whichever place is specified in Part Iof this Charter. If a General Average statement is required, it shall be prepared at such port or place in the United States or United Kingdom, whichever country is specified in Part I of this Charter, as may be selected by the Owner, unless otherwise mutually agreed, by an Adjuster appointed by the Owner and approved by the Charterer. Such Adjuster shall attend to the settlement and the collection of the General Average, subject to customary charges. General Average Agreements and / or security shall be furnished by the Owner and / orCharterer and / or Owner and / or Consignee of cargo, if requested. Any cash deposit being made as security to pay General Average and / or salvage shall be remitted to the Average Adjuster and shall be held by him at his risk in a special account in a duly authorized and licensed bank at the place where the General Average statement is prepared.

(iv) Both to Blame

If the Vessel comes into collision with another ship as a result of the negligence of the other ship and any act, neglect or default of the Master, mariner, pilot or the servants of the Owner in the navigation or in the management of the Vessel, the owners of the cargo carried hereunder shall indemnify the Owner against all loss or liability to the other or non-carrying ship or her owners in so far as such loss or liability represents loss of, or damage to, or any claim whatsoever of the owners of said cargo, paid or payable by the other or recovered by the other or non-carrying ship or her owners as part of their claim against the carrying ship or Owner. The foregoing provisions shall also apply where the owners, operators or those in charge of any ships or objects other than, or in addition to, the colliding ships or object are at fault in respect of a collision or contact.

(v) Limitation of Liability

Any provision of this Charter to the contrary not withstanding, the Owner shall have the benefit of all limitations of, and exemptions from, liability accorded to the owner or chartered owner of vessels by any statue or rule of law for the time being inforce.

(vi) War Risks

a) If any port of loading or of discharge named inthis Charter Party or to which the Vessel may properly be ordered pursuant to the terms of the Bills of Lading be blockaded, or

b) If owing to any war, hostilities, war like operations, civil war, civil commotions, revolutions or the operation of international law —

   (i) entry to any such port of loading or of discharge or the loading or discharge of cargo at any such port be considered by the Master or Owners in his or their discretion dangerous or prohibited or

   (ii) it be considered by the Master or Owners in his or their discretion dangerous or impossible for the Vessel to reach any such port of loading or discharge - the Charterers shall have the right to order the cargo or such part of it as may be affected to be loaded or discharged at any other safe port of loading or discharge within the range of loading or discharging ports respectively established under the provisions of the Charter

Party (provided such other port is not blockaded or that entry thereto or loading or discharge of cargo thereat is not in the Master's or Owner's discretion dangerous or prohibited). If in respect of a port of discharge no orders be received from Charterers within 48 hours after they or their agents have received from the Owners a request for the nomination of a substitute port, the Owners shall then be at liberty to discharge the cargo at anysafe port which they or the Master may in their or his discretion decide on (whether within the range of discharging ports established under the provisions of the Charter Party or not) and such discharge shall deemed to be due fulfillment of the contract or contracts ofaffreightment so far as cargo so discharged is concerned.

In the eventof the cargo being loaded or discharged at any such other port within the respective range of loading or discharging ports established under the provisions of the Charter Party, the Charter Party shall be read in respect of freight and all other conditions whatsoever as if the voyage performed were that originally designated. In the event, however, that the Vessel discharges the cargo at a port outside the range of discharging ports established under the provisions of the CharterParty, freight shall be paid as for the voyage originally designated and all extra expenses involved in reaching the actual port ofdischarge and or discharging the cargo thereat shall be paid by theCharterers or Cargo Owners. In the latter event the Owners shall have alien on the cargo for all such extra expenses.

c) The Vessel shall have liberty to comply with any directions or recommendations as to departure, arrival, routes, port sof call, stoppages, destinations, zones, waters, delivery or in anyotherwise whatsoever given by the government of the nations under whose flag the Vessel sails or any government or local authority including any de facto government or local authority or by any person or body acting or purporting to act as or with the authority of any such government or authority or by any committee or person having under the terms of the war risk insurance on the vessel the right to give any such directions or recommendations. If by reason of or in compliance with any such directions or recommendations, anything is done or is not done such shall not be deemed a deviation.

If by reason of or in compliance with any such direction or recommendation the Vessel does not proceed to the port or ports of discharge originally designated or to which she may have been ordered to the terms of the Bills of Lading, the Vessel may proceed to any safe port of discharge which the Master or Owners in his or their discretion may decide on and there discharge the cargo. Such discharge shall be deemed to be due fulfillment of the contract or the contracts of affreightment and the Owners shall be entitled to freight as if discharge has been effected at the port or ports originally designated or to which the vessel may have been ordered pursuant to the terms ofthe Bills of Lading. All extra expenses involved in reaching and discharging the cargo at any such other port of discharge shall be paid by Charterers and / or Cargo Owners and the Owners shall have a lien on the cargo for freight and all such expenses.

(vii) Deviation Clause

The Vessel shall have liberty to call at any ports in any order, to sail with or without pilots, to tow or to be towed, to go to the assistance of vessels in distress, to deviate for the purpose of saving life or property or of landing any ill or injured person onboard, and to call for fuel at any port or ports in or out of theregular course of the voyage. Any salvage shall be for the sole benefit of the Owner.

21. Lien

The Owner shall have an absolute lien on the cargo for all freight, deadfreight, demurrage and costs, including attorney fees, of recovering the same, which lien shall continue after deliveryof the cargo into the possession of the Charterer, or of the holders of any Bills of Lading covering the same or of any storageman.

22. *Agents*

The Owner shall appoint Vessel's agents at all ports.

23. *Breach*

Damages for breach of this Charter shall include all provable damages, and all costs of suit and attorney fees incurred in any action hereunder.

24. *Arbitration*

Any and all difference and disputes of whatsoever nature arising out of this Charter shall be put to arbitration in the City of New York or in the City of London whichever place is specifiedin Part I of this charter pursuant to the laws relating to arbitration there in force, before a board of three persons, consisting of one arbitrator to be appointed by the Owner, one by the Charterer, and one by the two so chosen. The decision of any two of the three on any pointor points shall be final.

Either party hereto may call for such arbitration by service upon any officer of the other, wherever he maybe found, of a written notice specifying the name and address of the arbitrator chosen by the first moving party and a brief description ofthe disputes or differences which such party desires to put to arbitration. If the other party shall not, by notice served upon anofficer of the first moving party within twenty days of the service of such first notice, appoint its arbitrator to arbitrate the dispute or differences specified, then the first moving party shall have the right without further notice to appoint a second arbitrator, who shall be adis-interested person with precisely the same force and effect as if said second arbitrator has been appointed by the other party. In the event that the two arbitrators fail to appoint a third arbitrator within twenty days of the appointment of the second arbitrator, either arbitrator may apply to a Judge of any court of maritime jurisdictionin the city above-mentioned

25. *Sublet*

Charterer shall have the right to sublet the Vessel.However, Charterer shall always remain responsible for the fulfillment of this Charter in all its terms and conditions.

26. *Oil Pollution Clause*

Owner agrees to participate in Charterer's program covering oil pollution avoidance. Such program prohibits discharge overboard of all oily water, oily ballast or oil in any form of apersistent nature, except under extreme circumstances whereby safety of the vessel, cargo or life at sea would be imperiled.Upon notice being given to the Owner that Oil Pollution Avoidance controls are required, the Owner will instruct theMaster to retain on board the vessel all oily residues from consolidated tank washings, dirty ballast, etc., in one compartment, after separation of all possible water has taken place. All water separated to be discharged overboard.If the Charterer requires that demulsifiers shall be used for the separation of oil / water, such demulsifiers shall be obtained by the Owner and paid for by the Charterer.The oil residues will be pumped ashore at the loadingor discharging terminals, either as segregated oil, dirty ballast orco-mingled with cargo as it is possible for Charterer's to arrange.

- If it is necessary to retain the residue on board co-mingled with or segregated from the cargo to be loaded, Charterers shall pay for any deadfreight so incurred.Should it be determined that the residue is to beco-mingled or segregated on board, the Master shall arrange that the quantity of tank washings be measured in conjunction with cargo suppliers and a note of the quantity measured made in the vessel's ullage record.The Charterer agrees to pay freight as per the terms of the Charter Party on any consolidated tank washings, dirty ballast,etc., retained on board on Charterer's instructions during the loaded portion of the voyage up to a maximum of 1% of the total deadweight of the vessel that could be legally carried for such voyage. Any extra expenses incurred by the vessel at loading or discharging port in pumping ashore oil residues shall be for Charterer's account, and extratime, if any, consumed for this operation shall count as used laytime.

Projection

Projectcon is a specially designed charter party for the tug and barge sector. It is designed to provide a single contractual platform to govern the entire commercial adventure involved in the use of a barge and tug to transport special or projects cargoes.

Prior to the development of Projectcon operators in the tug and barge sector have had to rely on using a series of different forms to cover the whole process. Despite the fact that the main forms used were BIMCO documents such as Towcon, bargehire and heavycon with elements of supplytime, it was generally considered to be an unsatisfactory situation by the trade. Without a seamless integration between the contracts used it often became difficult to resolve issues that might arise during the voyage.

In 2003 Bimco was approached by several companies asking for a new "hybrid" standard form to be developed. Projectcon has been produced by a team of industry experts drawn from companies such as Smit, Anchor Marine Transport and Ugland with assistance from shipbrokers Fearnley's and with P&I advice from the Standard Club.

Projectcon was approved by the Documentary Committee in Nice in November 2005. The new charter party will join the suite of other offshore related standard documents provided by BIMCO which includes Supplytime 2005, Towncon, Towhire and Heavycon.

The following notes provide a background to the thinking behind many of the provisions of the charter party and are provided as guiding notes to users:

Format

Projection is divided into two parts – Part I is a box layout form following the well-known BIMCO style. The box form provides a "summary" of the key variable information of the charter party – such as the names and contact details of the parties, agreed rates, and tug/barge and cargo details. Part II of the form contains the main terms and conditions. Where appropriate the boxes in Part I are cross-referenced to the relevant clauses in Part II and vice versa.

Additional clauses covering special provisions, if necessary and agreed for a particular contract, may be added as a Rider to the contract and the clauses should be referred to in Box 29 in Part I. It should be noted that the incorporation of additional clauses, as with amendments to the standard text, may alter the balance of responsibilities and liabilities between the parties in the pre-printed form and, potentially, prejudice P&I cover.

Clause 1 (Definitions)

This Clause contains a list of defined terms commonly used in the charter party.

It should be noted that the term "Vessels" is used collectively to cover both the tug and the barge. In addition, your attention is drawn to the definition of "Transportation" which does not include mobilisation/demobilisation elements. This is because these are considered as items built into the freight rate. The risk of delay in connection with mobilisation and demobilisation rests with the owners under PROJECTCON and such risk is intended to be reflected in the agreed freight.

Clause 2 (Voyage)

Clause 2(a) sets the scope of the voyage. The provision does not allow the vessels to lie "safely aground" – only "safely afloat". This is because the nature of the trade would require the preparation of the bed for the barge to sit aground. Consequently, if a situation arises where the parties want the barge to be able to sit safely aground they must provide for this separately in a rider clause.

It is important to note that in Clause 2(b) the owners are to exercise due diligence in making the vessels seaworthy before and at arrival at the loading port, but not at the commencement of the laden voyage (which would be the usual assumption under a conventional voyage charter party).

The special nature of the trade means that there are circumstances where the barge, after arrival at the loading port, is not in a seaworthy condition due to the loading operations. This applies not only to submersible barges when submerged but also to ballastable barges. In the latter case a ballastable barge may be trimmed excessively or ballasted below her marks to accommodate the requirements of the loading operation.

In addition the owners may not necessarily be required to be in attendance during loading operations as the tug is not involved in this part of the procedure. However, after arrival at the loading port, the barge must be "towworthy", the responsibility of which rests with the party responsible for loading the cargo onto the barge - usually the charterers.

While the owners may not be able to guarantee the seaworthiness of the barge, they will still be in breach of contract if the lack of seaworthiness of either the tug or barge results in the owners not being able to fulfil their contractual obligations. As in TOWCON, the owners are only obliged to exercise due diligence to tender the tug at the place of departure in a seaworthy condition; but the tugowner gives no warranties, express or implied, beyond this point.

Clause 3 (Deviation and Delays)

Clause 3(a) provides the normal liberty to deviate on the basis that the deviation must be reasonable.

Clause 3(b) takes account of the situation where the tug master decides to deviate for the purpose of the safety of the cargo, in which case additional compensation can be claimed from the charterers. The owners are obliged to inform the charterers promptly of any delay or deviation. Any claim for additional compensation must be supported by appropriate documentation. This is done to protect the charterers against potential abuse by an owner who could reduce speed to save bunkers and still be compensated for the delay caused.

Finally, Clause 3(c) deals with delays beyond the owners' control for which the charterers must pay compensation to the owners. However, such delays do not cover delays caused by the late or non-arrival of the tug for whatever reason.

Clause 4 (Barge Engineer)

This Clause has been inserted to deal explicitly with liability for ballasting the barge and the use of barge engineers. The Clause permits the charterers to use barge machinery and ballasting equipment provided they do so using a fully qualified barge engineer provided by the owners.

Clause 5 (Loading and Discharging)

In the tug and barge trade it is common practice that loading and discharging operations are carried out by and are the responsibility of the charterers. The only requirement that the owners have is to present the tug and barge load-ready at the nominated place. Clause 5 reflects this practice; Clause 5(a) requires the charterers to have the cargo ready by the agreed delivery date and Clause 5(b) requires the owners to present the barge in load-ready condition with relevant certificates, class and equipment.

Clause 5(c) puts an obligation on the charterers to place the cargo on board the barge and position it to the full satisfaction of the owners and the Marine Warranty Surveyor. Furthermore, Clause 5(c) provides the procedures to be followed in case the parties have agreed to load the cargo by means of the "float-on" method.

Clauses 5(d) and (e) are the equivalent provisions concerning the discharging operations and, again, it is important to note that the operations must be done to the full satisfaction of the Marine Warranty Surveyor.

Finally, Clause 5(f) sets out clearly that all charges, dues, expenses, and the cost for loading, seafastening, release, discharging and "clean off" are for the charterers' account.

It is important to note that Clause 5 must be read in conjunction with Clause 9 (Commencement of Loading/ Cancelling) which regulates the owners' obligation to present the vessels to the charterers.

Clause 6 (Permits/Licences)

This clause requires the charterers to arrange at their cost all necessary permits and licences relating to the Transportation, as required, and also deals with the loss of time if there is a delay in providing such permits/licences. The owners are obliged to assist the charterers in obtaining licenses and permits if so required by the charterers.

Clause 7 (Taxes)

Clause 7 provides a balanced approach to the issue of taxes. A Box-reference is included in the clause whereby the owners are responsible for the taxes stated in the relevant box in Part I and the charterers are responsible for all other taxes. If the box in Part I is left blank the charterers are responsible for all taxes. This approach has been taken so that the tax burden is clear from the outset.

Clause 8 (Quarantine)

This clause is a standard provision and stipulates how time lost as a result of quarantine formalities and/or health restrictions is to be dealt with between the parties.

Clause 9 (Commencement of Loading/Cancelling)

Whereas the term "Vessels" is used throughout the form, it will be noted that it is only the "barge" that is mentioned in this clause. This is so because there is no particular requirement for the tug to be delivered before the commencement of loading of the barge.

It is common practice for tug and barge charters to be entered into well in advance of the charter period and actual dates being known. The parties, therefore, typically agree on an Initial Delivery Period (the so-called "delivery window" referred to in Clause 9(a)) with an option for the charterers to specify subsequently their firm requirements. In order to match the charterers' requirements for a wide initial period with the owners' need to ensure that the barge is efficiently utilised, Clause 9(b) provides a built-in mechanism for narrowing down the period within which the barge is eventually to be placed at the Charterers' disposal.

Non-delivery of a barge by the owners, or even a small delay, may have serious consequences for the charterers, not least when they are engaged in large construction projects in the offshore industry. However, it appears to be common practice in the industry to contractually limit the owners' liability towards the charterers in the event of non-fulfilment of their obligations to deliver the barge which results in claims made against the charterers by third parties.

Therefore, contrary to what is normally found in BIMCO standard documents, this Clause effectively limits the owners' liability in the event they fail to deliver the barge as agreed.

A distinction has been made between claims for damages caused by late delivery of the barge and those caused by non-delivery resulting in subsequent cancellation of the charter. Accordingly, Clause 9(c) provides that late delivery entitles the charterers to an agreed daily compensation capped at no more than the number of days stated in Box 14. Such compensation is deemed liquidated damages for the purposes of this charter and is the charterers' sole remedy for late delivery.

In the event of non-delivery of the barge within the number of days stipulated in Box 14, Clause 9(d) provides that the charterers shall have the option of cancelling the charter party.

An "interpellation" provision in Clause 9(e) sets out that if the owners are unable to meet the cancelling date they are to give the charterers notice as soon as possible of the revised readiness date and request confirmation from the charterers as to whether they intend to cancel the charter. If the charterers do not react within 48 hours of receipt of the notice, the notified new readiness date becomes the new cancelling date. It should be realised that the procedure in Clause 9(e) are also be helpful to the charterers because it may allow them to re-arrange their loading schedules.

In case the charterers choose to cancel the charter party according to Clause 9(d), Clause 9(f) exonerates the owners from responsibility for any loss or damages incurred by the charterers.

Clause 9(g) gives the owners the right to cancel the charter party if the cargo, for reasons beyond their control, is not loaded within fourteen days from tendering notice of readiness.

Clause 10 (Notices to the Charterers)

Clause 10(a) sets out the procedures for tendering notice of readiness. Notices can be given at any time of day or night. If the vessel is discharging offshore the tug will take instructions from the offshore installation as to how close the tug should approach. Once that point has been reached the tug will tender NOR. Similarly in the case of ports it is not always considered prudent to have a tug and barge anchored amongst other ships in the waiting area or steaming close to the port entrance. In such circumstances it is the practice in the trade to tender NOR at a time when the vessel would have arrived at the customary waiting area.

Clause 10(b) stipulates that the owners must keep the charterers duly advised of the expected time of arrival of the barge at the loading port and Clause 10(c) requires the owners to keep the charterers advised on a daily basis of the estimated time of arrival at the discharging port.

Clause 11 (Marine Warranty Surveyor(s)/Approval of the Vessels and Condition of the Cargo)

A careful study of this clause is strongly recommended as the Marine Warranty Surveyor(s)' role is of great importance in the tug and barge trade.

Clause 11(a) takes into account that it is invariably the charterers who appoint the surveyor. However, the appointment is made subject to the owners' approval which is not to be unreasonably withheld.

Clause 11(b) provides that the marine warranty surveyor is to approve the suitability of the vessels for the transportation. In the event that approval is not given by the agreed date, either party has the right to terminate the charter party.

Clauses 11(c) and (d) emphasise that the marine warranty surveyor is a servant of the charterers and that the charterers are to arrange and pay for all the marine warranty surveyors' services.

Finally, the provisions of Clause 11(e) provide for charterers to warrant that the full description of the cargo (as per Box 5) is correct. If the cargo does not comply with the description then the owners have the option to terminate the charter party.

Clause 12 (Freight)

Clause 12 provides that freight must be paid in instalments according to an agreed payment schedule (as stated in Box 17). The freight payment provisions further stipulate that freight is fully and irrevocably earned when due and is non-returnable whether cargo or vessels are lost or not lost.

Clause 13 (Free Time/Delay Payment)

In most other trades the recognised term for expressing time allowed for loading and discharging is "laytime". In the tug and barge trade, however, the term "free time" is more commonly used, so it has been adopted in PROJECTCON. In addition, the term "delay payment" is used in place of the traditional shipping term "demurrage".

According to Clause 13(a), "free time" starts counting as soon as notice of readiness has been tendered, unless loading/discharging has commenced earlier. Furthermore, the provisions stipulate that any time lost in waiting for a berth counts as "free time" or "time on delay", whereas time used for the actual loading and discharge operations in connection with float-on/float-off method will not count subject to certain exceptions.

"Free time" also includes the removal of seafastenings and lashings and the cleaning of the deck to ensure that the barge is in all respects ready for sea.

Clause 13(b) states that the Delay rate, referred to in Box 20, will be calculated per day or pro rate for part of a day.

According to Clause 13(c), time lost on account of other reasons, such as strike or lockout of master, officers or crew, or breakdown of the vessels or of the owners' equipment, will not count.

Clause 14 (Canal Transit)

This clause gives clear rules as to time counting, tolls, etc. if the transportation is scheduled to pass through a canal. Clause 14(b) also regulates the situation of an increase of canal tolls in excess of the amount indicated in Box 21; whereas Clause 14(c) contains provisions to cover the situation where a canal transit becomes impossible for reasons beyond the owners' control.

Clause 15 (Bunker Escalation)

This clause has been drafted on the basis that it works both ways depending on whether the price per ton for bunker oil stated in Box 22 goes up or down.

Clause 16 (Ice)

This clause is identical to the BIMCO General Ice Clause for Voyage Charter Parties with the exception of a few amendments needed to reflect the specific characteristics of the Projection Charter, such as "Vessels" being used in plural and the fact that bills of lading are not be issued under Projection. The BIMCO General Ice Clause for Voyage Charter Parties was adopted by the Documentary Committee in November 2004 and more information on this clause can be found in BIMCO Bulletin No. 6/2004 page 42.

Clause 17 (Dangerous Cargo)

This clause covers various contingencies if part of the cargo is of a dangerous nature.

Clause 18 (Lien)

The wording of this Clause is identical to Heavycon Clause 18 (Lien) and reflects current commercial practice.

Clause 19 (Substitution)

This Clause provides the owners with the opportunity to substitute the vessels with other similar vessels if such substitution has been approved by the charterers in advance and given that the substituting vessels have been approved by the Marine Warranty Surveyor.

Clause 20 (Termination)

Whether the charterers have the right to terminate the contract is subject to negotiation in each particular case and, depending on such negotiations, Box 23 may or may not be filled in. If not filled in, Clause 20 does not apply.

As freight is usually paid according to a schedule as the job progresses and as some of it may even be paid during the ballast voyage, the termination fee payable by the charterers must be paid in full without deduction of any pre-paid freight. The termination fee is meant to compensate the owners for the loss of earning opportunities as they are unlikely to be able to find any immediate new business if terminated (due to the long term planning involved in this trade). If the termination fee was calculated less any earned freight, the owners would be hit twice: firstly from the loss of business and secondly from not being compensated for the work already undertaken.

Clause 21 (Liability and Indemnity)

The provisions contained in Clause 21 take care of the allocation of liabilities as between owners and charterers.

Clause 21(a) contains an owners' group and charterers' group structure. This has been done to help make the clause easier to read and understand.

Clauses 21(b) and (c) set out owners' liability and charterers' liability in a knock-for-knock liability regime (based on similar provisions found in SUPPLYTIME 89 and the new SUPPLYTIME 2005). This means that each party pays the claims of its own group following an accident. The principle applies irrespective of blame and seeks to save time and expense in connection with casualties.

Clause 21(d) concerns performance claims under the charter party and a mutual obligation for each party to defend the other if a claim for which the other party is liable is claimed from the non-liable party. The obligation is extended both to claims under knock-for-knock and performance claims under the charter party.

Clause 22 (Bills of Lading, Cargo Notes and Receipts)

In the tug and barge sector it is common for the cargoes being carried to belong to the charterers and it is rarely the case that third party cargoes are carried. As a result, bills of lading or cargo receipts are rarely issued and Clause 22(a) reflects this practice. Should a cargo note or receipt be issued at the request of charterers then Clause 22(c) provides for the terms and conditions and dispute resolution clause of PROJECTCON to prevail in the event of a conflict of conditions.

Clause 23 (Insurance)

Closely related to the matters covered by Clause 21 (Liability and Indemnity) are the provisions concerning insurance. The clause is derived from HEAVYCON Clause 22 (Insurance) with the addition of a qualifying statement to avoid potential problems with "mis-directed arrow" on co-insurance.

Clause 24 (Himalaya Clause)

This clause is for the protection of all servants and agents of the owners and/or charterers (including independent contractors and sub-contractors) participating in the performance of the transportation and is not limited to stevedores. It is designed to afford such servants or agents at least the same protection as the owners and/or charterers have under the charter party or by any applicable statute, rule or regulation.

Clause 25 (Both-to-Blame Collision Clause)

Although this standard clause rarely comes in to play its incorporation into charter parties is required under the Club rules of P&I Clubs in the International Group of P&I Clubs. Consequently, the clause is included in Projection.

Clause 26 (General Average and New Jason Clause)

This is a standard clause which forms part of many standard charter parties. As will be seen, in accordance with other General Average Clauses, General Average is to be adjusted in London and in accordance with York-Antwerp Rules 1994, unless otherwise agreed. Although a new set of York-Antwerp Rules were published in 2004, BIMCO's Documentary Committee feels that the new rules are less favourable to owners and that, as a result, all new and revised charter parties should maintain the reference to the York-Antwerp Rules 1994. For further information please refer to BIMCO Special Circular No. 2, 24 February 2005.

Clause 27 (War Risks – VOYWAR 2004)

This is BIMCO's VOYWAR 2004, adopted by the Documentary Committee in November 2004. The clause makes reference, inter alia, to acts of terrorism. More information on this clause can be found in BIMCO Bulletin No. 6/2004 page 58.

Clause 28 (Interests)

This Clause provides a mechanism for interest to be paid on amounts due which are outstanding.

Clause 29 (Agency)

This Clause requires the owners to use for the vessels agents appointed and paid for by the charterers at both the loading and discharging ports.

Clause 30 (Brokerage)

The stipulation in the second paragraph of this Clause covers the brokers against loss of brokerage in the event of breach of contract by either of the parties.

Clause 31 (BIMCO Dispute Resolution Clause)

This clause is the latest edition of BIMCO's standard suite of dispute resolution provisions. In addition to BIMCO's Law and Arbitration Clause 1998, the provision incorporates a mediation clause. The mediation provision is designed to function in conjunction with the chosen arbitration option, whether that is English law, London arbitration; US law, New York arbitration; or law and arbitration as agreed. Mediation is a technique that is recognised as offering savings in costs and time over traditional methods of dispute resolution for certain types of disputes. BIMCO's mediation provision is only triggered once arbitration proceedings have commenced and then runs in parallel with those proceedings, if the parties so choose. This has been done to ensure that one party cannot invoke mediation as a delaying tactic. It also provides for the parties to mediate on all or just some of the issues being arbitrated.

Clause 32 (BIMCO ISPS/MTSA Clause for Voyage Charter Parties)

This clause is the BIMCO ISPS/MTSA Clause for Voyage Charter Parties 2005, adopted by the Documentary Committee in May 2005. More information on this clause can be found in BIMCO Builetin No. 3/2005 page 30.

Clause 33 (BIMCO Notices Clause)

This is a standard BIMCO clause dealing with the methods to be used for writing and sending notices. It should be noted that the Clause permits the use of e-mail as an acceptable method of written communication for the purposes of giving notices under the charter party.

LAYTIME

In commercial shipping, laytime is the amount of time allowed (in hours or days) in the Contract of Affreightment or Charter Party for the loading and unloading of cargo. If the laytime is exceeded, demurrage is incurred.

Demurrage

Demurrage (from demur, French demeurer, to delay, derived from Latin, mora) is a general term used to indicate a surcharge for delays in delivering a product. It has application in a variety of fields.

In industries where items are sold in rented containers, demurrage is synonymous with the free rental of the container for a given period of time. The assumption is that a given amount of free time using the container is built into the cost of the item.

In commercial shipping, demurrage is a term that applies to the time used for loading or off-loading cargo beyond the contractually agreed laytime for such operations. If the delay(s) causing the vessel to incur demurrage are the fault of the vessel's charterer, the shipowner is compensated for the time lost.

Unreasonable Deviation

The shipping industry began using containers during the 1960s to expedite cargo-handling. Today much of the cargo transported in international liner service is carried aboard container-ships specifically designed to stow containers in their holds and on their decks.

The practice of carrying containers on deck is described in the 1990 book "Ocean Container Transportation an Operational Perspective." According to the book, "the carrying capacity of the vessel is enhanced when cargo is stored in containers because deck space may be utilized more extensively. Modern containerships often carry containers up to five high on deck, held in position by a combination of corner locking devices and lashings. By utilizing the deck, approximately 30 per cent more cargo can be carried by average containership than if the ship's holds alone were used."

Determining Unreasonable Deviation

Recently, the Ninth Circuit Court of Appeals in the M/V Sea-Land Consumer case (1995 AMC 1065) attempted to determine whether an ocean carrier deviated from its contract of carriage by stowing containerized cargo on the deck of a containership without the agreement of the shipper.

In the Sea-Land Consumer case, the shipper and the ocean carrier entered into a bill-of-lading contract for the carriage of containerized cargo from Japan to the United States. The contract did not contain a statement that an option for deck stowage had been exercised. The container fell overboard during the voyage, and the shipper sued in federal district court for the loss. The district court granted summary judgement in the shipper's favor based upon an unreasonable-deviation theory, and the carrier appealed.

The concept of deviation originally was used in admiralty law to describe the vessel's wandering from its customary course. The meaning was later expanded to include any variation in the vessel's operation that increased voyage risks.

Unreasonable deviations invalidate bills of lading and strip carriers of defenses, such as the Cogsa (Carriage of Goods by Sea Act) package limitation. A common example of an unreasonable deviation involves unauthorized deck stowage of cargo. This is considered such a fundamental breach that the vessel becomes liable for cargo damage, unless deck stowage was customary in a particular port or trade or was expressly agreed upon. Conversely,, reasonable deviations, such as those intended to save life, carry no penalties.

In the Sea-Land Consumer case, the appeals court's determination that the shipper was entitled to below-deck stowage where the bill of lading did not specify deck stowage and the carrier failed to present evidence of an agreement or custom permitting deck stowage. The appeals court found that the carrier submitted evidence sufficient to raise an issue of fact so as to defeat summary judgment and mandate a trial.

Case sent back for fact-finding

The carrier also argued that, given the prevalence of containerization, deck stowage should not be considered an unreasonable deviation. It cited Second Circuit legal authority in support of its position. The Second Circuit recognizes that while clean bills of lading imply below-deck stowage, nevertheless, stowage elsewhere will be held an unreasonable deviation only when the ship's hold is the ordinary and contemplated stowage area.

The Ninth Circuit went on to note that "although we might be inclined to follow the (Second Circuit's) rationale based upon our own general knowledge of shipping developments over the years, that knowledge is not a substitute of an accurate record before the trial court."

The case has been remanded to the district court for further fact-finding, and its decision is pending. Meanwhile, it now appears certain that a cargo owner is not entitled to recover for containerized cargo lost overboard on a containership solely on the strength of a clean bill of lading not specifying on-deck stowage.

Chapter 4

Contract for the Use of Ships

CHARTER CONTRACT

1. Introductory Notes

Tourist agency "Adriatic.hr", located at Washingtonova 5, 21000 Split (Adriatic.hr onwards), guaranties the truthfulness of the information in connection with the charter offer presented on its web pages, www.adriatic.hr, and also for the truthfulness of the conditions under which the charter fleet is offered. Adriatic.hr takes care and maintains the offered vessels with the attention of a good host and guaranties that they are technically in order and in good condition.

The person who pays in advance (the client onwards), and thus confirms his reservation for one or more vessels from the Adriatic.hr's offer, establishes a legal relationship with Adriatic.hr by which he consents that he agrees with the general terms of renting vessels and with the terms that are herein given for his consideration. All data announced in these conditions presents legal obligation, both for the client and for Adriatic.hr. These conditions are the foundation for resolving eventually arisen disputes between the client and Adriatic.hr; therefore you are obliged to read them carefully.

2. Bookings

Applications for booking a vessel are accepted via e-mail by way of filling out the intended form on the Adriatic.hr web site. Bookings may also be done in the office of our agency, or in the offices of the Adriatic.hr partner-agencies that are authorized to sell the services we offer. During the application process, the client is obliged to give all information requested in the intended reservation form. The same applies during the client's application in our office, or in the offices of the Adriatic.hr authorized representatives to whom he must present all documents necessary for carrying out the regulated procedures.

If the client has not performed the above-mentioned steps during reservation of the vessel, 2 weeks before the beginning of the renting period, he is obliged to give Adriatic.hr the crew-list with their full names, addresses, dates of birth and the kind of valid identification documents.

3. Price List

The prices are expressed in euros. Adriatic.hr reserves its right of changing the prices, in case the owners of the vessels alter their prices.

All listed prices refer to a seven-day rent, from Saturday to Saturday.

Depending on the model, the year of making and the season of renting, the prices presented on the Adriatic.hr web pages may vary from one vessel to another and are therefore especially emphasized by each one of them.

The listed prices include: a technically in order, clean and dry vessel with full tanks of gas and water; using the vessel and its devices; an obligatory vessel insurance; a comprehensive insurance that exceeds the value of the deposit defined by the contract; Croatian sailing license, and a charter license of the vessel. All this information is presented on our web pages during reservation of the yacht.

The listed prices of the vessels do not cover port expenses (port and berth taxes in the main harbor, sojourn and other tariffs), additional vessel equipment, gas expenses, all other necessities, Adriatic.hr crew compensations and all other services, such as health and accident insurance for the crew, as it is also presented on our web pages during reservation.

Should there be any changes in the prices for certain vessel after the application has been filled out and before the preliminary payment, Adriatic.hr is obligated, immediately after realizing that, to notify the client about the change and, with his agreement, to send him a new settlement.

Should there be any changes in the prices after the preliminary payment, Adriatic.hr guarantees that the client will pay the rest of the amount according to the settlement on the bases of which he had decided to reserve certain vessel.

4. Payment Dynamics

In order to confirm the requested reservation of the vessel, the client has to make a preliminary payment that equals 50,00 % of the complete arrangement. The rest of the sum has to be paid 6 weeks before the beginning of the renting, at the latest.

The client can take over the reserved vessel only under the condition that he has regulated all necessary payments.

By paying in advance, the client confirms that he is completely familiar with all characteristics and conditions under which the certain vessel is offered to him. By paying in advance, all that is mentioned in these conditions becomes legal obligation, both for the client and Adriatic.hr.

The final settlement will be made together with the Adriatic.hr representative, or with the owner of the vessel, upon returning it, at the end of the renting period in the harbor agreed as the vessel's final destination.

5. The Client's Right of Changes and Cancellation

If the client wants to cancel the reserved vessel, he must do that in writing and send it to Adriatic.hr by e-mail, fax or regular mail.

The date, when Adriatic.hr receives the written cancellation request, presents the basis of calculating the cancellation coasts in the following way:

- for cancellations up to two months before the beginning of the renting period, Adriatic.hr charges

30 % of the whole arrangement. The rest of the money will be returned to the clients at his own expense.

- for cancellations up to one month before the beginning of the renting period, Adriatic.hr charges 50 % of the whole arrangement, i.e., it keeps the complete deposit.
- for cancellations within a month before the beginning of the renting period, Adriatic.hr charges the whole 100 % of the renting cost.
- for cancellations after taking over the vessel, Adriatic.hr keeps all 100% of the renting price and charges the client with all expenses that may occur due to that cancellation.

If the client who is canceling the rented vessel finds another user who is willing to overtake his rights and duties for the same reservation, Adriatic.hr only charges for the expenses caused by the change.

If cancellation is caused by force majeure, i.e., due to objective reasons on the client's side (death in the family, health reasons, terrible accident,...), the already-paid amount will not be returned to him but Adriatic.hr will offer a vessel at his disposal during the first free period, or in the next season.

The return of money will be done immediately after confirming its exact amount that has to be returned to the client. The payment can be done exclusively to the giro or foreign currency account of the client. When it comes to the currency transfer, the expenses of wiring the money to a foreign country are billed to the client.

6. Deposit

During checking-in, the client must leave an obligatory deposit as a warranty that he will compensate all possible losses and damages occurred during the renting period, even if they are not covered by the insurance policy. The deposit must be in cash, cheques, or by way of a slip with the imprint of the client's credit card. The modalities and amounts of the deposit are shown on our internet pages during presentation of the vessel.

The deposit will be returned to the client after the Adriatic.hr representative establishes that the vessel has been returned in the appointed time and at the appointed place, tidy and undamaged, with full tanks of gas and water and under the condition that there are no further requests from a third party, nor there are announced ones, concerning the client that are connected to the his usage of the rented vessel.

In case of brutal negligence, i.e., damaging the vessel and/ or the equipment, and in case of a loss of one or more parts, the client takes responsibility of all expenses. Adriatic.hr will keep the amount from the deposit that corresponds to the value of the repair, the acquiring and/or purchasing of the equipment, or separate parts of the vessel. If due to a damage, loss of the vessel or the equipment, renting it is not possible anymore, the value that Adriatic.hr will keep from the deposit will equal the value of the lost goods.

Leaving the deposit is obligatory also in cases when the vessel is rented along with a skipper hired by Adriatic.hr. In this case, the set down deposit cannot be used for covering the expenses caused by the skipper's negligence, bad steering of the vessel and bad management of the equipment.

7. Taking Over the Vessel

The vessels can be taken over in the appointed time and place, from 17.00 to 20.00 hours.

If the client does not take the vessel within 48 hours from the appointed time without previously announcing it, Adriatic.hr is authorized to one-sidedly break the renting contract and the client has no right to subsequently ask for compensation.

If due to whatever reasons Adriatic.hr is not able to deliver the reserved vessel in the appointed time and place, the agency has a 24 hour time-limit, from the appointed time of taking over the vessel, to provide the client with another vessel with the equal or better characteristics. If Adriatic.hr does not succeed in doing so, the client has the right to break the contract and to be compensated with the already-paid funds.

If the client decides to wait for a substitutive vessel more than the previously agreed 24 hour limit of overtaking of the same, he can be refunded the sum that equals the worth of the rent for the number of days he was not able to use the vessel. The responsibility of Adriatic.hr for amounts higher than the previously agreed for the rent, as well as for any other right of the client for compensation, is excluded.

When taking over the vessel, the client is obliged to submit to the Adriatic.hr representative an authenticated voucher which designates that the whole amount of the rent has been completely settled.

Adriatic.hr is obliged to give out to the client a technically proper and completely equipped vessel with full tanks of water and gas, clean and dry, ready for sailing.

When taking over the vessel, the client is obliged to carefully test its condition and the equipment and in order to verify whether the inventory checklist corresponds to reality. Eventual objections are presented exclusively before the beginning of the journey. Eventually concealed defects of the vessel and/or the equipment, which were not known to Adriatic.hr when submitting the vessel, as well as damages and defects after returning the vessel that Adriatic.hr could not foresee, do not give the client the right to ask for reduction of the rent.

8. Returning the Vessel

The client is obliged to return the vessel in the appointed time and place (9:00AM at the latest) to the defined port mentioned in the contract, clean and neatly, with full tanks of gas and water, ready for further sailing, i.e., in the same condition he overtook it.

If due to whatever reasons during the trip further sailing is not possible and/or exceeding the negotiated date of return is inevitable, further instructions should be given by contacting the base manager and Adriatic.hr. The information about the announcement must be written in the vessel's diary. Adverse weather conditions cannot justify the exceeding of the negotiated return date of the vessel. Exceeding is only justified in cases caused by force majeur.

When it comes to exceeding the negotiated date of return, the client guarantees that for a 3-hour delay he will pay additional daily rent. For delays over 3 hours and beginning a new calendar day, the client must pay triple daily rent multiplied by the additional expenses that have come up due to the late returning of the vessel. Therefore, returning the vessel to the designated port in the evening hours of the day before checking it out is obligatory. Deviations from this rule are possible but exclusively upon previous agreement with the client and Adriatic.hr.

When returning the vessel to a port that is not negotiated as final, the client must reimburse Adriatic.hr for all expenses connected with taking it back to the negotiated port, a delay fine, if such has occurred, as well as for all damages that occur during transferring back the vessel and that are not covered by the insurance policy.

When returning the vessel, an Adriatic.hr representative will perform a complete check-up of its general condition and the equipment and compare the present inventory and equipment with the inventory list.

The client is obliged to report to the Adriatic.hr representative eventual defects and damages. If damages have occurred on the underwater part of the vessel, or if there is such suspicion, a detailed check-up needs to be done with the help of a crane or a diver. Adriatic.hr decides in which way the check-up will be performed. However, the client is charged with the expenses of the procedure.

If the client tries to hide any damage or loss that has occurred during the renting of the vessel, he must pay a fine to Adriatic.hr in the amount of 300 € and to compensate for the committed damages.

The expenses for lost and damaged parts of the vessel, or the equipment, caused by negligence or bad management on the client's side, or his crew, are billed to the client. Adriatic.hr will compensate that sum from the deposit of the client.

In case that the vessel is returned dirty and untidy, Adriatic.hr will use the client's deposit for the special cleaning of the yacht. Adriatic.hr will also charge for gas supplementation and in a case the client does not return the vessel with full tanks.

During the time of renting, the vessel remains possession of Adriatic.hr or the owner with whom the agency has signed a cooperation contract. Until the moment of proper returning of the vessel, it is considered to be rented to the client.

9. Extending the Renting Period

If due to whatever reason the client wants to extend the renting period, he has to sail back to the designated port and contact the Adriatic.hr representative and in written form to ask for a permission for a new time of disembarkation and a new designated port.

10. Documents of the Vessel

The vessel is submitted to the client's usage with all proper documents necessary for renting (permit, registration, concession...), as well as with all other supplements found in the vessel's folder (list of port authorities, gas stations...). The client is obliged to handle and keep all received documents with extra care.

When returning the vessel, the client must give back all received documents and their supplements.

The client is obliged to keep records in the vessel's dairy.

11. Obligation of the Agency

Adriatic.hr is obliged to take care of the realization of the offered services with the attention of a good manager and to watch after the rights and interests of the clients, in accordance with the good Croatian tourist tradition.

Adriatic.hr is obliged to make sure that the guest receives all the services he paid for in the reserved term, and thus is responsible to him for any possible unfulfillment of the services, or a part of them.

In case of changes or unfulfillment of the services caused by force majeure (war, riots, strikes, terrorist activities, sanitary disorders, adverse weather, government official, etc.), Adriatic.hr refuses any responsibility.

12. Client's Obligations

The client is bound to and declares that:

1. Owns a valid passport. The client bears all expenses of document loss or their theft.
2. He will attain and study the published material for proper usage of the vessel
3. He will consciously and carefully handle the vessel, the inventory and the equipment, especially that he will not run it under the influence of alcohol or narcotics, and that in every way he will behave responsibly to the pleasure of his crew.
4. He will sail in the territorial borders of the Republic of Croatia. Leaving the territorial waters of the Republic of Croatia is possible only by means of previous written permission by Adriatic.hr.
5. He will not sail in forbidden sailing zones.
6. He will not sail and plan routes (itinerary) without previously studying the navigation charts, potential routes, nautical guides and all other guides found aboard, especially that he will not sail in areas that are not satisfactory researched and insufficiently covered by the nautical maps.
7. When taking over the vessel, he will let Adriatic.hr know about the approximate route of sailing (itinerary). In reasonable time periods he is to report to Adriatic.hr using a GSM, or the available radio-station, about his position and the condition of the vessel and his crew, as well as for all possible breakdowns and damages
8. He will carefully plan and maintain his itinerary so that the place of turning around and heading towards

the port of departure be, at the most, two days of sailing from the that port, which is approximately 40 NM.

9. He will not sail at night without the use of navigation lights; he will sail with the adequate watching over the deck and with the necessary attention directed toward potential obstacles.
10. He will sail in safe weather condition, in good visibility, and that he will avoid obviously dangerous areas.
11. Depending on the atmospheric conditions, he will taken in the sails in time, and for the purpose of comfortable sailing, he will not allow unnecessary damages on the mast, the sails and the lines.
12. He will not leave port or the anchoring place if the current wind intensity is, or is soon expected to be more than 23 knots, or when the general weather conditions are unstable.
13. He will not leave port or the anchoring place if the vessel or part of the equipment (such as the engine, the mast, the lines, the bilge pump, the sail equipment, the compass, the navigation lights, the safety equipment...) is not properly functioning.
14. He will not leave harbor if port authorities have issued a sailing prohibition, in case of insufficient gas supply, and in case of sickness of any crew member.
15. He will not use the vessel for commercial purposes (transporting goods and people for a compensation), professional fishing, sailing school and similar activities.
16. He will not further rent the vessel or give it away to a third party.
17. He will not take more passengers onboard more than the vessel is intended for, and that there will be no more people onboard than the ones listed on the crew list.

18. He will not participate in a regatta or other competitions without the agreement of Adriatic.hr.
19. He will not tow another vessel, except in emergency cases.
20. He will take all prevention measures in order to avoid situations in which the rented vessel needs to be towed. If such situations occur, the price of towing needs to be negotiated with the captain of the other vessel before towing, for which the client needs to ask for the Adriatic.hr's permission.
21. He will respect all customs and other regulations of the Republic of Croatia and that he will not take onboard any objects undeclared to the customs.
22. He will personally watch that he himself and all crew members behave in accordance with all valid laws and regulations of the Republic of Croatia, especially obeying fishing and diving laws; and that no archeological valuable objects should be found onboard.
23. He agrees that the renting contract is cancelled, if it is established that some crew member has broken any valid regulation and/or a law of the Republic of Croatia, which means that the vessel should be at Adriatic.hr's disposal, without any right of compensation on the client's side. Furthermore, it is hereby specially established that Adriatic.hr will be free of any responsibility before any government officials because, for all committed violations and/or criminal offences, the client is wholly responsible before the government organs.
24. He will overtake full responsibility and thus compensate Adriatic.hr for all expenses for which it has been established that have been caused by actions and failures on the client's side and for which Adriatic.hr is materially and criminally responsible to a third party.

25. The responsibility of the client for breaking any rules of sailing and all other rules, performed during the renting of the vessel, does not stop after the end of the renting period.
26. In case of damaging the vessel, accident or breakage, he should record the course of happening and immediately report to Adriatic.hr. He should also file a report of the sea accident to the closest port authorities, doctors or corresponding authorities so that he can get their attest.
27. In case of any defect of the vessel, or its equipment, caused by the natural expenditure of the vessel or the equipment, he should immediately report to Adriatic.hr. The agency is obliged to fix the defect within 24 hours upon receiving the report. If Adriatic.hr fixes the defect within 24-hour period, the client has no right to any compensation. The contact telephone numbers, which should be used in case of breakage, are listed in the vessel's documentation.
28. He will fully compensate Adriatic.hr for any damage performed in negligence and/or by the unconscious actions of the client, which are not covered by the insurance, and for which Adriatic.hr is responsible to a third party.
29. In case of disappearance of the vessel and its accompanying equipment, inability of sailing of the vessel, expropriating of the vessel and/or its confiscation, or prohibition by government officials or a third party, the client must immediately report to the competent authorities and Adriatic.hr and ask for a copy of the police report.
30. In case of confiscating the vessel by any government officials due to irresponsible or illegal actions (commercial fishing, extracting antiquities from the sea bottom...) performed during its renting period, he will take full responsibility.

31. He alone is responsible for contaminating the sea during filling the gas tank of or disposing of garbage or waste in forbidden areas outside the regulated places.
32. He will check the level of oil in the engine every day. The client is fully responsible for damages caused by an oil shortage.
33. He will correctly run the vessel's diary and leave it onboard after the rental period
34. He will take aboard home pets (dogs, cats, birds...) only with the permission of Adriatic.hr. Taking home pets aboard is not permitted. Exceptions are possible upon previous agreement.

    If he decides to act differently than hereby stated, the client alone takes upon himself all material and criminal responsibility.

13. Sailing Permit

The client must possess necessary nautical knowledge and skills and a valid sailing permit for running the vessel at open sea, as well as a confirmation of finished course on handling the radio station. If the client does not posses the required documents, knowledge and skills, he is obliged to let the vessel be run exclusively by a crew member who owns such documents.

The client, or the person appointed as a skipper by him, may be asked by an Adriatic.hr representative to demonstrate his knowledge and skills. The client is billed for the testing expenses. The time spent for testing is included in the renting period.

If during testing the Adriatic.hr representative establishes that the client, or the person appointed as a skipper by him, does not possess enough knowledge, experience and/or valid sail permits, then an Adriatic.hr skipper will join the crew at additional cost, in accordance with the official price-list. If the client does not accept the appointed skipper, Adriatic.hr can exercise its right to forbid sailing out of the vessel, to cancel the contract and to keep the whole amount of the deposit. In this case, the client has no right to be compensated.

If the client knows in advance that he will need the service of the official Adriatic.hr skipper, he ought to notify the Adriatic.hr personnel about that during reservation.

14. Insurance

The insurance is defined by the conditions established by the insurance company with whom the owner of the vessel, or Adriatic.hr, has signed the policy.

The insurance of the vessel covers damages inflicted to and by a third party up to the amount of the reported value of the vessel (obligatory insurance). The vessel is also covered by a comprehensive boat insurance that equals the amount of the reported value of the vessel. The comprehensive boat insurance covers damages that exceed the amount of the deposit and are caused by force majoure, but not damages caused intentionally or by negligence.

The client, the crew and their personal belongings are not insured and therefore we suggest that he should do that on his own. All damages and/or losses must be reported to Adriatic.hr immediately upon occurrence. When there is a greater damage, as well as in the case when more vessels participate in the accident, it must be reported to the competent port authorities and to ask for the corresponding document that will additionally be handed over to the insurance company. Damages covered by the insurance policy that were not immediately reported to Adriatic.hr, to the competent authorities, to the insurance company, and for which all necessary documents do not exist, will not be acknowledged, according to the conditions of the insurance. Therefore, the client is personally responsible for all damages and will be charged with all restoration expenses.

When the vessel is damaged, the client will be charged with all expenses in accordance with the conditions of the comprehensive boat insurance but only to the amount of the deposit. The expenses of all damages of the vessel and/or its equipment caused by negligence and/or loss of one or more equipment parts are born in full amount by the client.

The sails are not insured and thus the client will be charged with all repair expenses. The responsibility of the client is excluded only in case of natural wearing our of one or more sails, or in case of damages caused by breaking of the mast.

Engine damages caused by the oil shortage are not covered by the insurance; thus, the client will be charged personally for all repair expenses

The client takes full material responsibility for damages caused by anchoring and docking into ports and small ports that are known as being unsafe.

15. Responsibility for Expenses Orginated during Renting Period

The client himself is charged with all expenses or defects that have occurred while the vessel was his responsibility and that are not connected with the natural wearing out if the vessel. Before the process of reparation, the client has to come to an agreement with Adriatic.hr concerning the technical justification of the necessary repair.

Adriatic.hr covers all damages or defects that have occurred, or originated during the renting period, and that are connected with the natural wearing out of the vessel. Before the process of reparation, the client has to come to an agreement with Adriatic.hr concerning the technical justification of the necessary repair. The client is to pay the bill right at the repair place and to keep it so that, when returning the vessel, he may be refunded with the whole amount.

16. Breakages and Damages

The client is obliged to inform Adriatic.hr about all breakages and damages immediately after their occurrence, no matter what their cause may be. Adriatic.hr will instruct the client in what ways to perform all necessary activities and/

or change of equipment. The client will be charged with all unauthorized repairs and changes of parts of the equipment.

17. Property Loss

Adriatic.hr is not responsible for losses and/or damaging the property of the client and the rest of the crew, someone else' property that have been laid down and kept on the vessel, in the transportation vehicle, in the Adriatic.hr office or in the owner's vessel. By paying the necessary deposit and agreeing to the general conditions of renting a vessel, the client renounces his rights of requesting a compensation from Adriatic.hr, or from the owner of the vessel for losses and/or damages of his personal and/or someone else's property.

18. Photographs of the Vessels

If the photographs of the vessels presented on our web pages have the Adriatic.hr copyright sign, then these pictures correspond to the real vessel the client will be renting.

We want to especially emphasize that photographs of the vessels that do not have the Adriatic.hr's copyright sign are not the exact vessels the client will reside in, but only representative pictures of the vessel's maker, which still refer to the required model. The photographs of the vessels are published exclusively for orientation purposes and in order to help our users. It is possible that the client may notice some irregularities between the photographs and the real state of the vessel; however, these irregularities cannot serve as valid reasons for the client's request of a substitutive vessel nor for requesting any kind of compensation, if the real offered model corresponds to the rented one.

The presentation of the vessels we offer contains a plan of their different variations, depending on the number of cabins. Adriatic.hr is obliged to visibly emphasize the real number of cabins. We kindly ask the client to pay attention to the number of cabins of the vessel he is about to rent. All possibilities of later complaints from the client containing that he has been given a vessel with smaller number of cabins than presented by the plan on the internet, are excluded.

19. Complaints

If any client feels that the already-paid services are not completely and/or qualitatively performed, he has the right to address a complaint to Adriatic.hr. The client may request a proportional compensation only if during checking-out of the vessel he files a written complaint and encloses all corresponding documentation. Both the client and the Adriatic.hr representative should sign the written complaint. Adriatic.hr will not consider additionally received and incomplete documented complaints.

Adriatic.hr is obliged to come up with a written solution to the accepted complaint within 14 days upon receiving it. The agency can postpone the solution period for maximum another 14 days for the purpose of collecting data and verifying of the complaint that, directly or indirectly, concerns the involved persons cited in it.

The client renounces any mediation by any other person, the arbitration of the Association of Croatian Tourist Agencies, law institution or giving information to the means of mass meadia until Adriatic.hr comes up with a solution of the complaint. If the client breaks this regulation, because of the violation of the procedure, no matter his assertions, he loses the right of compensation. Adriatic.hr has the right to ask for a compensation from the client due to the harm he has done to the agency.

The highest amount of compensation can equal the amount of the advertised service but cannot comprise of the already used services or the whole amount of the rent. This excludes the client's right for a compensation of non-material damages.

20. Court Competence

If the client is not satisfied with the Agency's solution and cannot find a peaceful and reasonable agreement with it, he has the right to court arbitration. The court in Split is authorized for applying all Croatian law regulations in such cases.

21. Data Change

All changes and additions to these general conditions of renting a vessel are possible and valid exclusively in written form and signed by both the client and the agency.

THE CHARTER PATY AND SHIP

Chartering is part of the shipping industry. A charterer owns the cargo and employs a shipbroker to find a shipowner to deliver the cargo for a certain freight rate.

Cargo

Cargo is a term used to denote goods or produce being transported generally for commercial gain, usually on a ship, plane, train or truck. Nowadays containers are used in all intermodal long-haul cargo transport.

Marine Cargo Types

There is a wide range of marine cargoes at seaport terminals operated. The primary types are these:

- Containers are the largest and fastest growing cargo category at most ports worldwide. Containerized cargo includes everything from auto parts and machinery components to shoes, toys, and frozen meat and seafood.
- Automobiles are handled at many ports.
- Project cargoes and heavy lift cargoes may include items such as manufacturing equipment, factory components, power equipment such as generators and wind mills, military equipment or almost any other oversized or overweight cargo too big or too heavy to fit into a container.
- Break bulk cargo is typically material stacked on wooden pallets and lifted into and out of the hold of a vessel by cranes on the dock or aboard the ship itself. The volume of break bulk cargo has declined dramatically worldwide as containerization has grown.

- Bulk Cargoes, such as salt, oil, tallow and scrap metal, are usually defined as commodities that are neither on pallets nor in containers, and which are not handled as indiv

Bulk Cargo

Bulk cargo is cargo that is unpacked (un-bundled or un-bound) and is of the same or a similar kind or nature (homogeneous). These cargos are usually dropped or poured, with a spout or shovel bucket, as a liquid or solid, into a bulk carrier's hold, railroad car, or truck/trailer/semi-trailer body. Bulk cargos are classified as liquid or dry.

The largest bulk carrier cargo ship in the world is the iron ore carrier Berge Stahl, weighing a massive 364,768 dead-weight-tons (metric).

The busiest bulk cargo port in the world is the New Orleans-area based Port of South Louisiana.

- Dry bulk cargos:
  - Coal
  - Grain (wheat, maize, rice, barley, oats, rye, sorghum, soybeans, etc.)
  - Iron ore (ferrous and non-ferrous ores, ferroalloys, pig iron, scrap metal, etc.)
  - Wood chips
  - Cement
  - Chemicals (fertilizer, plastic granules and pellets, resin powder, synthetic fiber, etc.)
  - Dry edibles (for animals or humans: alfalfa pellets, citrus pellets, livestock feed, flour, peanuts, raw or refined sugar, seeds, starches, etc.)
  - Bulk mine (sand and gravel, copper, iron, (ores in pellet form) , salt, etc.)
- Liquid bulk cargos:
  - Oil
  - Liquefied natural gas (LNG)
  - Gasoline

  - Chemicals
  - Liquid edibles (vegetable oil, cooking oil, fruit juices, etc.)
- Large bulk sea-going companies:
  - Aasen Shipping & Aasen Chartering (Norway) Homepage
  - ALL-Transport A/S (Norway) Homepage
  - American Steamship Company (United States)
  - Canada Steamship Lines (Canada)
  - Commercial Trading & Discount (Greece)
  - Czech Ocean Shipping (Czech Republic)
  - Daeyang Shipping (China - Greece - Japan)
  - Fednav (Canada)
  - Gearbulk (Norway - Japan)
  - M/S Fjordbulk (Norway)
  - NOL Services (Singapore)
  - OAM Coal Trade and Bulk Shipping (Germany)
  - Österströms Rederi AB (Sweden)
  - SMC Marine Services (Singapore)
  - Samsun Logix (South Korea)
  - The Skaarup Group (United States) Homepage
  - Zhejiang Ocean Shipping Company (China)
- Large ports specializing in bulk cargo:
  - Port of South Louisiana
  - Port of Rotterdam
- Only monthly magazine for the dry bulk industry
  - Dry Cargo international

CONTAINERIZATION

Containerization is a system of intermodal freight transport cargo transport using standard ISO containers (also known as isotainers) that can be loaded and sealed intact onto container ships, railroad cars, planes, and trucks.

Container Dimensions

There are five common standard lengths, 20 ft (6.1 m), 40 ft (12.2 m), 45 ft (13.7 m), 48 ft (14.6 m), and 53 ft (16.2 m). US domestic standard containers are generally 48 ft and 53 ft (rail and truck). Container capacity is measured in twenty-foot equivalent units (TEU, or sometimes teu). A twenty-foot equivalent unit is a measure of containerized cargo capacity equal to one standard 20 ft (length) × 8 ft (width) × 8 ft 6 in (height) container. In metric units this is 6.10 m (length) × 2.44 m (width) × 2.59 m (height), or approximately 39 m^3. These sell at about US$2,500 in China, the biggest manufacturer.[1]

Most containers today are of the 40-ft (12.2 m) variety and are known as 40 foot containers. This is equivalent to 2 TEU. 45 foot (13.7 m) containers are also designated 2 TEU. Two TEU are equivalent to one forty-foot equivalent unit (FEU). High cube containers have a height of 9 ft 6 in (2.9 m), while half-height containers, used for heavy loads, have a height of 4 ft 3 in (1.3 m). When converting containers to TEUs, the height of the containers typically is not considered.

History

Containers produced a huge reduction in port handling costs, contributing significantly to lower freight charges and, in turn, boosting trade flows. Almost every manufactured product humans consume spends some time in a container. Containerization is an important element of the innovations in logistics that revolutionized freight handling in the 20th century.

Efforts to ship cargo in containers date to the 19th century. By the 1920s, railroads on several continents were carrying containers that could be transferred to trucks or ships, but these containers were invariably small by today's standards. From 1926 to 1947, the Chicago North Shore and Milwaukee Railway carried motor carrier vehicles and shippers' vehicles loaded on flatcars between Milwaukee and Chicago. Beginning in 1929, Seatrain Lines carried railroad boxcars on its sea vessels to transport goods between New York and Cuba. In the mid-1930s, the Chicago Great Western Railway and then the New Haven railroad began "piggy-back" service (transporting highway freight trailers on flatcars) limited to their own railroads. By 1953, the CB&Q, the Eastern Illinois and the

Southern Pacific railroads had joined the innovation. Most cars were surplus flatcars equipped with new decks. By 1955, an additional 25 railroads had begun some form of piggy-back trailer service.

The first vessels purpose-built to carry containers began operation in Denmark in 1951. Ships began carrying containers between Seattle and Alaska in 1951. The worlds first truly intermodel container system used purpose-built container ship theClifford J. Rodgers built in Montreal in 1955 and owned by the White Pass & Yukon Route. Its first trip carried 600 containers between North Vancouver, British Columbia and Skagway, Alaska on November 26, 1955; in Skagway, the containers were unloaded to purpose-built rail cars for transport north to the Yukon, in the first intermodal service using trucks, ships and rail cars. Southbound containers were loaded by shippers in the Yukon, moved by truck, rail, ship and truck to their consignees, without opening. This first intermodal system operated from November 1955 for many years.

The US container shipping industry dates to 1956, when U.S. trucking entrepreneur Malcom McLean put 58 containers aboard a refitted tanker ship, the "Ideal-X," and sailed them from Newark to Houston. What was new about McLean's innovation was the idea of using large containers that were never opened in transit between shipper and consignee and that were transferable on an intermodal basis, among trucks, ships and railcars. McLean had initially favored the construction of "trailerships" - taking trailers from large trucks and stowing them in a ship's cargo hold. This method of stowage, referred to as Roll On/Roll Off, was not adopted because of the large waste in potential cargo space onboard the vessel, known as broken stowage. Instead, he modified his original concept into loading just the containers, not the chassis, onto the ships, hence the designation container ship or "box" ship.

In the United States, at first, containerization grew through cracks in the rigid regulatory structure of the 1960s.

But the United States' present fully integrated systems became possible only after the Interstate Commerce Commission's regulatory oversight was cut back (and later abolished in 1995), trucking and rail were deregulated in the 1970s and maritime rates were deregulated (with very little fanfare) in 1984.

Containerization has revolutionized cargo shipping. Today, approximately 90% of non-bulk cargo worldwide moves by containers stacked on transport ships; 26% of all containers originate from China. As of 2005, some 18 million total containers make over 200 million trips per year. There are ships that can carry over 11,000 TEU ("Emma Mærsk", 1,300 feet long, launched August 2006), and designers are working on freighters capable of 14,000 TEU. It has even been predicted that, at some point, container ships will be constrained in size only by the Straits of Malacca, one of the world's busiest shipping lanes. Such a ship would be as long as one-quarter of a mile (400 m) and 190 feet (58 m) wide.

However, few initially foresaw the extent of the influence containerization would bring to the shipping industry. In the 1950s, Harvard University economist Benjamin Chinitz predicted that containerization would benefit New York by allowing it to ship industrial goods produced there more cheaply to the Southern United States than other areas, but did not anticipate that containerization might make it cheaper to import such goods from abroad. Most economic studies of containerization merely assumed that shipping companies would begin to replace older forms of transportation with containerization, but did not predict that the process of containerization itself would have some influence on producers and the extent of trading.

The widespread use of ISO standard containers has driven modifications in other freight-moving standards, gradually forcing removable truck bodies or swap bodies into the standard sizes and shapes (though without the strength needed to be stacked), and changing completely the worldwide use of freight pallets that fit into ISO containers or into commercial vehicles.

Improved cargo security is also an important benefit of containerization. The cargo is not visible to the casual viewer and thus is less likely to be stolen and the doors of the containers are generally locked (or rather "sealed") so that tampering is more evident. This has reduced the "falling off the truck" syndrome that long plagued the shipping industry.

Use of the same basic sizes of containers across the globe has lessened the problems caused by incompatible rail gauge sizes in different countries. Most of the trains in the world operate on 1435 mm (4 ft 8½ in) gauge track known as standard gauge but many industrialized countries like Australia, Russia, Finland and Spain use broader gauges while many countries in Africa and South America use narrower gauges on their networks. The use of container trains in all these countries makes trans-shipment between different gauge trains easier, with automatic or semi-automatic equipment.

Some of the largest global companies containerizing containers today are Patrick Global Shipping, Bowen Exports and Theiler & Sons Goods, LLC.

Double Stack Containerization

Most flatcars cannot carry more than one standard 40 foot container, but a well car can accept a container and still leave enough clearance for another container on top, on most North American rail routes that don't have overhead electric power. Pacer International, under its chief executive officer Donald Orris, introduced this Double Stack principle under the name of Stacktrain rail service in 1984. It saved money, and now accounts for almost 70 percent of intermodal freight transport shipments there.

CARGO SHIP

A cargo ship or freighter is any sort of ship or vessel that carries cargo, goods and materials from one port to another. Thousands of cargo carriers ply the world's seas and oceans each year; they handle the bulk of international trade. Cargo ships are usually specially designed for the task, being equipped with cranes and other mechanisms to load and unload, and come in all sizes.

Types

Specialized types of cargo vessels include container ships and bulk carriers (technically tankers and supertankers are cargo ships, although they are routinely thought of as a separate category).

History

The earliest records of waterborne activity mention the carriage of items for trade; the evidence of history and archaeology shows the practice to be widespread by the beginning of the 1st millennium BC. The desire to operate trade routes over longer distances and at more seasons of the year motivated improvements in ship design during the Middle Ages.

Before the middle of the 19th century, the incidence of piracy resulted in most cargo ships being armed, sometimes quite heavily, as in the case of the Manila galleons and East Indiamen.

Piracy

Piracy is still quite common in some waters, particualarly around Asia, most notably in the Malacca Straits, a narrow channel between Indonesia and Singapore / Malaysia. In 2004, the governments of those three nations agreed to provide better protection for the ships passing through the Straits. Also piracy prone are the waters off Somalia and Nigeria, while smaller vessels are also in danger along parts of the South American coasts.

Definitions

While the definitions have become "cross-pollinated" over the years, "cargo" technically refers to the goods carried aboard the ship for hire, while "freight" refers to the compensation the ship or charterer receives for carrying the cargo.

Generally, the modern ocean shipping business is divided into two classes:

1. Liner business: typically (but not exclusively) container vessels (wherein "general cargo" is carried in 20 or 40-foot "boxes"), operating as "common carriers", calling a regularly-published schedule of ports. A common carrier refers to a regulated service where any member of the public may book cargo for shipment, according to long-established and internationally agreed rules.
2. Tramp-tanker business: generally this is private business arranged between the shipper and receiver and facilitated by the vessel owners or operators, who offer their vessels for hire to carry bulk (dry or liquid) or break bulk (cargoes with individually handled pieces) to any suitable port(s) in the world, according to a specifically drawn contract, called a charter party.

Larger cargo ships are generally operated by shipping lines: companies that specialize in the handling of cargo in general. Smaller vessels, such as coasters, are often owned by their operators.

Merchant vessels usually carry the designation M/V for "Motor Vessel" (oil/Diesel). It is used as part of a ship's name, such as "M/V Independence", similarly to how "SS" (now seldom used) stands for "Steam Ship" (coal) in names such as SS Uganda.

Famous cargo ships would include the Liberty ships of World War II, which were prefabricated all over the USA and then assembled by the coast in an average of 6 weeks and as little as 4 days. These ships allowed the allies to replace older cargo vessels with ones that were faster then the Kriegsmarine's U-boats could sink and contributed significantly to the ability of the Allies to keep Britain in the war and build up troops and equipment for the D-Day landings.

Lake freighters built for the Great Lakes in North America differ in design from "salties" because of the difference in wave size and frequency in the lakes. A number of these boats are so large that they cannot leave the lakes because the do not fit into the locks on the Saint Lawrence Seaway.

Sizes of Cargo Ships

Cargo ships are categorized partly by their capacity, partly by their weight, and partly by their dimensions (often with reference to the various canals and canal locks through which they can travel). Some common categories include:

- Small Handy size, carriers of 20,000-28,000 deadweight tonnage
- Handy size, carriers of 28,000-40,000 deadweight tonnage
- Handymax, carriers of 40,000-50,000 dwt
- Seawaymax, the largest size which can traverse the St Lawrence Seaway
- Aframax, oil tankers between 75,000 and 115,000 dwt. This is the largest size defined by the average freight rate assessment (AFRA) scheme.
- Suezmax, the largest size which can traverse the Suez Canal
- Panamax, the largest size which can traverse the Panama Canal (generally: vessels with a width smaller than 32.2 meter)
- Capesize, vessels larger than Panamax and Suezmax, which must traverse the Cape of Good Hope and Cape Horn in order to travel between oceans
- VLCC (Very Large Crude Carrier), supertankers between 150,000 and 320,000 dwt
- ULCC (Ultra Large Crude Carrier), enormous supertankers between 320,000 and 550,000 dwt

STEVEDORE

The words stevedore, docker, and longshoreman can have various waterfront-related meanings concerning loading and unloading ships, according to place and country.

The word "stevedore" (and Dutch stuwadoor) was brought from Spain or Portugal by sailors. It started as a phonetic spelling of Spanish estibador or Portuguese estivador = "a man who stuffs", here in the sense of "a man who loads ships", which was the original meaning of "stevedore"; compare Latin stipâre = "to stuff".

As a result, the word "stevedore" has become proverbial for a man with a lot of muscle, as in "The ballet troupe found that in the off-season their best male dancer had been working on an oil rig for the money and came back looking like a stevedore."

The work of the men who load and unload ships

In Britain, such men are usually called dockers while in the U.S. the term longshoreman is used, derived from "along-the-shore man".

Loading and unloading ships is skilled work that needs operating loading equipment, the proper techniques for lifting and stowing cargo, and correct handling of hazardous materials.

In earlier days, men who load and unload ships had to tie down cargoes with rope. A special form of stop knot is called the stevedore's knot. The methods of securely tying up parcels of goods is called stevedore lashing or stevedore knotting.

While loading a general cargo vessel, they use dunnage, which are pieces of wood (or nowadays sometimes strong inflatable bags) set down to keep the cargo out of any water that might be lying in the hold or are placed as shims between cargo crates to keep them from shifting during a voyage.

They are expected to be physically strong and able to follow orders.

Traditionally, stevedores would have no fixed job and turn up at the docks in the morning hoping to find someone willing to employ them for the day. London dockers and Deal porters called this practice "standing on the stones". In Britain, due to changes in employment laws, such jobs have either become permanent or have been to converted to temping jobs.

USA Word Usage

In usual present-day USA waterfront word usage, a stevedore is a man or a company who manages the operation of loading or unloading a ship. A stevedore typically owns equipment used in the loading or discharge operation and hires longshoremen who load and unload cargo under the direction of a stevedore superintendent.

Sometimes the word "stevedore" is still used to mean "man who loads and unloads a ship", as British "docker".

Because they work outdoors in all types of weather, these workers adopted a type of cap that has a snug fit, is warm, and is easily put away in a pocket. These are a type of beanie or watch cap called variously stevedore's cap or stevedore's hat.

Today, a commercial stevedoring company also may contract with a terminal owner to manage all terminal operations. Many large containership operators have established in-house stevedoring operations to handle cargo at their own terminals and to provide stevedoring services to other container carriers.

Two unions within the AFL-CIO represent longshoremen in the United States: the International Longshoremen's Association, which represents longshoremen on the East Coast, on the Great Lakes and connected waterways and along the Gulf of Mexico, and the International Longshore and Warehouse Union, which represents longshoremen along the West Coast, in Hawaii and Alaska, and, through an affiliate, in Canada.

UK Word Usage

In the United Kingdom, the definition of a stevedore varies from port to port. In some ports, only the highly skilled master of a loading gang is referred to as a "stevedore".

"Docker" is the usual general term used in the UK for a man who loads or unloads ships and performs various other jobs required at a sea port.

Australian Word Usage

In Australia, stevedores / dockers were historically referred to as wharf labourers and were colloquially called wharfies. The Maritime Union of Australia has coverage of these workers, and fought a substantial industrial battle in the 1998 Australian waterfront dispute to prevent the contracting out. of work to non-union contractors.

New Zealand Usage

New Zealand usage is highly similar to the Australian version; waterfront workers are also known as "wharfies." The 1951 New Zealand waterfront dispute, involving New Zealand stevedores, was the largest and bitterest industrial dispute in the country's history.

Famous Stevedores

Famous ex-stevedores include comedian Artie Lange (although he refers to himself as an ex-longshoreman), Irish-American author Frank McCourt, actor Chief Dan George, and author / philosopher Eric Hoffer.

The film, On the Waterfront starring Marlon Brando, is a famous portrayal of longshoremen and their working conditions. It is thought to be partially based on real events.

Chapter 5

Marine Accidents and Law

Marine accident frequencies reported in 20 different sources have been studied and compared. Further than this, comparisons were made with an analysis done by the present authors. There seems to be consistency within the sources in the use of the terms total loss, casualty and accident/incident. The rates were observed to decrease by an order of magnitude going from accident/incident to casualty and likewise from casualty to total loss. The overall frequencies were found to be in the range of 0.009 to 0.07 total losses per 10 Ship miles, 0.03 to 1 casualties per 10[6] ship miles, and 0.5 to 13 accidents/incidents per 10 ship miles. It was found that the frequency depends on visibility, brightness, geographical environment, age of vessel and size of vessel.

Collision and grounding frequencies were found to increase with decreasing visibility, brightness and more restricted waters. Collision frequencies were found to increase with increasing size of vessel. Fire/explosion and structural damage frequencies were found to increase with increasing age, and collisions to decrease with increasing age. No firm trend was found from the effect of flag state or type of vessel.

Maritime accidents include accidents are those accidents that happen on the high seas and can involve recreational boaters, jet skiers, seamen, military sailors, and/or cruise ship passengers. Seamen are the most legally represented group for injuries sustained at sea. These injuries can be caused from something as simple as a slick deck or as complicated as a collision with another vessel. Seamen are mainly protected legally by two acts: the Jones Act and the Longshoremen's and Harbor Workers Compensation Act.

The Marine Accident Inquiry Agency (MAIA) clarifies the causes of marine accidents through lawsuit-like procedures called "marine accident inquiry", in order to contribute to the prevention of such accidents.

Should a marine accident be determined to be the result of intentional acts or negligence by marine technicians, pilots or small boat skippers, those judged responsible will be subjected to disciplinary punishment. Should the accident be ascribed to causes related to other persons (shipping or shipbuilding companies, etc.) concerned in the marine accident, such persons may be given recommendations to maintain beter safety standards.

Ships have greatly increased in size in the last five decades. Average length, beam and draft has doubled and sea-going commerce has tripled - accounting for 98% of all U.S. trade by weight. Half of this cargo consists of hazardous materials. Transport of these materials and other goods require safe handling and safe navigation to prevent accidents leading to increased risk to life, property, and the environment. This is especially important today due to our growing dependence on foreign oil and the potential for oil spill disasters resulting from marine accidents. Ships must be able to transport cargoes to their destinations safely and efficiently in and out of our ports and harbors. With the proper tools and services, marine accidents can be minimized and the safety and efficiency of maritime vessel traffic can be assured. Up-to-date nautical charts, the most fundamental tool, are essential for safe navigation as well as for the safety of life and property.

Houseboat Carbon Monoxide Hazards- Coast Guard Recall

February 23, the Coast Guard began issuing mandatory recall notices to houseboat manufacturers who may have built vessels equipped with swim platforms and electrical generator exhaust systems vented into a stern cavity. This design has been found to permit lethal concentrations of carbon monoxide to build up in the vicinity of the swim platform. The directed recall was addressed to those houseboat manufacturers who had not responded to the Coast Guard's December 21, 2000 letter notifying them of this design defect, which has been linked to a large number of carbon monoxide [CO] poisonings. Six houseboat manufacturers have agreed to voluntarily recall all of their boats with the design problem.

Cruise Ship Passengers at Risk

Nearly six million passengers boarded cruise ships from U.S. ports in 1999. However, these passengers are every day placed in danger because the ships lack an important safety item, a local sounding smoke alarm. Historically, most fire-related deaths do not result from burn injuries, but from smoke inhalation.

MARINE VHF RADIO

Marine VHF radio is installed on all large ships and most motorized small craft. It is used for a wide variety of purposes, including summoning rescue services and communicating with harbours and marinas, and operates in the VHF frequency range, between 156 to 174 MHz. Although it is widely used for collision avoidance, its use for this purpose is contentious and is strongly discouraged by some countries, including the UK.

A marine VHF set is a combined transmitter and receiver and only operates on standard, international frequencies known as "channels". Channel 16 (156.8 MHz) is the calling and emergency channel. Transmission power ranges between 1 and 25 watts, giving a maximum range of up to about 60 nautical miles (111 km) between aerials mounted on tall ships and hills, and 5 nautical miles (9 km) between aerials mounted on small boats at sea-level.

Marine VHF mostly uses "simplex" transmission, where communication can only take place in one direction at a time. A transmit button on the set or microphone determines whether it is operating as a transmitter or a receiver. The majority of channels, however, are set aside for "duplex" transmissions channels where communication can take place in both directions simultaneously . Each duplex channel has two frequency assignments. This is mainly because, in the days before mobile phones and satcomms became widespread, the duplex channels could be used to place calls on the public telephone system for a fee via a marine operator. This facility is still available in some areas, though its use has largely died out. In US waters, Marine VHF radios can also receive NOAA Weather Radio broadcasts, where they are available, on receive-only channels wx1, wx2, etc.

Sets can be fixed or portable. A fixed set generally has the advantages of a more reliable power source, higher transmit power, a larger and more effective aerial and a bigger display and buttons. A portable set can be carried to a lifeboat in an emergency, has its own power source and is more easily water-proofed.

Marine radios can be "voice-only" or can include "Digital Selective Calling". Voice-only equipment is the traditional type, which relies totally on the human voice for calling and communicating.

Digital Selective Calling equipment, a part of GMDSS, provides all the functionality of voice-only equipment and, additionally, allows several other features:

- A transmitter can call a receiver automatically using Digital Selective Calling on Channel 70, using a telephone-type number known as a Maritime Mobile Service Identity or MMSI
- A distress button, which automatically sends a digital distress signal identifying the calling vessel and the nature of the emergency
- A connection to a GPS receiver allowing the digital distress message to contain the distressed vessel's position

The MMSI is a nine digit number identifying a VHF set or group of sets. The left hand digits of MMSI indicate the country and type of station. For examples, here are MMSI prefixes of 4 types of station:

- Ship : 23 is the United Kingdom – e.g. a UK ship : 232003556
- Coast : 00 – e.g. Solent Coastguard : 002320011
- Group of stations : 0 – e.g. 023207823
- Portable DSC equipment : for UK 2359 - e.g. 235900498

Operating procedures

Proper operating procedures for marine radio include:

- Listening before transmitting
- Using Channel 16 only to establish communication (if necessary) and then switching to a different channel
- Using a set of international "calling" procedures such as the "Mayday" distress call and the "Pan-pan" urgency call
- Using "pro-words" based on the English language such as Acknowledge, All after, All before, All stations, Confirm, Correct, Correction, In figures, In letters, Over, Out, Radio check, Read back, Received, Repeat, Say again, Spell, Standby, Station calling, This is, Wait, Word after, Word before, Wrong
- Using the NATO phonetic alphabet: Alpha, Bravo, Charlie, Delta, Echo, Foxtrot, Golf, Hotel, India, Juliet, Kilo, Lima, Mike, November, Oscar, Papa, Quebec, Romeo, Sierra, Tango, Uniform, Victor, Whiskey, X-ray, Yankee, Zulu
- Using a phonetic numbering system based on the English language: Wun, Too, Tree, Fow-er, Fife, Six, Sev-en, Ait, Nin-er, Zero, Decimal

Marine VHF radio is sometimes illegally operated inland. Since enforcement is often the job of the local coast guard, enforcement away from the water is sometimes difficult.

AIS System

AIS (short for automatic identification system), was mandated by the Maritime Security Act of 2002. As a result of this act, any cargo vessel, oil tanker, tug boat, and passenger vessel permitted to carry more than 150 passengers; must carry a Coast Guard approved AIS system. A typical AIS is an integral VHF radio and GPS unit that sends out data from your own ship and receives data from other AIS equipped ships in your area. A typical AIS transmits:

1. Your ship's name 2. Your ship's type such as cargo vessel, passenger ferry, tug, yacht, tanker. 2. Your ship's length, beam and draft 3. Your ship's MMSI (mobile marine service identity) 4. Your ship's destination, estimated time of arrival, course and speed 5. Your ship's navigational status such as, Underway, Berthed, Aground, At Anchor, Moored, etc.

The idea of AIS is that your information is transmitted to all AIS equipped ships within range of the AIS signal. An AIS equipped vessel can either, call your vessel on VHF radio or send a text message to your ship if there is a conflicting traffic situation developing between two or more vessels. In an area that is controlled by a VTS (vessel traffic system), the VTS operators can aid mariners in crowded shipping lanes.

MARITIME SECURITY ACT OF 2002

The Maritime Transportation Security Act of 2002 (MTSA), signed on November 25, 2002 by the President of the United States, is designed to protect ports and waterways from a terrorist attack. This law is the U.S. equivalent of the International Ship and Port Facility Security Code (ISPS), and was fully implemented on July 1, 2004. It requires vessels and port facilities to conduct vulnerability assessments and develop security plans that may include passenger, vehicle and baggage screening procedures; security patrols; establishing restricted areas; personnel identification procedures; access control measures; and/or installation of surveillance equipment. By creating a consistent security program for all our nation's ports, we are better able to identify and deter threats.

Developed using risk-based methodology, the MTSA security regulations focus on those sectors of maritime industry that have a higher risk of involvement in a transportation security incident, including various tank vessels, barges, large passenger vessels, cargo vessels, towing vessels, offshore oil and gas platforms, and port facilities that handle certain kinds of dangerous cargo or service the vessels listed above.

MTSA also required the establishment committees in all the nation's ports to coordinate the activities of all port stakeholders, including other federal, local and state agencies, industry and the boating public. These groups, called Area Maritime Security Committees, are tasked with collaborating on plans to secure their ports so that the resources of an area can be best used to deter, prevent and respond to terror threats

Chapter 6

Marine Salvage

Marine salvage is the process of rescuing a ship, it's cargo and sometimes the crew from peril. Salvage encompasses rescue towing, refloating a grounded ship or patching or repairing a ship. Today the protection of the envionment from cargoes such as oil is often is considered a higher priority the saving the ship or cargo.

"Salvors" are seamen and engineers who carry out salvage to vessels that are not owned by themselves. When salvaging large ships, they may use cranes, floating dry docks and divers to lift and repair ships for short journeys to safety towed by a tugboat. The aim of the salvage may be to repair the vessel at a harbour or dry dock. Another reason for salvage may be to prevent pollution or damage to the marine environment. Alternatively the vessel or valuable parts of the vessel or its cargo may be recovered for its resale value, or for scrap.

Types of Salvage

There are two type of salvage, contract salvage and pure salvage. Contract salvage occurs when a contract is made prior to commencement of salvage operations, the amount of compensation is fixed and the salvor is paid regardless if the salvage is sucessful. When a ship or boat has been rescued or salvaged without prior agreement between the owner salvor or an agreement is made but not for a fixed amount, this is pure salvage. In this case the salvor can legally claim recompense or a salvage claim. It is also pure salvage when the ship's master signs an open form salvage agreement with no fixed compensation.This is a contingency contract that leaves the value of the salvage operation to be decided at a later date and both parties agree to binding arbitration in the case of a dispute.

The best-known open form is the Lloyd's Open Form salvage contract, which was developed by Lloyd's of London and states "no cure - no pay".Although this rule seems to the disadvantage of the owner of the ship, its purpose is to encourage potential salvors to risk their vessels and use their working time for the benefit of both themselves and the ship owner. In order for a claim to be awarded three requirments must be meet: The vessel must be in peril, the services must be rendered voluntarily, in other words there is no contractual obligation, and finally the salvage must be sucessful.

Ship salvage and the law

Salvage law has as a basis that a salvor should be rewarded for risking his life and property to rescue the property of another from peril. A vessel is consider in peril if it is in danger or could become in danger. Examples of a vessel in peril are when it is aground or in danger of going aground.

Prior to a salvage attempt the savor receives permission from the owner or the master to assist the vessel. If the vessel is abandoned no permission is needed.

The amount of the award depends on, in part, the value of the salved vessel, the degree of risk involved and the degree of peril the vessel was in. Legal disputes do arise from the claiming of salvage rights. To reduce the amount of a claim after an accident, boat owners or skippers often remain on board and in command of the vessel; they do everything possible to minimise further loss and seek to minimize the degree of risk the vessel is in. If another vessel offers a tow and the master or owner negotiates an hourly rate the before accepting then salvage does not apply.

Some maritime rescue organisations, such as Britain's Royal National Lifeboat Institution, insist the crews of their lifeboats renounce their right to claim compensation for salvage.

Jetsam are goods that were thrown off a ship, which was in danger, to save the ship. Flotsam are goods that floated off the ship while it was in danger or when it sank. Ligan are goods left in the sea on the wreck or tied to a buoy so that they can be recovered later by the owners. Derelict is abandoned vessels or cargo.

In the United Kingdom under the Merchant Shipping Act 1995, jetsam, flotsam, lagan and all other cargo and wreckage remain the property of their original owners. Anyone, including recreational divers and beachcombers, removing those goods must inform the Receiver of Wreck to avoid the accusation of theft. As the leisure activity of Wreck diving is common, there are laws to protect historic wrecks of archaeological importance and to protect war graves.

The 1910 Brussels Convention for the Unification of Certain Rules with Respect to Assistance and Salvage at Sea reflects the traditional legal principles of marine salvage. The 1989 International Convention on Salvage incorporated the essential provisions of the 1910 Convention, and added some new provisions, as well. The 1989 Salvage Convention entered force on July 14, 1996, with nearly twenty parties. It replaces the 1910 Convention for states which are parties to both where the two conventions' provisions are incompatible.

Chapter 7

Monitor Compliance with Legislative Requirements

1966 Load Line Convention

The Minister may, at the request of the Government of a country to which the Load Line Convention applies, issue a Load Line Convention certificate in respect of an international load line ship of that country if he is satisfied in like manner as in the case of a Saorstát Eireann ship that he can properly issue the certificate, and where a certificate is issued at such a request, it shall contain a statement that it has been so issued.

With a view to determining the validity in Saorstát Eireann of certificates purporting to have been issued in accordance with the Load Line Convention in respect of Load Line Convention ships not registered in Saorstát Eireann, the Minister shall make such regulations as appear to him to be necessary for the purpose of giving effect to Article seventeen of the Load Line Convention, and, for the purpose of the provisions hereafter contained in this Part of this Act relating to Load Line Convention ships not registered in Saorstát Eireann, the expression "a valid Load Line Convention certificate" means a certificate complying with such of those regulations as are applicable in the circumstances.

For many years the wish to amend the 1966 Load Line Convention has been frustrated by the need for explicit approval of all amendments by two-thirds of the states which have ratified the original convention. In such cases the 'inertia factor' invariably seems to rule the day, and amendments sit on the shelf gathering dust.

To circumvent the problem a Protocol to the 1966 Convention was adopted in 1988, but that too has been lying stagnant for ten years awaiting ratification. Recently, however, the necessary tonnage level has at last been achieved and the Protocol will enter into force in February 2000. An all-important provision in the Protocol is the tacit acceptance amendment procedure, which should ensure that necessary amendments will not in future be delayed by procedural difficulties.

The danger now is that the flood gates will open, and that over the coming months it will be difficult to restrain the enthusiasts who are already talking about the need for a wholesale revision of the Convention. Some changes may be needed, but the load line concept has stood the test of time and ICS will encourage caution in the discussions ahead.

STCW CONVENTION

The International Convention on Standards of Training, Certification and Watchkeeping for Seafarers (STCW), 1978, as amended, sets qualification standards for masters, officers and watch personnel on seagoing merchant ships. STCW was adopted in 1978 by conference at the International Maritime Organization (IMO) in London, and entered into force in 1984. The Convention was significantly amended in 1995.

The 1978 STCW Convention was the first to establish basic requirements on training, certification and watchkeeping for seafarers on an international level. Previously the standards of training, certification and watchkeeping of officers and ratings were established by individual governments, usually without reference to practices in other countries. As a result standards and procedures varied widely, even though shipping is the most international of all industries.

The Convention prescribes minimum standards relating to training, certification and watchkeeping for seafarers which countries are obliged to meet or exceed.

The Convention did not deal with manning levels: IMO provisions in this area are covered by regulation 13 of Chapter V of the International Convention for the Safety of Life at Sea (SOLAS), 1974, whose requirements are backed up by resolution A.890(21) Principles of safe manning, adopted by the IMO Assembly in 1999, which replaced an earlier resolution A.481(XII) adopted in 1981.

One especially important feature of the Convention is that it applies to ships of non-party States when visiting ports of States which are Parties to the Convention. Article X requires Parties to apply the control measures to ships of all flags to the extent necessary to ensure that no more favourable treatment is given to ships entitled to fly the flag of a State which is not a Party than is given to ships entitled to fly the flag of a State that is a Party.

The difficulties which could arise for ships of States which are not Parties to the Convention is one reason why the Convention has received such wide acceptance. By December 2000, the STCW Convention had 135 Parties, representing 97.53 percent of world shipping tonnage.

U.S. Proposal for Revision

In December 1992, as details of the grounding of the M/V Aegean Sea on rocks outside the Spanish port of La Corunna were being reported, the IMO's Maritime Safety Committee (MSC) agreed to a U.S. proposal to conduct a comprehensive review of the 1978 Convention. In making the proposal, the U. S. suggested that the review should specifically consider criteria used for insuring fitness of watchstanders and the role of the human element in maritime casualties. During the ensuing discussions, some delegations expressed agreement that the time had come for the organization to concentrate on areas relating to people, training and operational practices rather than on issues dealing with improving ship construction and equipment standards. Consequently, the MSC directed one of its subordinate committees, the Standards of Training and Watchkeeping (STW) Sub-Committee, to take the human element into account, and further that the Sub-Committee should complete the revision by 1996.

In 1993, the IMO embarked on this comprehensive revision of STCW to establish the highest practicable standards of competence to address the problem of human error as the major cause of maritime casualties. A small number of special consultants developed a document identifying categories of behavioral conditions which, in their view, could be improved to some degree with proper training and enhanced shipboard practices and arrangements. After considering these conditions in terms of the effects of the human element in marine casualties, the consultants prepared a preliminary draft of suggested amendments to the STCW Convention, including a number of proposals directly addressing the human element. They also included a proposal to develop a new STCW Code, which would contain the technical details associated with provisions of the Convention. The amendments were discussed and modified by the STW Subcommittee over the following two years.

The most significant amendments concerned:

a) Enhancement of port state control;
b) Communication of information to IMO to allow for mutual oversight and consistency in application of standards,
c) Quality standards systems (QSS), oversight of training, assessment, and certification procedures,
d) Placement of responsibility on parties, including those issuing licenses, and flag states employing foreign nationals, to ensure seafarers meet objective standards of competence, and
e) Rest period requirements for watchkeeping personnel.

Amendments Adopted

On July 7, 1995, a conference of parties to the Convention, meeting at IMO headquarters in London, adopted the package of amendments to STCW. The amendments entered force on February 1, 1997. The Coast Guard subsequently took steps necessary to implement the revised requirements, ensuring that U.S. licenses and documents would be issued in compliance with the 1995 Amendments.

Full implementation was required by February 1, 2002. Mariners already holding licenses had the option to renew those licenses in accordance with the old rules of the 1978 Convention during the period ending on February 1, 2002. Mariners entering training programs after August 1, 1998 are required to meet the competency standards of the new 1995 Amendments.

Training Requirements

The Amendments require that seafarers be provided with "familiarization training" and "basic safety training" which includes basic fire fighting, elementary first aid, personal survival techniques, and personal safety and social responsibility. This training is intended to ensure that seafarers are aware of the hazards of working on a vessel and can respond appropriately in an emergency.

STCW, as amended, will require all training and assessment activities to be "continuously monitored through a quality standards system to ensure achievement of defined objectives, including those concerning the qualifications and experience of instructors and assessors." The 1995 amendments require those responsible for instruction and assessment of the competence of seafarers to be qualified for the type and level of training or assessment involved. Persons performing these roles are expected to have received guidance in instructional techniques and assessment methods. The Coast Guard has drafted policy guidance for use in qualifying and managing training and assessment personnel.

Like all treaties, the STCW Convention is an agreement between countries. As of November 1998, there were 133 countries which had formally expressed their commitment to the obligations expressed by the STCW Convention. Virtually every maritime country is a "party" to this agreement. Following is a summary of the articles of the STCW Convention.

Article I - General Obligations

The first article contains three important principles. The Parties are to give effect to the convention and the Annex; any reference to the convention is understood to be a reference to the Annex as well; and Parties are to take all steps necessary to give the convention "full and complete effect."

Article II - Definitions

Certain terms as used in the convention are defined to ensure everyone has a common understanding of what is meant. For example:

A "party" is "a State for which the convention has entered into force" but an "Administration" is "the Government of the Party whose flag the ship is entitled to fly" (i.e., flag State). "Certificate" means " a valid document, by whatever name it may be known, issued by or under the authority of the Administration or recognized by the Administration authorizing the holder to serve as stated in this document or as authorized by national regulations."

One of the most important definitions pertains to "seagoing ship" because that affects where the requirements of the convention will apply. "Seagoing ship" means "a ship other than those which navigate exclusively in inland waters or in waters within, or closely adjacent to, sheltered waters or areas where port regulations apply." This becomes very significant for an understanding of Article III.

Article III - Application

This article contains two fundamental principles. First, the convention applies to seafarers serving on board seagoing ships entitled to fly the flag of a Party. Second, it limits this broad application by excepting specific classes: warships and those otherwise entitled to sovereign immunity; fishing vessels (i.e., those which catch fish or other living resources); pleasure yachts; and wooden ships of primitive build.

Most importantly, as a consequence of this Article and the broad definition of "seagoing ship" in Article II, the convention must be understood to apply to vessels which operate on the ocean whether they are engaged in domestic or international voyages.

Article IV - Communication of Information

Under this Article, Parties are required to submit certain information to the Secretary-General of the IMO "as soon as practicable" after becoming Parties. The information should include texts of laws and regulations on matters that lie within the scope of the convention; contents of study courses; details on examination requirements for certificates issued in compliance with the convention; and samples of certificates which are issued.

Additional discussion of this subject can be found in section 4 of this handbook, under the heading "Regulation I/7 -Communication of Information."

Article V - Other Treaties and Interpretation

Three important principles are reflected in this article. First, Parties are to ensure that there is no conflict in their commitments if there happen to be other treaties between them which relate to standards of training, certification or watchkeeping for seafarers. Second, matters which are not expressly addressed in the STCW convention are left to the discretion of the Parties. Third, the convention was intended to be understood in the context of the UN Convention on Law of the Sea.

Article VI - Certificates

Article VI contains the two most important obligations in the convention. First, certificates are to be issued to masters, officers and ratings when they meet the requirements for service, age, medical fitness, training, qualification and examinations in accordance with the Annex.

Second, certificates issued to masters and officers are to be endorsed using the form prescribed in regulation I/2 of the Annex. The endorsement must be available in or translated into English. This form is discussed in more detail in section 4 of this handbook, under the heading "Regulation I/2 - Certificates and Endorsements."

Article VII - Transitional Provisions

When a country first becomes a party to the STCW convention, this article permits it to continue to issue certificates of competency in accordance with its previous practices for five years.

The 1995 Amendments to STCW provide a special set of transitional arrangements to allow some new requirements to be phased in between February 1, 1997 and February 1, 2002. This arrangements are discussed in section 4 of this Handbook, under the heading "Regulation 1/15 -Transitional provisions."

Article VIII - Dispensations

This article permits flag States to issue a "dispensation which permits a specific seafarer (except master and chief engineer), in exceptional circumstances, to serve up to six months in a capacity immediately above the one for which the seafarer is qualified. Parties are required to provide IMO with an annual report of the number of dispensations issued during the year.

Article IX - Equivalents

Parties are permitted by this article to adopt educational and training arrangements which are different from those required by the Convention, including those involving seagoing service and shipboard organization. However, these arrangements must ensure a degree of safety at sea and pollution prevention "at least equivalent to the requirements of the Convention."

This article takes into account that experts may differ on how best to train a seafarer, but the ultimate objectives are the same: to provide for safety of life and property, and to protect the marine environment.

Article X - Control

While Article VI requires flag States to ensure that seafarers hold certificates, Article X provides an enforcement mechanism by allowing Port States to verify that seafarers serving on board hold any required certificates, and to detain a ship when certain officers are not properly certificated. The port control aspects of STCW are discussed in more detail in section 4 of this handbook, under the heading "Regulation I/4 - Control Procedures."

Article XI - Promotion of Technical Cooperation

This Article takes into account the fact that some countries may have difficulty in meeting their obligations under the convention, due to a lack of financial resources, technical expertise, or administrative personnel. The article expresses a commitment by all Parties to work together, through 1MG, to support Parties which request technical assistance. 1MG coordinates technical assistance projects which are funded through contributions from member countries, other UN organizations, such as the UN Development Program, and other interested organizations.

Article XII - Amendments

An international agreement is subject to change under any procedures that might be contained in the agreement. Article XII of the STCW Convention sets out alternative procedures for revising the articles and the Annex. IMO is identified as the organization to consider and adopt proposed amendments or to convene a conference of all parties to consider and adopt such amendments.

Article XIII - Signature. Ratification. Acceptance. Approval and Accession

This article sets out all the possible ways for a country to formally commit itself to complying with the requirements of the convention. The specific process will depend on the legal and political system in the particular country which is planning to become a Party to the convention.

Article XIV - Entry into Force

When the STCW Convention was adopted by a conference at IMO in 1978, the conference had to agree on the conditions which had to be met before the new agreement could come into force. Article XIV provided that the convention would enter into force 12 months after 25 countries had given their formal commitment to IMO. However, the 25 countries had to represent at total of at least 50% of the tonnage of the world's merchant ships of 100 gross register tons or more. The STCW Convention came into force on April 28, 1984, when these condition were met. As noted earlier, there are 133 countries which are party to the convention (as of November 1998).

Article XV - Denunciation

In the event a country wanted to withdraw from the convention, this article requires that a denunciation be sent to the Secretary-General of IMO. The denunciation could take effect not earlier than 12 months after the Secretary-General has received this notification.

Article XVI - Deposit and Registration

This article identifies the IMO as being responsible for keeping custody of the convention and for sending certified copies to countries which sign the convention or formally indicate their intent to become a Party.

Article XVII - Languages

The text of the convention is officially maintained at IMO in seven languages: Arabic, Chinese, English, French, German, Russian and Spanish. The Chinese, English, French, Russian and Spanish versions are considered to be "equally authentic" for purposes of legal interpretation.

As noted earlier, none of the articles was changed by the amendments to the STCW convention adopted in 1995. Those amendments resulted in changes to the regulations in the Annex and adoption of a new STCW Code, as discussed in the remaining sections of this handbook.

INTERNATIONAL CONVENTION FOR THE PREVENTION OF POLLUTION OF THE SEA BY OIL, 1954

The Governments represented at the International Conference on Pollution of the Sea by Oil held in London from 26 April 1954 to 12 May 1954,

Desiring to take action by common agreement to prevent pollution of the sea by oil discharged from ships, and considering that this end may best be achieved by the conclusion of a Convention,

Have Accordingly appointed the undersigned plenipotentiaries, who, having communicated their full powers, found in good and due form, Have Agreed as follows:

Article I

(1) For the purposes of the present Convention, the following expressions shall (unless the context otherwise requires) have the meanings hereby respectively assigned to them, that is to say:

"The Bureau" has the meaning assigned to it by Article XXI;

"Discharge" in relation to oil or to an oily mixture means any discharge or escape howsoever caused;

"Heavy diesel oil" means marine diesel oil, other than those distillates of which more than 50 percent by volume distils at a temperature not exceeding 340C when tested by ASTM Standard Method D.158/53;

"Mile" means a nautical mile of 6080 feet or 1852 metres;

"Oil" means crude oil, fuel oil, heavy diesel oil and lubricating oil, and "oily" shall be construed accordingly.

(2) For the purposes of the present Convention the territories of a Contracting Government mean the territory of the country of which it is the Government and any other territory for the international relations of which the Government is responsible and to which the Convention shall have been extended under Article XVIII.

Article II

The present Convention shall apply to sea-going ships registered in any of the territories of a Contracting Government, except

(i) Ships for the time being used as naval auxiliaries;

(ii) Ships of under 500 tons gross tonnage;

(iii) Ships for the time being engaged in the whaling industry;

(iv) Ships for the time being navigating the Great Lakes of North America and their connecting and tributary waters as far east as the lower exit of the Lachine Canal Montreal in the Province of Quebec, Canada.

Article III

(1) Subject to the provisions of Articles IV and V, the discharge from any tanker, being a ship to which the Convention applies, within any of the prohibited zones referred to in Annex A to the Convention in relation to tankers of-

(a) Oil;

(b) Any oily mixture the oil in which fouls the surface of the sea, shall be prohibited.

For the purposes of this paragraph the oil in an oily mixture of less than 100 parts of oil in 1,000,000 parts of the mixture shall not be deemed to foul the surface of the sea.

(2) Subject to the provisions of Articles IV and V, any discharge into the sea from a ship, being a ship to which the Convention applies and not being a tanker, of oily ballast water or tank washings shall be made as far as practicable from land. As from a date three years after the date on which the Convention comes into force, paragraph (1) of this Article shall apply to ships other than tankers as it applies to tankers, except that:

(a) The prohibited zones in relation to ships other than tankers shall be those referred to as such in Annex A to the Convention; and

(b) The discharge of oil or of any oily mixture from such ship shall not be prohibited when the ship is proceeding to a port not provided with such reception facilities as are referred to in Article VIII.

(3) Any contravention of paragraphs (1) and (2) of this Article shall be an offence punishable under the laws of the territory in which the ship is registered.

Article IV

(1) Article III shall not apply to:

(a) The discharge of oil or of an oily mixture from a ship for the purpose of securing the safety of the ship, preventing damage to the ship or cargo, or saving life at sea; or

(b) The escape of oil, or of an oily mixture, resulting from damage to the ship or unavoidable leakage, if all reasonable precautions have been taken after the occurrence of the damage or discovery of the leakage for the purpose of preventing or minimising the escape;

(c) The discharge of sediment:

(i) Which cannot be pumped from the cargo tanks of tankers by reason of its solidity; or

(ii) Which is residue arising from the purification or clarification of oil fuel or lubricating oil, provided that such discharge is made as far from land as is practicable.

(2) In the event of such discharge or escape as is referred to in this Article a statement shall be made in the oil record book required by Article IX of the circumstances of and reason for the discharge.

Article V

Article III shall not apply to the discharge from the bilges of a ship:

(a) Of any oily mixture during the period of twelve months following the date on which the Convention comes into force in respect of the territory in which the ship is registered;

(b) After the expiration of such period, of an oily mixture containing no oil other than lubricating oil.

Article VI

The penalties which may be imposed in pursuance of Article III under the law of any of the territories of a Contracting Government in respect of the unlawful discharge from a ship of oil or of an oily mixture into waters outside the territorial waters of that territory shall not be less than the penalties which may be imposed under the law of that territory in respect of the unlawful discharge of oil or of an oily mixture from a ship into such territorial waters.

Article VII

As from a date twelve months after the present Convention comes into force in respect of any of the territories of a Contracting Government all ships registered in that territory shall be required to be so fitted as to prevent the escape of fuel oil or heavy diesel oil into bilges the contents of which are discharged into the sea without being passed through an oily-water separator.

Article VIII

As from a date three years after the present Convention comes into force in respect of any of the territories of a Contracting Government, that Government shall ensure the provision in each main port in that territory of facilities adequate for the reception, without causing undue delay to ships, of such residues from oily ballast water and tank washings as would remain for disposal by ships, other than tankers, using the port, if the water had been separated by the use of an oily-water separator, a settling tank or otherwise. Each Contracting Government shall from time to time determine which ports are the main ports in its territories for the purposes of this Article, and shall notify the Bureau in writing accordingly indicating whether adequate reception facilities have been installed.

Article IX

(1) There shall be carried in every ship to which the Convention applies an oil record book (whether as part of the ship's official log-book or otherwise) in the form specified in Annex B to the present Convention. The appropriate entries shall be made in that book, and each page of the book, including any statement under paragraph (2) of Article IV, shall be signed by the officer or officers in charge of the operations concerned and by the master of the ship. The written entries in the oil record book shall be in an official language of the territory in which the ship is registered, or in English or French.

(2) The competent authorities of any of the territories of a Contracting Government may inspect on board any such ship while within a port in that territory the oil record book required to be carried in the ship in compliance with the provisions of the Convention, and may make a true copy of any entry in that book and may require the master of the ship to certify that the copy is a true copy of such entry. Any copy so made which purports to have been certified by the master of the ship as a true copy of an entry in the ship's oil record book shall be made admissible in any judicial proceedings as evidence of the facts stated in the entry. Any action by the competent authorities under this paragraph shall be taken as expeditiously as possible and the ship shall not be delayed.

Article X

(1) Any Contracting Government may furnish to the Contracting Government in the territory of which a ship is registered particulars in writing of evidence that any provision of the Convention has been contravened in respect of that ship, wheresoever the alleged contravention may have taken place. If it is practicable to do so, the competent authorities of the former Government shall notify the master of the ship of the alleged contravention.

(2) Upon receiving such particulars the latter Government shall investigate the matter, and may request the former Government to furnish further or better particulars of the alleged contravention. If the Government in the territory of which the ship is registered is satisfied that sufficient evidence is available in the form required by law to enable proceedings against the owner or master of the ship to be taken in respect of the alleged contravention, it shall cause such proceedings to be taken as soon as possible, and shall inform the other Contracting Government and the Bureau of the result of such proceedings.

Article XI

Nothing in the present Convention shall be construed as derogating from the powers of any Contracting Government to take measures within its jurisdiction in respect of any matter to which the Convention relates or as extending the jurisdiction of any Contracting Government.

Article XII

Each Contracting Government shall send to the Bureau and to the appropriate organ of the United Nations:

(a) The text of laws, decrees, orders and regulations in force in its territories which give effect to the present Convention;

(b) All official reports or summaries of official reports in so far as they show the results of the application of the provisions of the Convention, provided always that such reports or summaries are not, in the opinion of that Government, of a confidential nature.

Article XIII

Any dispute between Contracting Governments relating to the interpretation or application of the present Convention which cannot be settled by negotiation shall be referred at the request of either party to the International Court of Justice for decision unless the parties in dispute agree to submit it to arbitration.

Article XIV

(1) The present Convention shall remain open for signature for three months from this day's date and shall thereafter remain open for acceptance.

(2) Governments may become parties to the Convention by-

(i) Signature without reservation as to acceptance;

(ii) Signature subject to acceptance followed by acceptance; or

(iii) Acceptance.

(3) Acceptance shall be effected by the deposit of an instrument of acceptance with the Bureau, which shall inform all Governments that have already signed or accepted the Convention of each signature and deposit of an acceptance and of the date of such signature or deposit.

Article XV

(1) The present Convention shall come into force twelve months after the date on which not less than ten Governments have become parties to the Convention, including five Governments of countries each with not less than 500,000 gross tons of tanker tonnage.

(2) (a) For each Government which signs the Convention without reservation as to acceptance or accepts the Convention before the date on which the Convention comes into force in accordance with paragraph (1) of this Article it shall come into force on that date. For each Government which accepts the Convention on or after that date, it shall come into force three months after the date of the deposit of that Government's acceptance.

(b) The Bureau shall, as soon as possible, inform all Governments which have signed or accepted the Convention of the date on which it will come into force.

Article XVI

(1) Upon the request of any Contracting Government a proposed amendment of the present Convention shall be communicated by the Bureau to all Contracting Governments for consideration.

(2) Any amendment communicated to Contracting Governments for consideration under paragraph (1) of this Article shall be deemed to have been accepted by all Contracting Governments and shall come into force on the expiration of a period of six months after it has been so communicated, unless any one of the Contracting Governments shall have made a declaration not less than two months before the expiration of that period that it does not accept the amendment.

(3) (a) A conference of Contracting Governments to consider amendments of the Convention proposed by any Contracting Government shall be convened by the Bureau upon the request of one-third of the Contracting Governments.

(b) Every amendment adopted by such a conference by a two-thirds majority vote of the Contracting Governments represented shall be communicated by the Bureau to all Contracting Governments for their acceptance.

(4) Any amendment communicated to Contracting Governments for their acceptance under paragraph (3) of this Article shall come into force for all Contracting Governments, except those which before it comes into force make a declaration that they do not accept the amendment, twelve months after the date on which the amendment is accepted by two-thirds of the Contracting Governments.

(5) Any declaration under this Article shall be made by a notification in writing to the Bureau which shall notify all Contracting Governments of the receipt of the declaration.

(6) The Bureau shall inform all signatory and Contracting Governments of any amendments which come into force under this Article, together with the date on which such amendments shall come into force.

Article XVII

(1) The present Convention may be denounced by any Contracting Government at any time after the expiration of a period of five years from the date on which the Convention comes into force for that Government.

(2) Denunciation shall be effected by a notification in writing addressed to the Bureau, which shall notify all the Contracting Governments of any denunciation received and of the date of its receipt.

(3) A denunciation shall take effect twelve months, or such longer period as may be specified in the notification, after its receipt by the Bureau.

Article XVIII

(1) (a) Any Government may, at the time of signature or acceptance of the present Convention, or at any time thereafter, declare by notification in writing given to the Bureau that the Convention shall extend to any of the territories for whose international relations it is responsible.

(b) The Convention shall, from the date of the receipt of the notification, or from such other date as may be specified in the notification, extend to the territories named therein.

(2) (a) Any Contracting Government which has made a declaration under paragraph (1) of this Article may, at any time after the expiration of a period of five years from the date on which the Convention has been so extended to any territory, give notification in writing to the Bureau, declaring that the Convention shall cease to extend to any such territory named in the notification.

(b) The Convention shall cease to extend to any territory mentioned in such notification twelve months, or such longer period as may be specified therein, after the date of receipt of the notification by the Bureau.

(3) The Bureau shall inform all Contracting Governments of the extension of the Convention to any territories under paragraph (1) of this Article, and of the termination of any such extension under paragraph (2) of this Article, stating in each case the date from which the Convention has been, or will cease to be, so extended.

Article XIX

(1) In case of war or other hostilities, a Contracting Government which considers that it is affected, whether as a belligerent or as a neutral, may suspend the operation of the whole or any part of the present Convention in respect of all or any of its territories. The suspending Government shall immediately give notice of any such suspension to the Bureau.

(2) The suspending Government may at any time terminate such suspension and shall in any event terminate it as soon as it ceases to be justified under paragraph (1) of this Article. Notice of such

termination shall be given immediately to the Bureau by the Government concerned.

(3) The Bureau shall notify all Contracting Governments of any suspension or termination of suspension under this Article.

Article XX

As soon as the present Convention comes into force it shall be registered by the Bureau with the Secretary-General of the United Nations.

Article XXI

The duties of the Bureau shall be carried out by the Government of the United Kingdom of Great Britain and Northern Ireland unless and until the Inter-Governmental Maritime Consultative Organisation comes into being and takes over the duties assigned to it under the Convention signed at Geneva on 6 March 1948, and thereafter the duties of the Bureau shall be carried out by the said Organisation.

In Witness Whereof the undersigned plenipotentiaries have signed the present Convention.

Done in London this twelfth day of May, 1954, in English and French, both texts being equally authoritative, in a single copy, which shall be deposited with the Bureau and of which the Bureau shall transmit certified copies to all signatory and Contracting Governments.

ANNEX A

Prohibited Zones

(1) Subject to paragraph (3) of this Annex, the prohibited zones in relation to tankers shall be all sea areas within 50 miles from land, with the following exceptions:

(a) The Adriatic Zones

Within the Adriatic Sea the prohibited zones off the coasts of Italy and Yugoslavia respectively shall each extend for a distance of 30 miles from land, excepting only the island of

Vis. When the present Convention has been in force for a period of three years the said zones shall each be extended by a further 20 miles in width unless the two Governments agree to postpone such extension. In the event of such an agreement the said Governments shall notify the Bureau accordingly not less than three months before the expiration of such period of three years and the Bureau shall notify all Contracting Governments of such agreement.

(b) The North Sea Zone

The North Sea Zone shall extend for a distance of 100 miles from the coasts of the following countries:

- Belgium
- Denmark
- the Federal Republic of Germany
- the Netherlands
- the United Kingdom of Great Britain and Northern Ireland,

but not beyond the point where the limit of a 100-mile zone off the west coast of Jutland intersects the limit of the 50-mile zone off the coast of Norway.

(c) The Atlantic Zone

The Atlantic Zone shall be within a line drawn from a point on the Greenwich meridian 100 miles in a north-north-easterly direction from the Shetland Islands; thence northwards along the Greenwich meridian to latitude 64deg. north; thence westwards along the 64th parallel to longitude 10deg. west; thence to latitude 60deg. north, longitude 14deg. west; thence to latitude 54deg. 30' north, longitude 30deg. west; thence to latitude 44deg. 20' north, longitude 30deg. west; thence to latitude 48deg. north, longitude 14deg. west; thence eastwards along the 48th parallel to a point of intersection with the 50-mile zone off the coast of France. Provided that in relation to voyages which do not extend seawards beyond the Atlantic Zone as defined above, and which are to ports not provided with adequate facilities for the reception of oily residue, the Atlantic Zone shall be deemed to terminate at a distance of 100 miles from land.

(d) The Australian Zone

The Australian Zone shall extend for a distance of 150 miles from the coasts of Australia, except off the north and west coasts of the Australian mainland between the point opposite Thursday Island and the point on the west coast at 20deg. south latitude.

(2) Subject to paragraph (3) of this Annex the prohibited zones in relation to ships other than tankers shall be all sea areas within 50 miles from land with the following exceptions:

(a) The Adriatic Zones

Within the Adriatic Sea the prohibited zones off the coasts of Italy and Yugoslavia respectively shall each extend for a distance of 20 miles from land, excepting only the island of Vis. After the expiration of a period of three years following the application of prohibited zones to ships other than tankers in accordance with paragraph (2) of Article III the said zones shall each be extended by a further 30 miles in width unless the two Governments agree to postpone such extension. In the event of such an agreement the said Governments shall notify the Bureau accordingly not less than three months before the expiration of such period of three years, and the Bureau shall notify all Contracting Governments of such agreement.

(b) The North Sea and Atlantic Zones

The North Sea and Atlantic Zones shall extend for a distance of 100 miles from the coasts of the following countries:

- Belgium
- Denmark
- the Federal Republic of Germany
- Ireland
- The Netherlands
- The United Kingdom of Great Britain and Northern Ireland.

but not beyond the point where the limit of a 100-mile zone off the west coast of Jutland intersects the limit of the 50-mile zone off the coast of Norway.

(3) (a) Any Contracting Government may propose:

(i) The reduction of any zone off the coast of any of its territories;

(ii) The extension of any such zone to a maximum of 100 miles from any such coast, by making a declaration to that effect and the reduction or extension shall come into force after the expiration of a period of six months after the declaration has been made, unless any one of the Contracting Governments shall have made a declaration not less than two months before the expiration of that period that its interests are affected either by reason of the proximity of its coasts or by reason of its ships trading in the area, and that it does not accept the reduction or extension, as the case may be.

(b) Any declaration under this paragraph shall be made by a notification in writing to the Bureau which shall notify all Contracting Governments of the receipt of the declaration.

INTERNATIONAL SAFETY MANAGEMENT CODE

Preamble

1. The purpose of this Code is to provide an international standard for the safe management and operation of ships and for pollution prevention.
2. The Assembly adopted resolution A.443(XI), by which it invited all Governments to take the necessary steps to safeguard the shipmaster in the proper discharge of his responsibilities with regard to maritime safety and the protection of the marine environment.

3. The Assembly also adopted resolution A.680(17), by which it further recognized the need for appropriate organization of management to enable it to respond to the need of those on board ships to achieve and maintain high standards of safety and environmental protection.
4. Recognizing that no two shipping companies or shipowners are the same, and that ships operate under a wide range of different conditions, the Code is based on general principles and objectives.
5. The Code is expressed in broad terms so that it can have a widespread application. Clearly, different levels of management, whether shore-based or at sea, will require varying levels of knowledge and awareness of the items outlined.
6. The cornerstone of good safety management is commitment from the top. In matters of safety and pollution prevention it is the commitment, competence, attitudes and motivation of individuals at all levels that determines the end result.

Part A - Implementation

1. General

- Definitions

  The following definitions apply to parts A and B of this Code.

- "International Safety Management (ISM) Code" means the International Management Code for the Safe Operation of Ships and for Pollution Prevention as adopted by the Assembly, as may be amended by the Organization.
- "Company" means the owner of the ship or any other organization or person such as the manager, or the bareboat charterer, who has assumed the responsibility for operation of the ship from the shipowner and who, on assuming such responsibility, has agreed to take over all duties and responsibility imposed by the Code.

- "Administration" means the Government of the State whose flag the ship is entitled to fly.
- "Safety management system" means a structured and documented system enabling Company personnel to implement effectively the Company safety and environmental protection policy.
- "Document of Compliance" means a document issued to a Company which complies with the requirements of this Code.
- "Safety Management Certificate" means a document issued to a ship which signifies that the Company and its shipboard management operate in accordance with the approved safety management system.
- "Objective evidence" means quantitative or qualitative information, records or statements of fact pertaining to safety or to the existence and implementation of a safety management system element, which is based on observation, measurement or test and which can be verified.
- "Observation" means a statement of fact made during a safety management audit and substantiated by objective evidence.
- "Non-conformity" means an observed situation where objective evidence indicates the non-fulfilment of a specified requirement.
- "Major non-conformity" means an identifiable deviation that poses a serious threat to the safety of personnel or the ship or a serious risk to the environment that requires immediate corrective action and includes the lack of effective and systematic implementation of a requirement of this Code.
- "Anniversary date" means the day and month of each year that corresponds to the date of expiry of the relevant document or certificate.

- "Convention" means the International Convention for the Safety of Life at Sea, 1974, as amended.
- Objectives
- The objectives of the Code are to ensure safety at sea, prevention of human injury or loss of life, and avoidance of damage to the environment, in particular to the marine environment and to property.
- Safety management objectives of the Company should, inter alia:
- provide for safe practices in ship operation and a safe working environment;
- Establish safeguards against all identified risks; and
- Continuously improve safety management skills of personnel ashore and aboard ships, including preparing for emergencies related both to safety and environmental protection.
- The safety management system should ensure:
- Compliance with mandatory rules and regulations; and
- That applicable codes, guidelines and standards recommended by the Organization, Administrations, classification societies and maritime industry organizations are taken into account.
- Application

  The requirements of this Code may be applied to all ships.
- Functional requirements for a safety management system

  Every Company should develop, implement and maintain a safety management system which includes the following functional requirements:
- A safety and environmental-protection policy;
- Instructions and procedures to ensure safe operation of ships and protection of the environment in

compliance with relevant international and flag State legislation;

- Defined levels of authority and lines of communication between, and amongst, shore and shipboard personnel;
- Procedures for reporting accidents and non-conformities with the provisions of this Code;
- Procedures to prepare for and respond to emergency situations; and
- Procedures for internal audits and management reviews.

2. *Safety and Environmental Protection Policy*

- The Company should establish a safety and environmental-protection policy which describes how the objectives given in paragraph 1.2 will be achieved.
- The Company should ensure that the policy is implemented and maintained at all levels of the organization, both ship-based and shore-based.

3. *Company Responsibilities and Authority*

- If the entity who is responsible for the operation of the ship is other than the owner, the owner must report the full name and details of such entity to the Administration.
- The Company should define and document the responsibility, authority and interrelation of all personnel who manage, perform and verify work relating to and affecting safety and pollution prevention.
- The Company is responsible for ensuring that adequate resources and shore-based support are provided to enable the designated person or persons to carry out their functions.

4. *Designated Persons*

To ensure the safe operation of each ship and to provide a link between the Company and those on board, every

Company, as appropriate, should designate a person or persons ashore having direct access to the highest level of management. The responsibility and authority of the designated person or persons should include monitoring the safety and pollution-prevention aspects of the operation of each ship and ensuring that adequate resources and shore-based support are applied, as required.

5. Master's Responsibility and Authority

- The Company should clearly define and document the master's responsibility with regard to:
- Implementing the safety and environmental-protection policy of the Company;
- Motivating the crew in the observation of that policy;
- Issuing appropriate orders and instructions in a clear and simple manner;
- Verifying that specified requirements are observed; and
- Reviewing the safety management system and reporting its deficiencies to the shore-based management.
- The Company should ensure that the safety management system operating on board the ship contains a clear statement emphasizing the master's authority. The Company should establish in the safety management system that the master has the overriding authority and the responsibility to make decisions with respect to safety and pollution prevention and to request the Company's assistance as may be necessary.

6. Resources amd Personnel

- The Company should ensure that the master is:
- properly qualified for command;
- Fully conversant with the Company's safety management system; and

- Given the necessary support so that the master's duties can be safely performed.
- The Company should ensure that each ship is manned with qualified, certificated and medically fit seafarers in accordance with national and international requirements.
- The Company should establish procedures to ensure that new personnel and personnel transferred to new assignments related to safety and protection of the environment are given proper familiarization with their duties. Instructions which are essential to be provided prior to sailing should be identified, documented and given.
- The Company should ensure that all personnel involved in the Company's safety management system have an adequate understanding of relevant rules, regulations, codes and guidelines.
- The Company should establish and maintain procedures for identifying any training which may be required in support of the safety management system and ensure that such training is provided for all personnel concerned.
- The Company should establish procedures by which the ship's personnel receive relevant information on the safety management system in a working language or languages understood by them.
- The Company should ensure that the ship's personnel are able to communicate effectively in the execution of their duties related to the safety management system.

7. Development of Plans for Shipboard Operations

The Company should establish procedures for the preparation of plans and instructions, including checklists as appropriate, for key shipboard operations concerning the safety of the ship and the prevention of pollution. The various tasks involved should be defined and assigned to qualified personnel.

8. Emergency Preparedness

- The Company should establish procedures to identify, describe and respond to potential emergency shipboard situations.
- The Company should establish programmes for drills and exercises to prepare for emergency actions.
- The safety management system should provide for measures ensuring that the Company's organization can respond at any time to hazards, accidents and emergency situations involving its ships.

9. Reports and Analysis of Non-Conformities, Accidents and Hazardous Occurrences

- The safety management system should include procedures ensuring that non-conformities, accidents and hazardous situations are reported to the Company, investigated and analysed with the objective of improving safety and pollution prevention.
- The Company should establish procedures for the implementation of corrective action.

10. Maintenance of the Ship and Equipment

- The Company should establish procedures to ensure that the ship is maintained in conformity with the provisions of the relevant rules and regulations and with any additional requirements which may be established by the Company.
- In meeting these requirements the Company should ensure that:
- Inspections are held at appropriate intervals;
- Any non-conformity is reported, with its possible cause, if known;
- Appropriate corrective action is taken; and
- Records of these activities are maintained.
- The Company should establish procedures in its safety management system to identify equipment and

technical systems the sudden operational failure of which may result in hazardous situations. The safety management system should provide for specific measures aimed at promoting the reliability of such equipment or systems. These measures should include the regular testing of stand-by arrangements and equipment or technical systems that are not in continuous use.

- The inspections mentioned in 10.2 as well as the measures referred to in 10.3 should be integrated into the ship's operational maintenance routine.

11. *Documentation*

- The Company should establish and maintain procedures to control all documents and data which are relevant to the safety management system.
- The Company should ensure that:
- Valid documents are available at all relevant locations;
- Changes to documents are reviewed and approved by authorized personnel; and
- Obsolete documents are promptly removed.
- The documents used to describe and implement the safety management system may be referred to as the Safety Management Manual. Documentation should be kept in a form that the Company considers most effective. Each ship should carry on board all documentation relevant to that ship.

12. *Company Verification, Review and Evaluation*

- The Company should carry out internal safety audits to verify whether safety and pollution-prevention activities comply with the safety management system.
- The Company should periodically evaluate the efficiency of and, when needed, review the safety management system in accordance with procedures established by the Company.

- The audits and possible corrective actions should be carried out in accordance with documented procedures.
- Personnel carrying out audits should be independent of the areas being audited unless this is impracticable due to the size and the nature of the Company.
- The results of the audits and reviews should be brought to the attention of all personnel having responsibility in the area involved.
- The management personnel responsible for the area involved should take timely corrective action on deficiencies found.

Part B - Certification and Verification

13. Certificationa dn Periodical Verification

- The ship should be operated by a Company which has been issued with a Document of Compliance or with an Interim Document of Compliance in accordance with paragraph 14.1, relevant to that ship.
- The Document of Compliance should be issued by the Administration, by an organization recognized by the Administration or, at the request of the Administration, by another Contracting Government to the Convention to any Company complying with the requirements of this Code for a period specified by the Administration which should not exceed five years. Such a document should be accepted as evidence that the Company is capable of complying with the requirements of this Code.
- The Document of Compliance is only valid for the ship types explicitly indicated in the document. Such indication should be based on the types of ships on which the initial verification was based. Other ship types should only be added after verification of the Company's capability to comply with the requirements of this Code applicable to such ship

types. In this context, ship types are those referred to in regulation IX/1 of the Convention.

- The validity of a Document of Compliance should be subject to annual verification by the Administration or by an organization recognized by the Administration or, at the request of the Administration, by another Contracting Government within three months before or after the anniversary date.
- The Document of Compliance should be withdrawn by the Administration or, at its request, by the Contracting Government which issued the Document when the annual verification required in paragraph 13.4 is not requested or if there is evidence of major non-conformities with this Code.
- All associated Safety Management Certificates and/or Interim Safety Management Certificates should also be withdrawn if the Document of Compliance is withdrawn.
- A copy of the Document of Compliance should be placed on board in order that the master of the ship, if so requested, may produce it for verification by the Administration or by an organization recognized by the Administration or for the purposes of the control referred to in regulation IX/6.2 of the Convention. The copy of the Document is not required to be authenticated or certified.
- The Safety Management Certificate should be issued to a ship for a period which should not exceed five years by the Administration or an organization recognized by the Administration or, at the request of the Administration, by another Contracting Government. The Safety Management Certificate should be issued after verifying that the Company and its shipboard management operate in accordance with the approved safety management system. Such a

Certificate should be accepted as evidence that the ship is complying with the requirements of this Code.

- The validity of the Safety Management Certificate should be subject to at least one intermediate verification by the Administration or an organization recognized by the Administration or, at the request of the Administration, by another Contracting Government. If only one intermediate verification is to be carried out and the period of validity of the Safety Management Certificate is five years, it should take place between the second and third anniversary dates of the Safety Management Certificate.
- In addition to the requirements of paragraph 13.5.1, the Safety Management Certificate should be withdrawn by the Administration or, at the request of the Administration, by the Contracting Government which has issued it when the intermediate verification required in paragraph 13.8 is not requested or if there is evidence of major non-conformity with this Code.
- Notwithstanding the requirements of paragraphs 13.2 and 13.7, when the renewal verification is completed within three months before the expiry date of the existing Document of Compliance or Safety Management Certificate, the new Document of Compliance or the new Safety Management Certificate should be valid from the date of completion of the renewal verification for a period not exceeding five years from the date of expiry of the existing Document of Compliance or Safety Management Certificate.
- When the renewal verification is completed more than three months before the expiry date of the existing Document of Compliance or Safety Management Certificate, the new Document of Compliance or the new Safety Management Certificate should be valid from the date of completion of the renewal verification for a period not exceeding five years from the date of completion of the renewal verification."

14. *Interim Certification*

- An Interim Document of Compliance may be issued to facilitate initial implementation of this Code when:
- a Company is newly established; or
- new ship types are to be added to an existing Document of Compliance, following verification that the Company has a safety management system that meets the objectives of paragraph 1.2.3 of this Code, provided the Company demonstrates plans to implement a safety management system meeting the full requirements of this Code within the period of validity of the Interim Document of Compliance. Such an Interim Document of Compliance should be issued for a period not exceeding 12 months by the Administration or by an organization recognized by the Administration or, at the request of the Administration, by another Contracting Government. A copy of the Interim Document of Compliance should be placed on board in order that the master of the ship, if so requested, may produce it for verification by the Administration or by an organization recognized by the Administration or for the purposes of the control referred to in regulation IX/6.2 of the Convention. The copy of the Document is not required to be authenticated or certified.
- An Interim Safety Management Certificate may be issued:
- To new ships on delivery;
- When a Company takes on responsibility for the operation of a ship which is new to the Company; or
- When a ship changes flag.

  Such an Interim Safety Management Certificate should be issued for a period not exceeding 6 months by the Administration or an organization recognized by the Administration or, at the request of the Administration, by another Contracting Government.

- An Administration or, at the request of the Administration, another Contracting Government may, in special cases, extend the validity of an Interim Safety Management Certificate for a further period which should not exceed 6 months from the date of expiry.
- An Interim Safety Management Certificate may be issued following verification that:
- The Document of Compliance, or the Interim Document of Compliance, is relevant to the ship concerned;
- The safety management system provided by the Company for the ship concerned includes key elements of this Code and has been assessed during the audit for issuance of the Document of Compliance or demonstrated for issuance of the Interim Document of Compliance;
- The Company has planned the audit of the ship within three months;
- The master and officers are familiar with the safety management system and the planned arrangements for its implementation;
- Instructions, which have been identified as being essential, are provided prior to sailing; and
- Relevant information on the safety management system has been given in a working language or languages understood by the ship's personnel.

15. *Verification*

- All verifications required by the provisions of this Code should be carried out in accordance with procedures acceptable to the Administration, taking into account the guidelines developed by the Organization.

16. Forms of Certificates

- The Document of Compliance, the Safety Management Certificate, the Interim Document of Compliance and the Interim Safety Management Certificate should be drawn up in a form corresponding to the models given in the appendix to this Code. If the language used is neither English nor French, the text should include a translation into one of these languages.
- In addition to the requirements of paragraph 13.3, the ship types indicated on the Document of Compliance and the Interim Document of Compliance may be endorsed to reflect any limitations in the operations of the ships described in the safety management system.

AN OVERVIEW OF THE PROPOSED CONSOLIDATED MARITIME LABOUR CONVENTION, 2006

The ILO and its Work in the Maritime Sector

Seafarers and the conditions of work and living that they experience have always been of special concern to the ILO.

- The ILO's earliest legal instruments were aimed at improving the working conditions of seafarers.
- One of the first legal instruments that the ILO adopted was a Recommendation (National Seamen's Code Recommendation, 1920 (No. 9)), a year after the ILO was created, foreseeing the importance of the establishment of an international seafarers' code, which would clearly set out the rights and obligations relevant to this sector.
- Matters relating particularly to the situation of seafarers have also, from the beginning, normally, been considered at a special session, a maritime session of the International Labour Conference.

- The first Maritime Session of the ILO took place in 1920. Since then there have been 9 maritime sessions. The last was in 1996.
- The next Maritime session in February 2006 will be the 94th International Labour Conference and the 10th Maritime session.
- At this 10th session the ILO will devote itself to the review and adoption of an important new legal instrument, the Maritime Labour Convention, 2006, which seeks to fulfil the ideas first foreseen in 1920 – a comprehensive code regarding seafarers' rights and the obligations of States with respect to these rights.

The ILO and Maritime Labour Standards

- Since 1920 the ILO has adopted more than 65 legal instruments (Conventions and Recommendations).
- Taken all together these instruments comprehensively address all aspects of working conditions for seafarers.
- Issues that are addressed include concerns central to securing conditions of "decent work" for seafarers such as the minimum age for work onboard ships, hours of work, occupational safety and health protection, standards for accommodation and catering, access to medical care, repatriation, labour inspections and social security.

Changes Needed to ILO Standard Setting

- The phenomenon described as "globalization", has required that the ILO review its standard setting and supervisory activity with a view to ensuring that its standards are designed to achieve universal acceptance and that issues such as effective enforcement and compliance are directly addressed.
- In 1998 the ILO engaged in an examination of the maritime labour instruments (international Conventions & Recommendations) as part of an overall review of its standards and standard setting practices.

- Changes in the maritime sector meant that changes in standards were needed.

Changes Needed to Modernize ILO Maritime Standards

- This led to the idea in 2001, of the Workers and Employers in the Joint Maritime Commission, for a new approach to ensure: (a) comprehensive and effective protection of the seafarers' rights to decent work and (b) a level playing field for Governments and Shipowners, with flexibility as to the means of delivering this protection and accommodating diversity.
- The Workers and Employers developed a number of preferred solutions or approaches to maritime labour standards, called the "Geneva Accord', which were supported by Governments.
- A number of factors affecting the maritime sector led the ILO Governing Body to agree with the ideas in the "Geneva Accord" and to conclude that there was a need for a major revision of the existing labour instruments in order to better meet the need for international standards for decent work in the maritime sector.

Reasons for Change

Reasons for change included the fact that:

- Many of the existing ILO instruments need to be updated
- Extensive structural change in the shipping industry, particularly in the last 25 years
- Emergence of the world's first genuinely global industry and workforce
- Changes in ownership, financing and the rise of ship management companies resulting in significant shifts in the labour market for seafarers
- Development of consciously composed mixed nationality crews in highly organized global network

linking shipowners, ship managers, crew managers, labour supplying agencies and training institutions

- Increased internationalization of ship registries and "flags of convenience"
- A need to provide a "level playing field" and avoid exploitation of workers
- Increased stress and complexity in the maritime work place has an impact on the health and social security of workers
- There is a relatively low ratification rate for some key Conventions
- A high level of detail combined with the large number of Conventions led to problems for inspections and enforcement
- Conditions of employment change rapidly but the process of updating Conventions in the ILO is expensive and lengthy

THE PURPOSE OF THE PROPOSED MARITIME LABOUR CONVENTION, 2006

In 2001, the ILO Governing Body took a decision to develop a new instrument that would:

- Consolidate nearly all existing maritime labour standards,
- Meet current and future needs,
- Address barriers to achieving universality in the acceptance of the standards, and
- Ensure better and more effective implementation of the standards.

An extensive consultation exercise stretching over more than four years and involving up to as many as 88 countries, developed the proposed Convention text.

The new Convention is seen as having two primary purposes:

- To bring the system of protection contained in existing labour standards closer to the workers concerned, in a form consistent with the rapidly developing, globalized sector;
- To improve the applicability of the system so that shipowners and governments interested in providing decent conditions of work do not have to bear an unequal burden in ensuring protection.

The draft Convention was reviewed in detail in September 2004 by a Preparatory Technical Maritime Conference (PTMC) involving over 500 delegates who adopted both the structure and the majority of the proposed Convention text.

A follow-up meeting in April 2005 developed additional text to address several specific areas that had been left unresolved by the PTMC and reviewed proposals for amendments that had not been considered at the PTMC because of time constraints.

The new draft convention adopted by the PTMC combines the "best of the old with the new".

It combines core standards found in existing Convention with an innovative format aimed at achieving universal acceptance and a new approach to securing ongoing compliance and to more rapidly updating of the technical standards.

Format of the Proposed Maritime Labour Convention, 2006

Three different but related parts:

- Articles
- Regulations
- A Code (Part A mandatory Standards, Part B non-mandatory Guidelines)

The proposed Convention is "vertically integrated" in presentation with the Regulations and Code provisions organised under 5 Titles:

- Title 1: Minimum requirements for seafarers to work on a ship
- Title 2: Conditions of employment
- Title 3: Accommodation, recreational facilities, food and catering
- Title 4: Health protection, medical care, welfare and social protection
- Title 5: Compliance and enforcement

Example of vertical integration (extracts):

Regulation 1.2 – Medical Certificate

Purpose: To ensure that all seafarers are medically fit to perform their duties at sea

1. Seafarers shall not work on a ship unless they are certified as medically fit to perform their duties.) ...

Standard A1.2 – Medical Certificate

1. The competent authority shall require that, prior to beginning work on a ship, seafarers hold a valid medical certificate attesting that they are medically fit to perform the duties they are to carry out at sea.

Innovations

Some innovative features of the new Convention include:

- A new system for effective enforcement and compliance - a certification system for labour standards (a Maritime Labour Certificate & a Declaration of Maritime Labour Compliance issued by the flag State)
- Flag State certification and a foreign port inspection system applies to ships above 500 GT engaged in international voyages or voyages between foreign ports, however the certificate system is available, on request by shipowners, to other ships
- The Certificate and Declaration will provide prima facie evidence of compliance with the requirements of the Convention

- Standards will still apply to most other ships (smaller ships can be exempted from some requirements) however, the port inspection provisions and certification requirements would not be mandatory.
- Accelerated Convention amendment procedures to update Code provisions to address changes in the sector
- Onboard and onshore complaint procedures to encourage rapid resolution of problems, if possible
- A complaint and inspection system that is linked with the well-established ILO supervisory system
- Provisions setting international standards for flag State delegation of some functions to a Recognized Organization
- A modernized management based approach to occupational safety and health

Conclusion

The Maritime Labour Convention, 2006 is needed because it will:

- Provide a modern system for improved and enforceable conditions for decent work in the maritime sector
- Create, as much as possible, a level playing field in a globalized industry by ensuring that competition is not based on unjust, exploitive and unfair labor practices

SOLAS CONVENTION

The SOLAS Convention in its successive forms is generally regarded as the most important of all international treaties concerning the safety of merchant ships. The first version was adopted in 1914, in response to the Titanic disaster, the second in 1929, the third in 1948 and the fourth in 1960.

The 1960 Convention - which was adopted on 17 June 1960 and entered into force on 26 May 1965 - was the first major task for IMO after the Organization's creation and it represented a considerable step forward in modernizing regulations and in keeping pace with technical developments in the shipping industry.

The intention was to keep the Convention up to date by periodic amendments but in practice the amendments procedure incorporated proved to be very slow. It became clear that it would be impossible to secure the entry into force of amendments within a reasonable period of time.

As a result, a completely new Convention was adopted in 1974 which included not only the amendments agreed up until that date but a new amendment procedure - the tacit acceptance procedure - designed to ensure that changes could be made within a specified (and acceptably short) period of time.

Instead of requiring that an amendment shall enter into force after being accepted by, for example, two thirds of the Parties, the tacit acceptance procedure provides that an amendment shall enter into force on a specified date unless, before that date, objections to the amendment are received from an agreed number of Parties.

As a result the 1974 Convention has been updated and amended on numerous occasions. The Convention in force today is sometimes referred to as SOLAS, 1974, as amended.

Amendment Procedure

Article VIII of the SOLAS 1974 Convention states that amendments can be made either:

After Consideration within IMO

Amendments proposed by a Contracting Government are circulated at least six months before consideration by the Maritime Safety Committee (MSC) - which may refer discussions to one or more IMO Sub-Committees - and amendments are adopted by a two-thirds majority of Contracting Governments present and voting in the MSC. Contracting Governments of SOLAS, whether or not Members of IMO are entitled to participate in the consideration of amendments in the so-called "expanded MSC".

Amendments by a Conference

Conference of Contracting Governments is called when a Contracting Government requests the holding of a Conference and at least one-third of Contracting Governments agree to hold the Conference. Amendments are adopted by a two-thirds majority of Contracting Governments present and voting.

In the case of both a Conference and the expanded MSC, amendments (other than to Chapter I) are deemed to have been accepted at the end of a set period of time following communication of the adopted amendments to Contracting Governments, unless a specified number of Contracting Governments object. The length of time from communication of amendments to deemed acceptance is set at two years unless another period of time - which must not be less than one year - is determined by two-thirds of Contracting Governments at the time of adoption.

Amendments to Chapter I are deemed accepted after positive acceptance by two-thirds of Contracting Governments.

Amendments enter into force six months after their deemed acceptance.

The minimum length of time from circulation of proposed amendments through entry into force is 24 months - circulation: six months, adoption to deemed acceptance date: 12 months minimum; deemed acceptance to entry into force: six months.

However, a resolution adopted in 1994 makes provision for an accelerated amendment procedure to be used in exceptional circumstances - allowing for the length of time from communication of amendments to deemed acceptance to be cut to six months in exceptional circumstances and when this is decided by a Conference. In practice to date, the expanded MSC has adopted most amendments to SOLAS, while Conferences have been held on several occasions - notably to adopt whole new Chapters to SOLAS or to adopt amendments proposed in response to a specific incident.

Technical Provisions

The main objective of the SOLAS Convention is to specify minimum standards for the construction, equipment and operation of ships, compatible with their safety. Flag States are responsible for ensuring that ships under their flag comply with its requirements, and a number of certificates are prescribed in the Convention as proof that this has been done. Control provisions also allow Contracting Governments to inspect ships of other Contracting States if there are clear grounds for believing that the ship and its equipment do not substantially comply with the requirements of the Convention - this procedure is known as port State control.The current SOLAS Convention includes Articles setting out general obligations, amendment procedure and so on, followed by an Annex divided into 12 Chapters.

Chapter I - General Provisions

Includes regulations concerning the survey of the various types of ships and the issuing of documents signifying that the ship meets the requirements of the Convention. The Chapter also includes provisions for the control of ships in ports of other Contracting Governments.

Chapter II-1 - Construction - Subdivision and Stability, Machinery and Electrical Installations

The subdivision of passenger ships into watertight compartments must be such that after assumed damage to the ship's hull the vessel will remain afloat and stable. Requirements for watertight integrity and bilge pumping arrangements for passenger ships are also laid down as well as stability requirements for both passenger and cargo ships.

The degree of subdivision - measured by the maximum permissible distance between two adjacent bulkheads - varies with ship's length and the service in which it is engaged. The highest degree of subdivision applies to passenger ships.

Requirements covering machinery and electrical installations are designed to ensure that services which are essential for the safety of the ship, passengers and crew are maintained under various emergency conditions. The steering gear requirements of this Chapter are particularly important.

Chapter II-2 - Fire protection, fire detection and fire extinction

Includes detailed fire safety provisions for all ships and specific measures for passenger ships, cargo ships and tankers.

They include the following principles: division of the ship into main and vertical zones by thermal and structural boundaries; separation of accommodation spaces from the remainder of the ship by thermal and structural boundaries; restricted use of combustible materials; detection of any fire in the zone of origin; containment and extinction of any fire in the space of origin; protection of the means of escape or of access for fire-fighting purposes; ready availability of fire-extinguishing appliances; minimization of the possibility of ignition of flammable cargo vapour.

Chapter III - Life-Saving Appliances and Arrangements

The Chapter includes requirements for life-saving appliances and arrangements, including requirements for life boats, rescue boats and life jackets according to type of ship.

The International Life-Saving Appliance (LSA) Code gives specific technical requirements for LSAs and is mandatory under Regulation 34, which states that all life-saving appliances and arrangements shall comply with the applicable requirements of the LSA Code.

Chapter IV - Radiocommunications

The Chapter incorporates the Global Maritime Distress and Safety System (GMDSS). All passenger ships and all cargo ships of 300 gross tonnage and upwards on international voyages are required to carry equipment designed to improve the chances of rescue following an accident, including satellite emergency position indicating radio beacons (EPIRBs) and search and rescue transponders (SARTs) for the location of the ship or survival craft.

Regulations in Chapter IV cover undertakings by contracting governments to provide radiocommunciation services as well as ship requirements for carriage of radiocommunications equipment. The Chapter is closely linked to the Radio Regulations of the International Telecommunication Union.

Chapter V - Safety of Navigation

Chapter V identifies certain navigation safety services which should be provided by Contracting Governments and sets forth provisions of an operational nature applicable in general to all ships on all voyages. This is in contrast to the Convention as a whole, which only applies to certain classes of ship engaged on international voyages.

The subjects covered include the maintenance of meteorological services for ships; the ice patrol service; routeing of ships; and the maintenance of search and rescue services.

This Chapter also includes a general obligation for masters to proceed to the assistance of those in distress and for Contracting Governments to ensure that all ships shall be sufficiently and efficiently manned from a safety point of view.

The chapter makes mandatory the carriage of voyage data recorders (VDRs) and automatic ship identification systems (AIS) for certain ships.

Chapter VI - Carriage of Cargoes

The Chapter covers all types of cargo (except liquids and gases in bulk) "which, owing to their particular hazards to ships or persons on board, may require special precautions".

The regulations include requirements for stowage and securing of cargo or cargo units (such as containers).

The Chapter requires cargo ships carrying grain to comply with the IMO International Grain Code.

Chapter VII - Carriage of Dangerous Goods

The regulations are contained in three parts:

Part A - Carriage of dangerous goods in packaged form or in solid form or in bulk - includes provisions for the classification, packing, marking, labelling and placarding, documentation and stowage of dangerous goods. Contracting Governments are required to issue instructions at the national level and the Chapter refers to International Maritime Dangerous Goods (IMDG) Code, developed by IMO, which is constantly updated to accommodate new dangerous goods and to supplement or revise existing provisions.

Part B covers Construction and equipment of ships carrying dangerous liquid chemicals in bulk and requires chemical tankers built after 1 July 1986 to comply with the International Bulk Chemical Code (IBC Code).

Part C covers Construction and equipment of ships carrying liquefied gases in bulk and gas carriers constructed after 1 July 1986 to comply with the requirements of the International Gas Carrier Code (IGC Code).

Part D includes special requirements for the carriage of packaged irradiated nuclear fuel, plutonium and high-level radioactive wastes on board ships and requires ships carrying such products to comply with the International Code for the Safe Carriage of Packaged Irradiated Nuclear Fuel, Plutonium and High-Level Radioactive Wastes on Board Ships (INF Code).

The chapter requires carriage of dangerous goods to be in compliance with the relevant provisions of the International Maritime Dangerous Goods Code (IMDG Code). The IMDG Code was first adopted by IMO in 1965 and has been kept up to date by regular amendments, including those needed to keep it in line with United Nations Recommendations on the Transport of Dangerous Goods which sets the basic requirements for all the transport modes.

Chapter VIII - Nuclear ships

Gives basic requirements for nuclear-powered ships and is particularly concerned with radiation hazards. It refers to detailed and comprehensive Code of Safety for Nuclear Merchant Ships which was adopted by the IMO Assembly in 1981.

Chapter IX - Management for the Safe Operation of Ships

The Chapter makes mandatory the International Safety Management (ISM) Code, which requires a safety management system to be established by the shipowner or any person who has assumed responsibility for the ship (the "Company").

Chapter X - Safety Measures for High Speed Craft

The Chapter makes mandatory the International Code of Safety for High-Speed Craft (HSC Code).

Chapter XI-1 - Special Measures to Enhance Maritime Safety

The Chapter clarifies requirements relating to authorization of recognized organizations (responsible for carrying out surveys and inspections on Administrations' behalves); enhanced surveys; ship identification number scheme; and port State control on operational requirements.

Chapter XI-2 - Special Measures to Enhance Maritime Security

The Chapter was adopted in December 2002 and entered into force on 1 July 2004. Regulation XI-2/3 of the new chapter enshrines the International Ship and Port Facilities Security Code (ISPS Code). Part A of the Code is mandatory and part B contains guidance as to how best to comply with the mandatory requirements. The regulation requires Administrations to set security levels and ensure the provision of security level information to ships entitled to fly their flag. Prior to entering a port, or whilst in a port, within the territory of a Contracting Government, a ship shall comply with the requirements for the security level set by that Contracting Government, if that security level is higher than the security level set by the Administration for that ship.

Regulation XI-2/4 confirms the role of the Master in exercising his professional judgement over decisions necessary to maintain the security of the ship. It says he shall not be constrained by the Company, the charterer or any other person in this respect.Regulation XI-2/4 confirms the role of the Master in exercising his professional judgement over decisions necessary to maintain the security of the ship. It says he shall not be constrained by the Company, the charterer or any other person in this respect.

Regulation XI-2/5 requires all ships to be provided with a ship security alert system, according to a strict timetable that will see most vessels fitted by 2004 and the remainder by 2006. When activated the ship security alert system shall initiate and transmit a ship-to-shore security alert to a competent authority designated by the Administration, identifying the ship, its location and indicating that the security of the ship is under threat or it has been compromised. The system will not raise any alarm on-board the ship. The ship security alert system shall be capable of being activated from the navigation bridge and in at least one other location.

Regulation XI-2/6 covers requirements for port facilities, providing among other things for Contracting Governments to ensure that port facility security assessments are carried out and that port facility security plans are developed, implemented and reviewed in accordance with the ISPS Code.

Other regulations in this chapter cover the provision of information to IMO, the control of ships in port, (including measures such as the delay, detention, restriction of operations including movement within the port, or expulsion of a ship from port), and the specific responsibility of Companies.

Chapter XII - Additional Safety Measures for Bulk Carriers

The Chapter includes structural requirements for bulk carriers over 150 metres in length.

The Protocol of 1978

Adoption: 17 February 1978
Entry into force: 1 May 1981

The 1978 Protocol was adopted at the International Conference on Tanker Safety and Pollution Prevention, which was convened in response to a spate of tanker accidents in 1976-1977.

The conference adopted measures affecting tanker design and operation, which were incorporated into both the SOLAS Protocol of 1978 as well as the Protocol of 1978 relating to the 1973 International Convention for the Prevention of Pollution from Ships (1978 MARPOL Protocol).

The 1978 SOLAS Protocol made a number of important changes to Chapter I, including the introduction of unscheduled inspections and/or mandatory annual surveys and the strengthening of port State control requirements. Chapter II-1, Chapter II-2 and Chapter V were also improved.

The main amendments included the following:

New crude oil carriers and product carriers of 20,000 dwt and above were required to be fitted with an inert gas system.

An inert gas system became mandatory for existing crude oil carriers of 70,000 dwt and above by 1 May 1983, and by 1 May 1985 for ships of 20,000-70,000 dwt.

In the case of crude oil carriers of 20-40,000 dwt there was provision for exemption by flag States where it was considered unreasonable or impracticable to fit an inert gas system and high-capacity fixed washing machines are not used. But an inert gas system is always required when crude oil washing is operated.

An inert gas system was required on existing product carriers from 1 May 1983 and by 1 May 1985 for ships of 40-70,000 dwt and down to 20,000 dwt which were fitted with high capacity washing machines.

In addition to requiring that all ships of 1,600 grt and above be fitted with radar, the Protocol required that all ships of 10,000 grt and above have two radars, each capable of being operated independently.

All tankers of 10,000 grt and above to have two remote steering gear control systems, each operable separately from the navigating bridge.

The main steering gear of new tankers of 10,000 grt and above to comprise two or more identical power units, and be capable of operating the rudder with one or more power units.

The 1981 amendments

Adoption: 20 November 1981
Entry into force: 1 September 1984

Chapters II-1 and II-2 were re-written and updated.

In Chapter II-1, the provisions of resolution A.325(IX) Recommendation concerning regulations for machinery and electrical installations in passenger and cargo ships (adopted in November 1975) were incorporated and made mandatory. Changes to regulations 29 and 30 on steering gear introduced the concept of duplication of steering gear control systems in tankers. These measures were agreed taking into account concerns following the 1978 Amoco Cadiz disaster and relevant provisions in the 1978 SOLAS Protocol.

Chapter II-2 was re-arranged to take into account strengthened fire safety requirements for cargo ships and passenger ships.

The revised Chapter II-2 incorporated the requirements of resolution A.327(IX) Recommendation concerning fire safety requirements for cargo ships, which included 21 regulations based on the principles of: separation of accommodation spaces from the remainder of the ship by thermal and structural boundaries; protection of means of escape; early detection, containment or extinction of any fire; and restricted use of combustible materials. Other amendments to Chapter II-2 related to provisions for halogenated hydrocarbon extinguishing systems, special requirements for ships carrying dangerous goods, and a new regulation 62 on inert gas systems.

Some important changes were also made to Chapter V, including the addition of new requirements concerning the carriage of shipborne navigational equipment, covering such matters as gyro and magnetic compasses; the mandatory carriage of two radars and of automatic radar plotting aids in ships of 10,000 grt and above; echo-sounders; devices to indicate speed and distance; rudder angle indicators; propeller revolution indicators; rate of turn indicators; radio-direction finding apparatus; and equipment for homing on the radiotelephone distress frequency.

In addition, a few minor changes were made to Chapter III; seven regulations in Chapter IV were replaced, amended or added and a number of small changes were made to Chapter VII.

The 1983 amendments

Adoption: 17 June 1983

Entry into force: 1 July 1986

The most extensive changes involved Chapter III, which was completely rewritten. The Chapter in the 1974 Convention differed little from the texts which appeared in the 1960 and 1948 SOLAS Conventions and the amendments were designed not only to take into account the many technical advances which had taken place since then but also to expedite the evaluation and introduction of further improvements.

There were also a few minor changes to Chapter II-1 and some further changes to Chapter II-2 (including improvements to the 1981 amendments) designed particularly to increase the safety of bulk carriers and passenger ships. Some small changes were made to Chapter IV.

Amendments to Chapter VII extended its application to chemical tankers and liquefied gas carriers by making reference to two new Codes, the International Code for the Construction and Equipment of Ships Carrying Dangerous Chemicals in Bulk (IBC Code) and the International Code for the Construction and Equipment of Ships Carrying Liquefied Gases in Bulk (IGC Code). Both apply to ships built on or after 1 July 1986.

The 1988 (April) Amendments

Adoption: 21 April 1988
Entry into force: 22 October 1989

In March 1987 the car ferry Herald of Free Enterprise capsized shortly after leaving Zeebrugge in Belgium and sank with the loss of 193 lives. The United Kingdom proposed a series of measures designed to prevent a recurrence, the first package of which was adopted in April 1988.

They included new regulations 23-2 and 42-1 of Chapter II-1 intended to improve monitoring of doors and cargo areas and to improve emergency lighting.

The 1988 (October) Amendments

Adoption: 28 October 1988
Entry into force: 29 April 1990

Some of these amendments also resulted from the Herald of Free Enterprise disaster and included details of how stability of passenger ships in a damaged condition should be determined and a requirement for all cargo loading doors to be locked before a ship leaves the berth.

The amendments also made it compulsory for passenger ships to have a lightweight survey at least every five years to ensure their stability has not been adversely affected by the accumulation of extra weight or any alterations to the superstructure.

Other amendments concerning the stability of passenger ships in the damaged condition were also adopted. These regulations had been in preparation before the Herald of Free Enterprise incident and their adoption was brought forward.

The 1988 Protocol (HSSC)

Adoption: 11 November 1988
Entry into force: 3 February 2000

The Protocol introduced a new harmonized system of surveys and certification (HSSC) to harmonize with two other Conventions, Load Lines and MARPOL 73/78. The aim is to alleviate problems caused by the fact that as requirements in the three instruments vary, ships may be obliged to go into dry-dock for a survey required by one convention shortly after being surveyed in connection with another.

By enabling the required surveys to be carried out at the same time, the system is intended to reduce costs for shipowners and administrations alike.

The 1988 (GMDSS) Amendments

Adoption: 11 November 1988
Entry into force: 1 February 1992

IMO had begun work on the Global Maritime Distress and Safety System (GMDSS) in the 1970s and its introduction marked the biggest change to maritime communications since the invention of radio.

The amendments which replaced the existing Chapter IV phased in the introduction of the GMDSS in stages between 1993 and 1 February 1999. The basic concept of the system is that search and rescue authorities ashore, as well as ships in the vicinity, will be rapidly alerted in the event of an emergency.

The GMDSS makes great use of the satellite communications provided by Inmarsat but also uses terrestrial radio.

The equipment required by ships varies according to the sea area in which they operate - ships travelling to the high seas must carry more communications equipment than those which remain within reach of specified shore-based radio facilities. In addition to distress communications, the GMDSS also provides for the dissemination of general maritime safety information (such as navigational and meteorological warnings and urgent information to ships).

The 1989 amendments

Adoption: 11 April 1989
Entry into force: 1 February 1992

The main changes concern Chapter II-1 and II-2 of the Convention and deal with ships' construction and with fire protection, detection and extinction.

In Chapter II-1, one of the most important amendments is designed to reduce the number and size of openings in watertight bulkheads in passenger ships and to ensure that they are closed in the event of an emergency.

In Chapter II-2, improvements were made to regulations concerning fixed gas fire-extinguishing systems, smoke detection systems, arrangements for fuel and other oils, the location and separation of spaces and several other regulations.

The International Gas Carrier Code - which is mandatory under SOLAS - was also amended.

The 1990 amendments

Adoption: May 1990

Entry into force: 1 February 1992

Important changes were made to the way in which the subdivision and stability of dry cargo ships is determined. They apply to ships of 100 metres or more in length built on or after 1 February 1992.

The amendments introduced a new part B-1 of Chapter II-1 containing subdivision and damage stability requirements for cargo ships based upon the so-called "probabilistic" concept of survival, which was originally developed through study of data relating to collisions collected by IMO.

This showed a pattern in accidents which could be used in improving the design of ships: most damage, for example, is sustained in the forward part of ships and it seemed logical, therefore, to improve the standard of subdivision there rather than towards the stern. Because it is based on statistical evidence as to what actually happens when ships collide, the probabilistic concept provides a far more realistic scenario than the earlier "deterministic" method, whose principles regarding the subdivision of passenger ships are theoretical rather than practical in concept.

Amendments were also made to the International Code for the Construction and Equipment of Ships Carrying Dangerous Chemicals in Bulk (IBC Code) and the International Code for the Construction and Equipment of Ships Carrying Liquefied Gases in Bulk (IGC Code).

The 1991 Amendments

Adoption: 24 May 1991
Entry into force: 1 January 1994

Chapter VI (Carriage of grain) was completely revised to extend it to include other cargoes and it was retitled Carriage of cargoes. The text is shorter, but the Chapter is backed up by two new Codes. The International Grain Code is mandatory while the Code of Safe Practice for Cargo Stowage and Securing is recommended. The Chapter also refers to the Code of Safe Practice for Ships Carrying Timber Deck Cargoes and the Code of Safe Practice for Solid Bulk Cargoes. In Chapter II-2, fire safety requirements for passenger ships were improved and other changes were made to Chapter III and Chapter V.

The April 1992 amendments

Adoption: 10 April 1992
Entry into force: 1 October 1994

New standards concerning the stability of existing ro-ro passenger ships after damage were included in amendments to Chapter II-1. They were based on measures to improve the damage stability of new ro-ro passenger ships which came into force on 29 April 1990 but were slightly modified. The measures were phased in over an 11-year period beginning 1 October 1994.

A number of other amendments to SOLAS were adopted, including improved fire safety measures for existing passenger ships carrying more than 36 passengers, including mandatory requirements for smoke detection and alarm and sprinkler systems in accommodation and service spaces, stairway enclosures and corridors. Other improvements involved the provision of emergency lighting, general emergency alarm systems and other means of communication.

Some of these measures became applicable for existing ships on 1 October 1994. Those dealing with smoke detection and alarm systems and sprinklers applied from 1 October 1997. Requirements concerning stairways of steel-frame construction, for fire-extinguishing systems in machinery spaces and for fire doors were mandatory from 1 October 2000.

The April 1992 amendments were particularly important because they applied to existing ships. In the past, major changes to SOLAS had been restricted to new ships by so-called "grandfather clauses". The reason for this is that major changes involve expensive modifications to most ships, and there had previously been a reluctance to make such measures retroactive.

The December 1992 amendments

Adoption: 11 December 1992
Entry into force: 1 October 1994

The most important amendments were concerned with the fire safety of new passenger ships. They made it mandatory for new ships (i.e. those built after 1 October 1994) carrying more than 36 passengers to be fitted with automatic sprinklers and a fire detection and alarm system centralized in a continuously-manned remote control station. Controls for the remote closing of fire doors and shutting down of ventilation fans must be located at the same place.

New standards for the fire integrity of bulkheads and decks were introduced and improvements made to standards for corridors and stairways used as a means of escape in case of fire. Emergency lighting which can be used by passengers to identify escape routes is required.

Other amendments affected the fire safety of ships carrying 36 passengers or less and also oil tanker fire safety.

Three Codes were also amended. Amendments to the International Code for the Construction and Equipment of Ships Carrying Dangerous Chemicals in Bulk (IBC Code) and the International Code for the Construction and Equipment of Ships Carrying Liquefied Gases in Bulk (IGC Code) entered into force on 1 July 1994 and affect ships built after that date.

Amendments to the Code for the Construction and Equipment of Ships Carrying Dangerous Chemicals in Bulk (BCH Code) entered into force on 1 July 1994. The Code is voluntary and applies to existing ships.

The May 1994 Amendments (Conference)

Adoption: 24 May 1994

Entry into force: 1 January 1996 (Chapters X, XI) 1 July 1998 (Chapter IX)

The Conference adopted three new SOLAS Chapters as well as a resolution on an accelerated amendment procedure.

Accelerated Amendment Procedure –

The Conference adopted a resolution on an accelerated amendment procedure to be used in exceptional circumstances. It states that a Conference of Contracting Governments can reduce the period after which an amendment to the technical Chapters of the Convention (which excludes the articles and Chapter I) is deemed to have been accepted from 12 months to six months, in exceptional circumstances.

Article VIII of SOLAS deals with the procedures for amending the Convention. The existing text says that proposed amendments have to be circulated to Governments at least six months prior to adoption and cannot enter into force until at least 18 months after adoption. This makes a total of 24 months, from circulation (six months), through adoption, to deemed acceptance date (12 months after adoption), to entry into force (six months after deemed acceptance date).

The resolution adopted by the conference states that the circulation period will remain at six months as will the period between the date on which the amendment is deemed to have been accepted and the date of entry into force. But the period between adoption and deemed acceptance date can be reduced to six months from 12. The total period between circulation of an amendment and its entry into force could thus be reduced from 24 months to 18 - in exceptional circumstances.

Index